African Traditional and Oral Literature as Pedagogical Tools in Content Area Classrooms

K-12

African Traditional and Oral Literature as Pedagogical Tools an Content Area Classrooms

K-12

Edited by

Lewis Asimeng-Boahene
Pennsylvania State University-Harrisburg

and

Michael Baffoe
University of Manitoba, Winnipeg, Canada

INFORMATION AGE PUBLISHING, INC.
Charlotte, NC • www.infoagepub.com

Library of Congress Cataloging-in-Publication Data

CIP data for this book can be found on the Library of Congress website http://www.loc.gov/index.html

ISBNs: Paperback: 978-1-62396-538-9
     Hardcover: 978-1-62396-539-6
     eBook: 978-1-62396-540-2

CONTENTS

ACKNOWLEDGMENTS

Behind every successful academic endeavor are lots of visible and invisible indispensable hands. This anthology of African traditional oral literature as pedagogical tools in content area classrooms would not have been possible without the support of our family, friends, colleagues, and administration and support staff.

For inspiration, support and stimulation of ideas, we owe a great debt of gratitude to Dr. Mary Napoli with whom we started the project. Her initial guidance and professional advice throughout the project deserve special acknowledgment.

We also wish to express our deep appreciation to Berea Henderson and Shedlmor Sevillo, Communications and Program Assistants, at the Faculty of Social Work, University of Manitoba for their painstaking formatting and editorial assistance.

We extend our sincere gratitude to Information Age Publishing for their offer to publish this work. We particularly wish to acknowledge the professional guidance of Amanda Uriarte of Information Age Publishing for her professional assistance throughout the project.

We wish to acknowledge the hard work of all the contributors for their meticulous efforts that made this project a reality.

Finally, a special appreciation to Ruth, Betty, Shirley, and Akwasi, for their patience, sacrifice, encouragement, unconditional love, and support for my academic odyssey [Lewis].

African Traditional and Oral Literature as Pedagogical Tools in
Contest Area Classrooms: K-12, pages vii–vii

INTRODUCTION

Asimeng-Boahene and Michael Baffoe

African oral literature defies single definition. It could be described as a collage of sociocultural practices. It refers to such genres as narratives, epics, lyrics, poetry, proverbs, drama, riddles or word play, song play, drums, poetry and historical contents (Finnegan, 1970; Okpewho, 1992). Thus, the term oral literature has been central to the analysis of the many unwritten forms in Africa that possess literary qualities. Consequently, African traditional oral literature could be seen as an integral part of the culture and history of an African local community, which is stored in various forms and transmitted through various modes. Traditional oral African literature, which is, passed from one generation to another, is usually by word of mouth and cultural rituals. This mode of education has by and large been used as a way of acquiring lifelong learning (Omolewa, 2007). By the mid-19th century, a few scholars and collectors were already using the term oral literature to describe African forms (see Finnegan, 1970).

The initial attention on African oral literature (folklore) is traceable to European travelers who wrote descriptions of the culture and essence of African kingdom they encountered in their wanderings in 1550. But the European travelers of this time who illuminated aspects of the African oral literature were not really concerned with the overall realization of oral literature) sometimes unconsciously swayed by such biased and uniformed

African Traditional and Oral Literature as Pedagogical Tools in Contest Area Classrooms: K-12, pages ix–xiii
Copyright © 2014 by Information Age Publishing

assumptions about the *descriptions* of literary traditions among nonliterate peoples (Ighile, n.d.). Thus, there is still the widely held myth of Africa as continent either devoid of literature until its *engagement with "civilized" nations* which precipitated publications in European languages, or having just *rudimentary* or unrefined literary construct not requiring systematic study (Finnegan, 1970). Thus, until recently, African oral literature was not placed in the context of literature as conceived by Western literary experts. It was classified as evolutionist, much in the tradition of Darwinist theory of natural selection or the preservation of favoured races in the struggle for life. Because of its being handed down by word of mouth, most European scholars in the tradition of Darwinism, believed that anything emanating from a primitive people might have lost some of its original qualities and therefore could not be considered authentic literature to qualify to be used as pedagogic tool in the mainstream academia (Okpewho, 1992).

Notwithstanding the overall minimal knowledge about Africa in the United States and other parts of the world, there is one glimmer of hope for transformation. For some time now, an African proverb, *it takes a whole village to raise a child* has become extensively used to inspire communities throughout the U.S. to contribute in the burden of educating U.S. children (Grant & Asimeng-Boahene, 2006). Therefore, "the village concept" can be evoked to encourage educators to accept and employ alternative paradigms of reality for nurturing and mentoring youth, many of whom are facing troubled childhoods and uncertain futures. I believe that, this recent attention to the African proverbs could provide modest springboard for teachers to utilize African proverbs as cultural/pedagogical tools.

African oral literatures are fundamental to the African ways of life. They are introduced to equip the citizens with the ability to function effectively in other areas of learning such as language acquisition, speech therapy, literacy, citizenship, critical thinking, social justice and other related themes (Omolewa, 2007). The unique characteristics of African traditional oral literature in terms of its definition, societal significance, and historical and today's perspectives need deeper exploration. This is the motivation behind this publication.

The book is therefore a bold attempt at advocating for the revision of existing pedagogic fora and the creation and addition of new fora that would provide for the inclusion of thoughts, perspectives and practices of African traditional oral literature in the pedagogical tools of content area classrooms especially in North America. The articles that are presented in this book provide theoretical frameworks for using African traditional oral literature and its various tenets as teaching tools. They bring together new voices of how African literature could be used as helpful tool in classrooms. Rationale for agitating for its use as ideal for pedagogic tool is the recurrent theme throughout the various articles presented.

The book explores how educators, literacy educators, learners, activists, policy makers, and curriculum developers can utilize the powerful yet untapped gem of African oral literature as pedagogical tools in content area classrooms to help expand educators repertoire of understanding beyond the "conventional wisdom" of their pedagogic creed. It is a comprehensive work of experienced and diverse, scholars, academicians, and educators who have expertise in multicultural education, traditional oral literature, urban education, children's literature and culturally responsive pedagogy that have become the focus of U.S. discourses in public education and teacher preparation.

We also believe that this anthology serves as part of the quest for multiple views about our "global village," emphasizing the importance of linking the idea of diverse knowledge with realities of global trends and development. Consequently, the goal and the basic thrust of this anthology is to negotiate for space for nonmainstream epistemology to share the pedagogical floor with the mainstream template, to foster alternative vision of reality for other knowledge production in the academic domain. The uniqueness of this collection is the idea of bringing the content and the pedagogy of most of the genres of African oral arts under one umbrella and thereby offering a practical acquaintance and appreciation with different African cultures. It therefore introduces the world of African mind and thoughts to the readers. In summary, this anthology presents an academic area which is now slowly gaining its long overdue recognition in the academia.

This book is divided into three parts: Part 1 explores oral literature as pedagogical tools that target six pre-K1-3. Here, contributing authors share their perspectives about Children's Oral Literature Through Singing Games, African Oral Literature Through Poetry, African Music as a Pedagogical Tool in the Classroom and Constructing Lessons Through Artifacts, Books, and Drama. The importance and use of poetry in pedagogy are highlighted by the authors of Chapters 2. The authors stress the fact that hearing poems read aloud helps children cultivate an appreciation for sound and language or that poetry's rhythm and rhyme delight children of every age. Poetry, according to the authors, also helps us see differently, validating individual human experiences and leading to self-understanding and understanding of those around us. They further remind us that reading poetry to children begins with us, teachers and librarians translates into reading poems as a part of our daily literacy routine, something heretofore unfamiliar to the preservice students who listened to the CD accompanying *Hip Hop Speaks to Children*.

Part 2 focuses on oral literature as pedagogical tools for Grades 4-8. In this section, the contributors share their thoughts on other aspects of African oral literature. They include an examination of the Influences of

African Cultural Naming Patterns on the Identity and Personality Development of Immigrant Children of African Descent in North American Classrooms. Others are the use of African Proverbs as Culturally Responsive Tools in Content Area in Social Studies Classrooms, and the use of "Riddles as Communicative and Pedagogical Tool to Develop a Multicultural Curriculum in Social Studies Classrooms.

African proverbs create a safe space to make use of critical thinking which can serve as literal, metaphorical, or psychological tonic. For example, *one head does not exchange ideas* (Akan, Ghana), which means two heads are better than one. Thus, African proverbs are valuable for education because they often create an imaginative space, where the mind is free to see alternative perspectives. Consequently, elders of African use proverbs as a tool to make a point, set examples, or explain situations. *He that has never travelled thinks his mother is the only good cook in the world (Kenya).*

Part 3 examines how oral literatures could be used as teaching tools in Grades 9-12 classrooms. Interesting discussions in this section include The Metaphor of Ghanaian Cloth: Decoding the Symbols in Ghanaian Wax Prints, and Utilizing Drama and Literature as Cultural Tools to address Culture and Context for Urban Students in the Content Classroom. Others are the Human Ingenuity as a Pedagogical Tool of Dialogic Performance and Competence Using African Ceremony of Libation.

The significance of Story-Telling and Drumming takes the next section of Part 3 in which the authors highlight the role of Story Telling in the context of Social Justice, Pedagogy, and Vision. Traditionally, Africans have revered good stories and story tellers from the past to the present. Ancient writing traditions do exist on the continent, but most Africans today, as in the past, are primarily oral peoples, and their art forms are oral rather than literary. Drawing insights from social justice, the authors of this chapter explore story-telling among the Veekuhane of Botswana, and more specifically, highlight the pedagogical potential of stories in the transmission of cultural ideas to school-going children to promote diversity, social harmony and justice in line with Botswana's Vision 2016 ideals.

The aspect of African oral literature through story-telling permeates most African cultures. With their fantasies, availability and entertainment value, stories are effective communication tools that teachers can readily employ to foster cultural fluency in multicultural educational environments. This is also exemplified by what the author of Chapter 13 articulates as Griots and Market Square Pedagogy: Call, Response and Performative Storytelling in the Classroom. As in most African cultures and ceremonies this section and the book closes with African drumming which the author poignantly presents as a Pedagogical Tool for Social Justice and Cultural Diversity in Urban Classrooms in the United States.

Concluding Thoughts

Every human culture in the world seems to create narratives as a way of universal features, however, the particular narrative meanings, themes, genres, and styles of storytelling around the world differ from culture to culture. Thus, if today's teachers can make good pedagogical choices, they must do so with the knowledge of not only local community but also global perspectives for, as Yokota (1993) opines, multicultural literature allows:

> Children to take part in experiences from cultures other than their own; and these experiences help them understand different backgrounds, thereby influencing their decisions about how they will live in this culturally pluralistic world. As we encourage teachers to choose books from other languages and cultures with guided discussions to help children develop an understanding of other people and their customs, we can provide a transformative effect in our curriculum. (as cited in Agbaw & Napoli, 2011, p. 267)

It can safely be assumed that the prime function of oral literature is to provide aesthetic pleasure and entertainment for the listeners, and this applies to all genres. Similarly it can reasonably be claimed that oral literature, like written literature, is of educational value, since being exposed to it enhances the listeners' verbal skills, enriches their vocabulary and enlarges their knowledge of their own society and its history.

This work is only the beginning of a long process of gaining recognition for African oral literature in content area classrooms. As it continues to attract interest of researchers and scholars around the world, because of its enduring esthetic appeal and relevance, we hope more publications will come out in this area to serve as additional pedagogical tools for North American classrooms and beyond.

REFERENCES

Finnegan, R. H. (1970). *Oral literature in Africa*. Oxford, England: Clarendon.

Grant, R., & Asimeng-Boahene, L. (2006). Culturally responsive pedagogy in citizenship education: using African proverbs as tools for teaching in urban schools. *Multicultural Perspectives, 8*(4), 17-24

Okpewho, I. (1992). *African oral literature: Background, character, & continuity*. Bloomington, IN: Indiana, University Press.

Yokota, J. (1993). Issues in selecting multicultural children's literature. In V. Yenika-Agbaw & M. Napoli (Eds.), *African American children's and adolescent literature in the classrooms: A critical guide* (p. 267). New York, NY: Peter Lang.

CHAPTER 1

CONSIDERING THE FUNCTIONS AND FORMS OF AFRICAN TRADITIONAL AND ORAL LITERATURE

Nancy L. Hadaway and Terrell A. Young

I was lucky to be given the gift of storytelling by my elders.
It was their wish that I not only learn from these stories, but that I
pass them on to the next generation and the generation after that.

—Baba Wague Diakité (2010, p. 8)

INTRODUCTION

As participants of our many group memberships—family, ethnic, regional, language, religious—we share a core of understandings that shape our communication, our ways of seeing life, and our ways of doing things. Our oral literature or folklore reflects these understandings through storytelling and traditional tales, rhymes, riddles, proverbs, and so on. In this way, folklore is part of a "universal language which can speak to people across

African Traditional and Oral Literature as Pedagogical Tools in
Contest Area Classrooms: K-12, pages 1–19
Copyright © 2014 by Information Age Publishing

human frontiers" (Smith, 2004, p. ix). Many Africans "still privilege their oral tradition over the written ones as a valuable and very practical multipurpose tool that enriches and gives meaning to their day-to-day communication. In addition to its entertainment value, the African oral tradition is also an encyclopedia of the various people's histories, cultural experiences, traditions, and values; a record of their feelings, attitudes, and responses to their experiences and environment; and also a tool for preserving and disseminating that knowledge both internally and globally" (Kizza, 2010, p. 7).

Unfortunately, folklore and oral traditions are being threatened by urbanization and technology coupled with the long term effects of colonization. As a result, there is deep concern about "the speed at which stories that anchor this oral tradition and the languages that sustain them are disappearing with the passing of each generation of Africans" (Kizza, 2010, p. 9). Raouf Mama (2006) nostalgically recalls evening story times in his native Benin when parents and elders shared legends as well as trickster and pourquoi tales, and he laments that by the time he was sixteen, those special evenings were no longer part of family life.

The purpose of this chapter is to consider the challenges in collecting and preserving African folklore as well as highlighting the functions this folklore serves. We will also classify a sample of African folktales based on those functions and explore how African oral and traditional literature can be used as a pedagogical tool to foster content area literacy and serve as a source of culturally relevant literature for a greater appreciation and comprehension of global issues.

Challenges in Collecting and Preserving African Folklore

Folklore survived for hundreds of years in oral form only passed from generation to generation. For several hundred years now, researchers have attempted to record the oral traditions and stories of various groups before that information is lost. Anthropologists and linguists often spend years studying groups and gathering their folklore, and they encounter challenges in collecting and preserving that oral literature. We discuss three of these challenges: the issue of translation from one language to another, capturing an oral performance on the written page, and the relevance of traditional stories today.

First, translation is complex process.

A translator is faced with the necessity of choosing between several meanings of a word in the source language and finding the adequate word in the target language. Further, translation implies not only conveying denotation (the literal, dictionary meaning of words), but also connotation, that is, contextual meaning that may change from text to text. (Nikolajeva, 2011, p. 407)

For folklore, however, the translation process is more than words on a page; there is a performance component for both the storyteller and the audience. Scheub (2005) argues that the major problem is not translating the African language to English; it is capturing an oral performance on the written page. "The creativity of the storyteller, gestures, facial expressions, tonal nuances, poses, the audience's responses, reactions, contributions, the actual environment. All of these are lost when transcribing an oral text into a written one" (Kizza, 2010, p. 188).

A final challenge is whether stories of such long duration can still be relevant today. However, one key aspect of folklore is that in the chain of transmission, the story is altered somewhat as each performer leaves an imprint, crafting the folklore to fit the audience and the setting. Kizza (2010) contends that,

> the stories being told are not fixed, unchangeable pieces as happens in the case of the written tradition; each storyteller is free to totally own the story one is telling and to try and make it relevant to one's audience through improvisation, omission, and addition of information as necessary. (p. 9)

Two examples of adapting folklore to contemporary life and audiences follow. In rural Africa, an innovative project involving folk performers using puppetry, storytelling, proverbs, role play, drumming, and dance communicated vital information for HIV/AIDS prevention (Panford, Nyaney, Amoah, & Aidoo, 2001). A second program in remote eastern Uganda trained traditional birth attendants to address serious health problems through the teaching power of songs and stories (Silver, 2001).

Another adaptation for current times is through modern technology. While technology can erode the prominence of traditional culture, it can also enhance the visibility of oral literature (Namullundah, 2011). The Internet is emerging as a new means of disseminating traditional lore (Hadaway, 2004). Promising websites offer not only written versions of traditional African tales, but also oral versions performed by storytellers utilizing multimedia.

Finally, it is important to note that there is really no single "African" oral literature. Africa is the second largest continent and as such, it is incredibly diverse. There are many countries and even more cultural and language groups on the continent, and the oral literature is a rich tradition among all those countries and groups of individuals. Moreover, many of the tales we discuss are found in similar versions across geographic and cultural boundaries. While we sometimes note the origin of a story, it is often impossible to determine with certainty the origin of any folklore.

Functions and Forms of Folklore: A Framework to Discuss African Oral Literature

Folklore both describes and prescribes. It reflects "what people do, how they think, live and have lived as well as their aspirations," … and it also reinforces "the status quo by consistently depicting societal and cultural norms" (Namullundah, 2011, p. xi). While the overarching functions of folklore are to educate and to entertain, more specifically, folklore serves the following functions (pp. 15-19):

- to reflect a group's cultural identity, cultural heritage, and geography
- to create, maintain, and negotiate boundaries between ethnic groups
- to provide an understanding of the social and material environment
- to share information about social roles and penalties for breaches
- to model rightful living and appropriate social interactions
- to portray a community's value for kinship ties, gender roles, the status of children, dietary habits, taboos, leisure
- to foster norms and values, desirable attitudes and behaviors that maintain communities, for example, obedience, diligence, social responsibility, determination, honesty, collectivity
- to act as moral sanctions on undesirable attitudes and behaviors without having to embarrass individual members
- to foster assessments of prevailing philosophies for life, justice, power, the world order
- to serve as a bonding ritual
- to lift the minds of narrator and listener

In considering these purposes, we synthesized the ideas and decided on five broad functions as a framework for analyzing and classifying different types of African folklore. Within each function, we grouped the different forms of folklore such as pourquoi or trickster tales that reflected that purpose. In the next section, we will discuss each of these five functions as well as the different types of folklore that fit within that function. The overall framework with functions and associated forms of folklore is as follows.

- Skill development: riddles, dilemma tales
- Social control: cautionary tales
- Explanation: etiological/pourquoi tales, myths
- Entertainment: trickster tales
- Education: songs, legends, proverbs, morality tales

African Folklore Classified by Function and Form

While the framework with functions and forms of folklore is a tool that helps to organize and discuss the oral literature examples, it is important to note that some of the folklore examples may fit in more than one function category. For instance, a trickster tale in addition to its classification as entertainment may also have etiological elements, explaining certain traits or events.

Skill development: There are some types of folklore that in addition to entertaining and educating are excellent for skill development. For instance, riddles "are frequently used to sharpen minds and cultivate oracy/orality" (Kizza, 2010, p. 51). One popular riddle format among the Baganda in Uganda is a type of call-response riddling known as *ebikokkyo* with "brief call statements, each with a specific one-word or one-phrase response" (p. 51). The audience knows they are being challenged when the initiator or caller utters *"kkoyi kkoyi;"* the audience indicates they are ready by replying *"lya."* Kizza provides examples including the following (p. 53):

> **CALLER:** A dwelling that is built by many people, but cannot be inhabited by more than one person:
> **AUDIENCE:** A grave.
> **CALLER:** A double-door with one supporting frame:
> **AUDIENCE:** Nose.

The second popular riddle format among the Baganda has more elaborate scenarios ending with a question. The audience must listen carefully to the scenario, paying attention to the details in order to answer the question following that scenario. Kizza's example of this riddle format follows.

> **SCENARIO:** Three people come to a river wanting to cross it. One sees the water and crosses the river without getting wet. One does not see the water, and that one too crosses without getting wet. The third sees the water, crosses the river, and is drenched. Who are these three people?
> **RESPONSE:** A pregnant woman crossing a river with a baby on her back. (p. 54)

Dilemma tales, common in African folklore, promote skills of argumentation and debate. The tales

are prose narratives that leave the listeners with a choice among alternatives, such as which of several characters have done the best, deserves a reward, or

should win an argument....The choices are difficult ones and usually involve
discrimination on ethical, moral, or legal grounds. (Bascom, 1975, p. 1)

The narrator ends the tale by stating the dilemma or a question, and then
the listeners debate the different points of view. At times, the narrator may
resolve the dilemma after a lively discussion has taken place, but that is
not always the case. As Bascom contends, "it is their intellectual function
and their relevance to ethical standards, rather than any literary merit,
that make dilemma tales interesting" (p. 3). In Cushman's (2010) translation of *Zarma Folktales of Niger*, "Betrayal" is an example of a dilemma tale.
In this story, a hunter finds a starving alligator who begs for help. If the
hunter helps, the alligator promises that no alligator will eat the hunter or
his family. The hunter agrees and carries the alligator to the middle of the
river. When the hunter tries to leave, the alligator prevents his departure
and plans to eat him. The hunter calls for help to a donkey, a cow, and a
horse on the shore, but they decline stating that they have been betrayed
by man. Finally, a hare agrees to help. He asks the hunter to demonstrate
how he saved the alligator. Once the hunter and alligator are out of the
water, the hunter overpowers the alligator and kills it. Upon witnessing
this, the hare hides. The hunter goes to the village and tells the children to
catch the hare and kill it. The hare is saved by a heron, but then the hare
kills the heron. The dilemma is posed at the end: "So, we must ask: was
it the alligator, the hunter, or the hare who betrayed the other?" (p. 25).

Social control: "Folktales caution children against strangers, the forest
and ogres, hostile neighbors and the environment" (Namullundah, 2011,
p. 147). Cautionary tales are especially common in the oral literature of
a group but perhaps less commonplace in written form. Such tales may
be shared as a means of warning and social control (e.g., what happens to
children who disobey their parents). In a cautionary tale, there is usually a
warning about some behavior (e.g., do not go outside at night), the forbid-
den act, and the consequences which are sometimes quite grisly.

"Shansa Mutongo Shima" from the collection, *A Pride of African Tales*
(Washington, 2004), is a cautionary tale from the Democratic Republic of
the Congo which warns about strangers and judging people by appearances alone. When Shansa, a handsome, clever stranger, comes to the village,
Bwayla accepts his proposal of marriage. The villagers initially feel that
she should not trust a stranger, but they become supporters when Shansa
proves himself to be a great hunter and brings the villagers many game
animals for a feast each day. All the while, they wonder how he manages
to kill so many animals. Bwayla becomes so suspicious that she follows her
intended into the jungle and discovers that he peels his human skin to become a lion. She must then convince her father and her uncle not to trust
Shansa, and they devise a trick that is put into action one night as Shansa

sleeps. The three of them disguise themselves as a giant with leopard skin and antelope antlers and sing that Bwalya wishes to kill Shansa and eat him. Shansa runs away and leaves Bwalya at the altar. The advice of this tale is "What lies inside a person is much more important than what you see on the outside. You must take your time, watch, and listen before you make your final decision about a person" (p. 36). As much as caution with regard to strangers and external appearances, an implicit function of this tale may also be to create, maintain, and negotiate boundaries between groups. The villagers would prefer that Bwalya marry within her group or village rather than marrying outside the village.

Fostering desirable attitudes and behaviors such as obedience to parents is a frequent theme of cautionary tales and is the focus of the next two tales. *Solma: Tales from Northern Ghana 6-12* (Agambila, 2002) is a collection of six tales, and "Kanwum and Bunsela" is a cautionary tale about a young girl of a single mother with a more contemporary setting. Kanwum goes dancing and stays so late that no one will walk her home. Along the way, a monster chases her, and the mother finds her daughter dead in the morning. The mother laments,

> I always said "Don't stay out late," but she never listened. Mothers, go and tell your children that Kanwum lost her heart because she would not listen to her mother.... Children, go home and listen to your mothers and fathers. (p. 8)

Minnie Postma shares "Mmadipetsane," a cautionary tale from Lesotho, in the collection, *Nelson Mandela's Favorite African Folktales* (2002). Mmadipetsane's mother sends the child to gather wild spinach. She walks for a long time before she sees a field with many wild roots, so she begins to dig. Suddenly, the ledimo, a huge, ugly monster appears and begins to yell at Mmadipetsane telling her she cannot dig in his field. The little girl continues digging and taunts the monster. When she returns home, she tells her mother where she found the wild roots and her mother exclaims, "What are you thinking, you disobedient child!" (p. 45). The child believes that she is more clever than the ledimo and because she is small, she can run and hide out of his reach. Unfortunately, the ledimo is crafty and he fills the hole—the child's hiding place—leaving her without a safe place to escape him. In the end, "the ledimo, the Giant, the Strong One, the Dangerous One, grabs the child who would not listen to her mother's warning" (p. 47), and he takes her home where he will eat her.

Explanation: Oral literature sometimes offers relief as in the case of etiological or pourquoi tales with their explanations of how certain things came to be. Humans are always seeking logical answers to their "why" questions even when there are apparently very few, if any, to be found. This is when etiological tales enter the picture to explain the logically inexplicable phenomena of our human existence without making us doubt our sanity or even negatively affecting our mental capacities. (Kizza, 2010, p. 101)

Cushman (2010) asserts that this type of tale is well known to Western audiences labeling them "how an animal got a trait" stories. "The Election of the Animal King" is one such example in Cushman's translation of *Zarma Folktales of Niger.*

How the Leopard Got His Claws (Achebe, 2011) is a pourquoi tale from Nigeria. Once upon a time all of the animals were friends, and the gentle and kind leopard was their king. Things changed when dog, which had teeth, attacked the leopard and became the new king. The story explains how the dog became man's servant, why the animals are no longer friends, why leopard attacks animals, and how leopard got his claws, teeth, and roar.

Two tales address the theme of color in the animal kingdom. First, in *Beautiful Blackbird* (Bryan, 2003), a tale from Zambia, Blackbird was the only bird of Africa who wasn't brightly colored. When Ringdove inquires who the most beautiful bird is, the other birds name Blackbird. At Ringdove's request, Blackbird brings blackening from his medicine gourd to decorate Ringdove's colored neck. As a result, the other birds also want trimming, so Blackbird paints dots and brushes lines and arcs until his gourd is empty. In a similar tale from the Yoruba of West Africa, *The Three Birds from Olongo* (Folarin & Folarin, 2001), readers learn that all birds originally lived in their own country, Olongo, which was exciting and colorful. When there is a drought, colors fade and there is little food. A bird suggests to the king and queen that some of them go to the land of the men to learn about irrigation, farming, and dyeing. When the birds go to earth, the king of men is enchanted by the colorful birds, and he agrees to teach them so long as they return after sharing this knowledge in Olongo. The birds return home, share their knowledge, and then return to earth. At first, the birds are welcomed but after some time, they are treated badly and hunted by men. This forces some birds to dye their feathers in black, brown, and gray as camouflage, and this is why some birds are dull in color but others such as the peacock and the macaw are still colorful.

The Orphan (Mollel, 2009) is a tale from the Maasai of East Africa. The tale explores the origin of Venus, called Kileken, the orphan boy. An old man encounters an orphan boy who comes to live with the old man and help him. The boy has mysterious powers; he is able to take starving cattle to graze and overnight, fat cattle return. The old man wishes to discover how this is done. However, the boy explains that so long as his abilities remain a secret, they will continue and he can stay with the old man. Curiosity gets the best of the old man who follows the boy as he herds the cattle to pasture. He sees the boy raise his arms toward the sky and a powerful glow spreads over the boy. Then, the drought ravaged land is covered in tall grass, green woods, and gushing springs. The man gasps, and the boy hears and knows that his power is no longer a secret. The boy explodes into a blinding star, Venus, and the land reverts to drought with starving cattle.

Folklore collections are a rich source for pourquoi tales. *The Zebra's Stripes and Other African Animal Tales* (Stewart, 2004) is a collection of animal tales; many are pourquoi tales including "Why Zebra Has No Horns," "How Leopard Got His Spots," "How Lion and Warthog Became Enemies." "The Zebra's Stripes" is from the San of Southern Africa and explains how the zebra got its stripes and why the baboon's bottom is bald. Another collection, *A Pride of African Tales* (Washington, 2004) has a variety of folklore types from many African countries. The one pourquoi tale, "The Boy Who Wanted the Moon," is from the Congo. "The Great Hunter" in *African Tales: A Barefoot Collection* (Mhlophe, 2009) is a tale from Swaziland that explains why the impala has been given special respect in that country. In her collection of Baganda folklore, Kizza includes numerous pourquoi tales such as "Why Cocks Crow at 3:00 A.M." and "Why Some Animals Are Prettier Than Others." Finally, "The Cat Who Came Indoors" from *Nelson Mandela's Favorite African Folktales* (Tracey, 2002) is a Shona story from Zimbabwe revealing how "cats become cherished inhabitants of human homes" (p. 12).

As noted earlier, there is sometimes overlap in the functions in folklore. We discovered several trickster tales that had etiological elements. These may or may not be a major focus of the tale, but there are both trickster elements such as deception and pranks as well as explanations for traits such as spider's bald head. There are many versions of the tale about Anansi and a pot of hot beans that burns the hair from his head including Anansi and the Pot of Beans (Norfolk & Norfolk, 2006), The Parade: A Stampede of Stories about Ananse, the Trickster Spider (Kojo, 2011), and "How Spider Got a Bald Head" from a collection of three Anansi tales, The First Adventures of Spider: West African Folktales (Arkhurst, 2012). In the latter book, Arkhurst shares two other Anansi tales with trickster and pourquoi components, "How Spider Got a Thin Waist" and "Why Spider Lives in Ceilings." In Anansi Goes Fishing (Kimmel, 1992), readers learn why today spiders everywhere weave webs. Finally, three tales, "How Ananse Stole All the Stories" from *Trick of the Tale: A Collection of Trickster Tales* (Matthews & Matthews, 2008), Anansi Does the Impossible (Aardema, 2000), and A Story, A Story (Haley, 1970/ 1988) share how Anansi tricks the Sky God, who is monopolizing all the stories, and thus, brings stories back to the world.

In addition to etiological or pourquoi tales,

> myths, though not as numerous as other types, play an important role in the African oral tradition. Like myths all over the world, African myths … artfully explain the creation of man, the universe and other creatures, the essence of their creator, and the nature of the relationships between these creatures and their creator, as well as the nature of human existence. (Kizza, 2010, pp. 13-14)

Hamilton (1988) explains "myths present themselves as truth and as accounts of actual facts no matter how different these facts or truths may be from our ordinary, "real" experience" (pp. ix-x). *Retold African Myths* (Tate, 1993) and *West African Myths* (Green, 2010) are helpful references for creation stories and myths explaining death, right, and wrong, and the commonality of beliefs across different cultural groups.

Entertainment: As Mama (2006) asserts folklore is a "great source of entertainment and spiritual nourishment " (p. ix). Stories can lift the minds of the narrator and the listener. Trickster tales, in particular, can help validate and serve as a bonding ritual for a group as they humorously portray protagonists who use wit, pranks, lies and deceit to triumph over their often more powerful foes. "Trickster figures are found worldwide. Although their prime role is to entertain, they also depict the weaknesses and strengths of human nature, especially the disadvantages of character traits such as vanity, greed and naivety. Often selfish and cruel, tricksters demonstrate an ability to outwit enemies who have an advantage over them. Sometimes the tricksters are small animals who appear to pose no threat to the larger animals of the kingdom and because they move quickly and jump well, they are often not caught" (Stewart, 2004, p. 11). Anansi the spider is a popular trickster figure, but other animals such as the clever and cunning hare or the jackal appear in African folktales.

In *Anansi and the Talking Melon* (Kimmel, 1994), Anansi uses a thorn to make a hole in a melon. He climbs into the melon and eats until he is too big to get out. Then, he tricks the animals into believing that it is a talking melon that they encounter. In *Anansi and the Magic Stick* (Kimmel, 2002), Anansi steals a magic stick that obeys the spider's orders to clear the yard, paint his house, and water his garden. Unfortunately, Anansi forgets how to stop the stick, the magic gets out of control, and the world is transformed. Anansi finds a "strange, moss-covered rock" in *Anansi and the Moss-Covered Rock* (Kimmel, 1988) and learns that whenever someone says "Isn't this a strange, moss-covered rock?" that they faint. He uses the rock to steal food from other animals until Little Bush Deer plays a trick on Anansi so the other animals can get their food. *The Parade: A Stampede of Stories about Ananse, the Trickster Spider* (Kojo, 2011) is a collection of trickster tales from Ghana. In the title story, "The Parade," readers learn how Ananse tricks the father of his future wife in order to gain permission to marry her. *The Pot of Wisdom: Ananse Stories* (Badoe & Diakite, 2001), another collection from Ghana, has a combination trickster and pourquoi tale "Why Pig Has a Short Snout." In the story, readers learn that Pig used to have a long elephant-like trunk and he was a money lender. Ananse had borrowed money from Pig to pay a dowry for his son's marriage, but he forgets to pay the money back and so, begs for a week extension. When Pig returns, Ananse lies and tells Pig that he has the money but has dropped it down a bamboo pole and cannot get it. Pig offers to thrust his trunk in the pole to get the money. When Pig does so, his trunk is caught. Finally, he shakes the pole, and it falls off but so does his trunk.

Turning to other trickster figures, in *The Clever Monkey* (Cleveland, 2006), two cats find a large piece of cheese. Each cat offers to divide the cheese, but neither trusts the other to do so fairly. They argue while a monkey watches. The monkey offers to divide the cheese, but once he does so, he tells the cats that the pieces are unequal. So he takes a bite of one piece and then continues to nibble from each piece to try to even them. Eventually there are just two tiny pieces remaining. The monkey leaves and the cats continue to argue about the cheese.

The hare is the trickster in the remaining three tales. The lion tells all the animals that he is in charge—the king—in *The Lion and the Hare: An East African Folktale* (Krensky, 2009), and he proceeds to hunt and eat the animals, sometimes several per day. The animals are afraid so they go to the lion and make an offer. They tell him that a king should not have to hunt; he should be able to sit in the sun and his prey should come to him. So, each day, one animal will come to the lion to be eaten. When the time comes for hare to be eaten, he tells the other animals he will not volunteer to be eaten and he devises his own plan. Hare tells the lion about a second lion who is eating his dinner. The lion is furious and asks the hare to take him to this new lion. The hare lures the lion to a well where the lion sees "the other lion" in his own reflection and jumps into the water. Once he lands in the well, the lion realizes he has been tricked. He becomes angry and while trying to escape, he hits his head and dies. "A Home of One's Own" from *Trick of the Tale: A Collection of Trickster Tales* (Matthews & Matthews, 2008) describes the rivalry between Leopard and Sungara the Hare. Both Sungara and Leopard are building a house—the same house—unbeknownst to each other. They believe that their ancestors are helping. Once the house is built, Sungara moves in but Leopard claims the house as well. Sungara offers to share the house. Leopard agrees but requires a wall between to separate the house. Despite the wall, Sungara is still afraid of Leopard, and he concocts a plan to frighten Leopard out of the house for good. Finally, Savory (2002) contributes "The Hare's Revenge" in *Nelson*

Mandela's Favorite African Folktales illustrating the principle that "those who are not strong must be clever instead" (p. 71).

Education: The most important function of folklore is education. Through sharing songs, legends, proverbs, and stories, a group shares their identity and heritage, their norms and values. As one type of folklore, songs create a sense of togetherness, and they are often used within tales for audience participation. However, songs "play a vital role in the preservation of the African people's history and traditions. Many important lessons, historical and traditional events, and activities are accurately chronicled in African songs" (Kizza, 2010, pp. 12-13). According to Medearis (1994), "the *griot* or praise singer was like a walking history book. The songs he sang traced the ancestors of the king or chief of the village, and hundreds of years of African history" (n.p.). Medearis' book, *The Singing Man* is based on a Yoruba folktale from Nigeria about such a singer.

Legends also serve to educate as they reveal stories of heroic deeds of historical figures. The people in legends really existed, but their lives and deeds may be embellished in the story. "These humans perform unimaginable feats like establishing kingdoms single-handedly, winning impossible wars with very little or no help, averting disasters—the list goes on" (Kizza, 2010, p. 14). Both Wisniewski (1999) and Eisner (2003) share legends that provide an account of how a young crippled child prince defeats an evil King who has taken over the land of Mali. Eventually the young boy becomes the king of Mali.

Proverbs may be used to comfort and to indoctrinate.

> African proverbs are also popular as age-tested knowledge banks, often used to preserve and to enforce societal values and beliefs; to an outsider, therefore, proverbs are a window into the cultural, social, and philosophical functions of a specific people. (Kizza, 2010, p. 11)

With one proverb per page, Bryan's (1999) collection of 26 African sayings, *The Night Has Ears: African Proverbs* provides an appetizing but small bite of African wisdom. Characterized by vivid concrete imagery and stunning gouache and tempera artwork, some selections deal with identity while others are cautionary. Most are readily understood, and a few have familiar counterparts, that is, "There is no one-way friendship" and "No one knows the story of tomorrow's dawn." Some sayings are serious and some are humorous but all will stimulate thought and discussion. Each is credited to a particular tribe, but no sources are cited. In *The Zebra's Stripes and Other African Animal Tales*, Stewart (2004) weaves proverbs from various groups after each folktale. For instance, in "How Leopard Got His Spots," she shares a Zulu proverb that translates: "The leopard eats by means of its spot" meaning "If one wants to succeed, one must develop characteristics that distinguish one from others" (p. 19).

Finally, one of the most important functions of folklore is to introduce and indirectly teach the rules of society, to impress upon individuals specific values, attitudes, and beliefs. To help with this function, African storytellers often use folktales which are "the central pillar of the African oral tradition" (Kizza, 2010, p. 12). Folktales suggest accepted means of social behavior, offer practical advice, and highlight the consequences of greed, pride, and untrustworthiness (Stewart, 2004, p. 10). Most of these folktales are classified as morality and character building tales, conveying specific messages to listeners (Kizza, 2010). At times, the moral is offered at the end of the story as in the collection *The Girl Who Married a Ghost and Other Tales from Nigeria* (Onyefulu, 2010), but other times, the moral or message must be inferred as in the collection *The Goddess of the Kitchen and Other Stories: Folktales from Africa* (Oyefeso, 2000).

In *The Tortoise's Gift: A Story from Zambia* (Don, 2012), Tortoise is able to use his natural characteristics (slow and steady) to solve a dilemma that proves to be beyond the talents of defter animals. A similar tale is found in *The Amazing Tree* (Kilaka, 2009). When a drought occurs, there is an amazing tree with ripe fruit that will not fall. Rabbit suggests that he ask the wise tortoise what to do. The animals agree, but they tell Rabbit he is too small to go. Instead, they send the big animals. The tortoise tells them to call the tree by its name. However, Elephant and Water Buffalo forget the name on the way home. This happens again and again until the animals finally send Rabbit who returns, utters the name, and the fruit falls from the tree. The animals state that they have learned a lesson: "Everyone is important here, no matter whether they are big or small" (n.p.).

Size is again an issue in "The Race" from *Hausaland Tales from the Nigerian Marketplace* (McIntosh, 2002). Frog and her family live by the river, but hippo takes no notice of them and often walks through the marsh stepping on the frogs and crushing them. Hippo is the fastest runner, so Frog challenges her to a race in order to get some attention. Frog devises a plan to win the race and Hippo is disgraced.

Friendship is at the heart of several tales. In *True Friends* (Kilaka, 2006), Rat and Elephant are best friends, but Rat is industrious, gathering and storing grain, while Elephant likes to relax. One year when the harvest is lean, Elephant worries that he may go hungry. Elephant convinces Rat to store his grain at Elephant's house but when Rat is hungry, Elephant will not share. Eventually, Elephant apologizes, and Rat imparts the moral of the story: "True friends don't think only of themselves, even when times are hard" (n.p.). *The Magic Gourd* (Diakité, 2003) pairs a rabbit struggling to feed his starving family and a chameleon trapped in a thorny bush. The rabbit saves the chameleon, and the chameleon gives the rabbit a magic gourd that when ordered to do so, fills itself with an object such as food. The rabbit shares with family and friends, but a greedy king steals the gourd and orders it to fill with gold. The rabbit is able to regain the gourd with the help of another reward from the chameleon. However, the rabbit shows generosity and leaves the king with all the gold and food he had created. The king learns, "Let us appreciate what we have been given" (p. 27) and the rabbit and the chameleon understand that "loyal friendships are the true treasures that make one rich" (p. 28). Finally, in *Fresh Fish* (Kilaka, 2005), Chimpanzee comes home with a boat full of fish and intends to share his catch with his friends, but Dog steals the fish. Chimpanzee and his friends take Dog to the village for a trial. He is found guilty, and for his sentence, he must plant twice as many trees on Tree Planting Day as the others. Dog works hard and completes the task before the others. All is forgiven in the end.

The perils of vanity are spotlighted in two tales. In *Mee-An and the Magic Serpent* (Diakité, 2007), Mee-An is beautiful and vain and searching for a suitor who is perfect, without blemishes. Unfortunately, a serpent learns this and disguises himself as a flawless suitor. When the disguised serpent is around, strange things happen which others feel are bad signs, but Mee-An pays no attention. She marries the serpent, and he takes Mee-An and her sister to his home. Later, the sisters discover the serpent in the river singing a song about fattening up the sisters so he can eat them. The two girls flee and return home with the help of a heron. Finally, in *Sense Pass King* (Tchana, 2002), a king becomes jealous of an exceptional young girl. She becomes known as Sense Pass King (meaning she is smarter than the king). The king sends his soldiers to kill her but she outwits them, so the king orders her to live with him in the palace to give him her counsel. When the king travels to a faraway kingdom to find a bride, Sense Pass King saves the expedition from a dragon with seven heads. When they return home, the king takes all the credit. The soldiers reveal the truth, so the people drive the king from the palace and make Sense Pass King their queen.

African Oral and Traditional Literature as a Pedagogical Tool

In keeping with our five functions of folklore framework, we have organized the instructional applications around these purposes. These activities should engage students with oral and traditional literature to promote content area literacy and a greater appreciation and comprehension of global issues.

Skill Development

Teachers can use the call and response technique with African riddles to foster both oral language development and inferential comprehension. Three resources for example riddles follow.

- *The House with No Door: African Riddle-Poems* (Swann, 1998)
- *Riddles of Abagusii of Kenya* (Okemwa, 2011)
- "African Riddles" at http://kwanzaaguide.com/2010/07/african-riddles/

Dilemma tales are excellent for building discussion and debate skills. Per Bascom (1975, p. 1) some "dilemma tales, which border on tall tales, ask the listeners to judge the relative skills of characters who have performed incredible feats." Teachers could have students compare and judge the characters in *Master Man: A Tale of Nigeria* (Shepherd, 2001) and *Sense Pass King: A story from Cameroon* (Tchana, 2002). "The Cowtail Switch" at http://www.ncsu.edu/chass/extension/ghanatalk/folktales/cow.html is an online example of a dilemma that can be used for discussion purposes. In addition, teachers can refer to dilemma tale examples adapted from Bascom (1975) and used in lesson plans on two websites: gailherman. net/documents/african_dilemma_tales08.doc (Herman, 2008) *and* https:// sites.google.com/site/bjohnsonsteachingportfolio/lesson-plans-1/english-ii/examples-of-differnt-unit-lesson-plans/lesson-plan-a (Cook, 2010).

Social Control: In the collection, *Misoso: Once upon a Time Tales from Africa,* Aardema (1994), shares a Liberian tale, "The Boogey Man's Wife." As she notes, the Liberians who were freed American slaves were probably familiar with the Boogey Man, a cautionary tale figure from America. In her afterword to the story, she states that such characters are common in many groups. The Ashanti have Sasabonsum, the Nandi warn children about Chemosit, and the San caution their children about Whitemouth. Students can research these figures using literature and web-based resources. Also, cautionary tales have been likened to urban legends. Students may want to compare and contrast African cautionary tales with various urban legends and discuss the similarities and differences.

Explanation: After reading numerous pourquoi tales, students can write their own "how an animal got a trait" story. Another option would be to have students search for pourquoi tales on YouTube and after listening to several of these, create their own video version and post it to the web.

Entertainment: Just as with cautionary tale figures, there are different tricksters in various parts of Africa and in other cultures. Students can research different tricksters and create a geographic display by region and country with the trickster's name and form, for example, spider, hare, and so forth. Too, students enjoy performing readers' theatre scripts and puppet shows. Pourquoi tales such as Aardema's (1975) *Why Mosquitos Buzz in People's Ears* and trickster tales like Eric Kimmel's (1988) *Anansi and the Moss-Covered Rock* are ideal for such purposes.

Education: *The Zebra's Stripes and Other African Animal Tales* (Stewart, 2004) is a good resource for cross curricular connections to help students learn about the wildlife in Africa. After each folktale there is a table with interesting facts about the animals highlighted in the tale, for example, habitats, physical characteristics, dietary habits, reproduction, and so forth. Similarly, in *African Tales: A Barefoot Collection* (Mhlophe, 2009), each tale is linked to a country which can help students expand their knowledge of the geography of Africa. The book begins with a map of Africa and some bulleted facts about the continent. Then, the book is organized with a basic introduction and bulleted facts about the country and a tale from that country.

Finally, one fascinating aspect of proverbs is their similarity across cultures and languages. The translations may vary somewhat, but the meaning—the values being stressed—is the same. Using *The Night Has Ears: African Proverbs* (Bryan, 1999) and *The Zebra's Stripes and Other African Animal Tales* (Stewart, 2004) as a starting point, students can map the proverbs cited and then conduct additional research for similar proverbs from other countries and languages.

Conclusion

As we noted at the beginning of this chapter, urbanization and more than a century of European colonization have resulted in the loss of both cultures and languages in Africa. As Diakité (2010) stresses, oral literature is a rich source of history and knowledge to connect Africans to their precolonial ancestors. Still, as with many cultures, the oral tradition is not valued in the same way as the written, and because of this, many stories and traditions will be lost. We hope that our analysis of the rich instructional possibilities within African folklore will encourage teachers to share these stories and to continue to educate and entertain future generations with oral literature.

REFERENCES

African Riddles. (2010). Kwanzaa guide. Retrieved from http://kwanzaaguide. com/2010/07/african-riddles/

Bascom, W. R. (1975). *African dilemma tales*. The Hague, the Netherlands: Mouton.

Cook, B. (2010). African Folktales Unit, Lesson Plan Example: Dilemmas. Retrieved from https://sites.google.com/site/bjohnsonsteachingportfolio/lesson-plans-1/english-ii/examples-of-differnt-unit-lesson-plans/lesson-plan-a

Hadaway, N. L. (2004). Collecting folklore in the home, school, and community. In T. A. Young (Ed.), *Happily ever after: Sharing folk literature to elementary and middle school children.* Newark, DE: International Reading Association.

Hamilton, V. (1988). *In the beginning: Creation stories from around the world.* San Diego, CA: Harcourt Brace Jovanovich.

Herman, G. N. (2008). African dilemma tales. Retrieved from gailherman.net/documents/african_dilemma_tales08.doc

Kizza, I. N. (2010). *The oral tradition of the Baganda of Uganda: A study and anthology of legends, myths, epigrams, and folktales.* Jefferson, NC: McFarland.

Mama, R. (2006). *Why monkeys live in trees and other stories from Benin.* Williamantic, CT: Curbstone Press.

Namullundah F. (2011). *The Bukusu of Kenya: Folktales, culture and social identities* Durha, NC: Carolina Academic Press.

Nikolajeva, M. (2011). Translation and crosscultural reception. In S. A. Wolf, K. Coats, P. Enciso, & C. A Jenkins (Eds.), *Handbook of research on children's and young adult literature* (pp. 404-418). New York, NY: Routledge.

Panford, S., Nyaney, M. O., Amoah, S. O., Aidoo, N. G. (2001). Using folk media in HIV/AIDS prevention in rural Ghana. *American Journal of Public Health, 91*, 1559-1562.

Scheub, H. (2005). *African tales.* Madison, WI: The University of Wisconsin Press.

Silver, D. (2001). Songs and storytelling: Bringing health messages to life in Uganda. *Education for Health: Change in Learning & Practice, 14*, 51-61.

Smith, A. M. (2004). *The girl who married a lion and other tales from Africa.* New York, NY: Pantheon.

The Cowtail Switch. (n.d.) Retrieved from at http://www.ncsu.edu/chass/extension/ghanatalk/folktales/cow.html

CHILDREN'S BOOKS CITED

Aardema, V. (1975). *Why mosquitos buzz in people's ears.* New York, NY: Dial.

Aardema, V. (1994). *Misoso: Once upon a time tales from Africa.* New York, NY: Scholastic.

Aardema, V. (2000). *Anansi does the impossible: An Ashanti tale.* New York, NY: Aladdin.

Achebe, C. (2011). *How the leopard got his claws.* Somerville, MA: Candlewick Press.

Agambila, G. A. (2002). *Solma: Tales from northern Ghana.* Accra: Ghana Universities Press.

Arkhurst, J. C. (2012). *The first adventures of spider: West African folktales.* New York, NY: Little Brown.

Badoe, A, & Diakite, B. W. (2001). *The pot of wisdom: Ananse stories.* Toronto, Canada: Groundwood.

Bryan, A. (1999). *The night has ears: African proverbs.* New York, NY: Simon & Schuster.

Bryan, A. (2003). *Beautiful blackbird*. New York, NY: Atheneum/Simon & Schuster.

Cleveland, R. (2006). *The clever monkey*. Atlanta, GA: August House.

Cushman, A. (Translator). (2010). *Zarma foktales of Niger*. Niantic, CT: Quale Press.

Diakité, B. W. (2003). *The magic gourd*. New York, NY: Scholastic.

Diakité, B. W. (2007). *Mee-An and the magic serpent*. Toronto, Canada: Groundwood.

Diakité, B. W. (2010). *A gift from childhood: Memories of an African boyhood*. Toronto, Canada: Groundwood.

Don, L. (2012). *The tortoise's gift: A story from Zambia*. Cambridge, MA: Barefoot.

Eisner, Will. (2003). *Sundiata: A legend of Africa*. New York, NY: NBM.

Folarin, A., & Folarin, M. (2001). *The three birds from Olongo*. Ibadan, Nigeria: Spectrum Books.

Green, J. (2010). *West African myths*. New York, NY: Gareth Stevens.

Haley, G. E. (1988). *A story, a story*. New York, NY: Aladdin. (Original work published 1970)

Kilaka, J. (2005). *Fresh fish*. Toronto, Canada: Groundwood.

Kilaka, J. (2006). *True friends*. Toronto, Canada: Groundwood.

Kilaka, J. (2009). *The amazing tree*. New York, NY: NorthSouth.

Kimmel, E. A. (1988). *Anansi and the moss-covered rock*. New York, NY: Holiday House.

Kimmel, E. A. (1992). *Anansi goes fishing*. New York, NY: Holiday House.

Kimmel, E. A. (1994). *Anansi and the talking melon*. New York, NY: Holiday House.

Kimmel, E. A. (2002). *Anansi and the magic stick*. New York, NY: Holiday House.

Kojo, K. P. (2011). *The parade: A stampede of stories about Ananse, the trickster spider*. New York, NY: Frances Lincoln.

Krensky, S. (2009). *The lion and the hare: An East African folktale*. Minneapolis, MN: Millbrook Press.

Matthews, J., & Matthews, C. (2008). *Trick of the tale: A collection of trickster tales*. Cambridge, MA: Candlewick.

McIntosh, G. (2002). *Hausaland tales from the Nigerian marketplace*. North Haven, CT: Linnet Books.

Medearis, A. S. (1994). *The singing man*. New York, NY: Holiday House.

Mhlophe, G. (2009). *African tales: A Barefoot collection*. Cambridge, MA: Barefoot Books.

Mollel, T. (2009). *The orphan boy*. Markham, Ontario: Fitzhenry & Whiteside.

Norfolk, B., & Norfolk, S. (2006). *Anansi and the pot of beans*. Atlanta, GA: August House.

Okemwa, C. (2011). *Riddles of Abagusii of Kenya*. Nairobi, Kenya: Nsemia.

Onyefulu, I. (2010), *The girl who married a ghost: And other tales from Nigeria*. New York, NY: Frances Lincoln.

Oyefeso, K. (2000). *The goddess of the kitchen and other stories: Folktales from Africa*. Ibadan, Nigeria: Spectrum.

Postma, M. (2002). Mmadipetsane. In N. Mandela (Ed), *Nelson Mandela's favorite African folktales* (pp. 43-47). New York, NY: W. W. Norton.

Savory, P. (2002). The hare's revenge. In N. Mandela (Ed), *Nelson Mandela's favorite African folktales* (71-73). New York, NY: W. W. Norton.

Shepherd, A. (2001). *Master man: A tale of Nigeria*. New York, NY: HarperCollins.

Stewart, D. (2004). *The zebra's stripes and other African animal tales*. Cape Town, SA: Struik.

Swann, B. (1998). *The house with no door: African riddle-poems*. Boston, MA: Brian Swann (Author)

Tate, E. E. (1993). *Retold African myths*. Logan, IA: Perfection Learning.

Tchana, K. (2002). *Sense Pass King: A story from Cameroon*. New York, NY: Holiday House.

Tracey, H. (2002). The cat who came indoors. In N. Mandela (Ed), *Nelson Mandela's favorite African folktales* (pp. 12-14). New York, NY: W. W. Norton.

Washington, D. L. (2004). A pride of African tales. New York, NY: HarperCollins/Amistad.

Wisniewski, D. (1999). Sundiata: Lion King of Mali. New York, NY: Sandpiper.

CHAPTER 2

WHAT'S IN A SINGING GAME?

Exploring Children's Oral Literature

Akosua Obuo Addo

INTRODUCTION

Students experience new cultures and think in new and stimulating ways when they perform African games in the K-12 classroom, yet there is scholarly writing on the connection between the language aspects of singing games and the elements of literature (Nyoni & Nyoni, 2013; Wiggins, 2007). Typically, African singing games are used in the music curriculum rather than across the curriculum. There are several successful examples on how and what to use, (Adzenyah, Maraire, & Tucker, 1997; Amoaku, 1991; Campbell, Williamson, & Perron, 1996; Serwadda, 1987; Kwami, 1999; Titon, 1997), as well as documentation on the value of African singing games in the United States of America's (U.S.) music curriculum, and in other parts of the world (Addo, 1997, 1998; Burns, 2009; Campbell, 1994; Harrop-Allin, 2011; Harwood, 1998; Kubitsky, 1998; Moore, 2002). Kubitsky (2002) uses the Orff-Schulwerk to frame her discussion on Ewe

African Traditional and Oral Literature as Pedagogical Tools in Contest Area Classrooms: K-12, pages 21–40

children's singing games in the music classroom. Carl Orff and Gunild Keetman developed the Orff Schulwerk, a creative and joyful approach to arts teaching and learning that promotes the use of music, language, and movement for an active learning experience that include speaking, singing, moving, playing, listening, and creativity. Series texts for the U.S. music curriculum (e.g., Spotlight on Music, Music and You) all feature singing games from different parts of Africa. Children, through singing games, express their individual and collective musical experiences in singing, listening, literacy, improvisation, analysis, and interpretation (Addo, 1995, 1996).

Turning to Africa, there is a growing body of literature on the role of indigenous knowledge systems (IKS), like African singing games as examples of culturally relevant materials for the African curriculum (Addo, 1995; Chikovore, Makusha, Muzvidziwa, & Richter, 2012; Mapara, 2009; Nyota & Mapara, 2008; Russell & Zembylas, 2007). Areas include early childhood (Marfo & Biersteker, 2011), mathematics (Mbusi, 2012; Chikodzi & Nyota, 2010; Tatira, Mutambara & Chagwiza, 2012) and movement education (Lyoka, 2007; Mwonga & Wanyama, 2012). Literature on the language and communication in singing games or play lore is emerging (Ogede, 1994), and how these provide foundations for literacy education is also unexplored scholarly literature about the African curriculum.

Mans, Dzansi-McPalm, and Agak (2003) clearly articulate the dimensions of play in African music pedagogy, and discuss forms of musical play that include, clapping with body action games, clapping and singing games, dancing play, music-drama play. I view these forms as play lore because they are oral arts traditions rich with literary perspectives reflecting neocolonial experiences, enabling histories, and shifting identities. Henceforth, I will use the expression play lore and singing games interchangeably. Songs and chants accompany these structured, recreational culturally situated expressions, owned and orally transmitted among children, employ their kinesthetic, sensory, intellectual, emotional, and social abilities; and are performed in the spaces they deem viable for play. In previous studies of children's play lore, I was drawn to the intersections of music, text, drama, and movement in performance, and the meanings children ascribe to these expressions as well as what we can learn about children's ways of knowing through their play performance (Addo, 1995, 1997). My conceptualization of play lore is significant when focusing on language and the elements of literature for literacy education. The purpose of this chapter is to highlight the value, depth and quality of the language and literature of singing games in supporting literacy development in the preschool, kindergarten to Grade 12 (pre-K-12) classroom.

Theoretical Framework

For literacy education to be meaningful, it needs to be creative, engaging, and reflective. Critical pedagogy offers a framework for students and teachers engaging in dialogue about play lore of various cultures with the aim of creating a global literate community. It is not my intention to go through the history and evolution of critical pedagogy in an attempt to establish children's play lore in literacy education. Nonetheless, increasing the motivation to learn, through engagement, creative experiences grounded in reflection, is the teacher's role. Therefore, Hake (1998) position on the interactive engagement of students as always heads-on and usually involving hands-on activities, which yield immediate feedback through discussions with peers and/or instructors is relevant to the critical pedagogy thesis. After all, literacy is much more than decoding and encoding texts on a page. It involves an active engagement with information in all its forms, understanding of this information and the creation of new information (Wink, 2010). Critical literacy, the expression often used when critical pedagogy and literacy education meet, seems to serve this purpose but to a lesser degree. Within the critical literacy framework, all knowledge is legitimate, and embracing diverse knowledge gives all children the opportunity to contribute to discussions, knowledge verification, and recreation (Wink, 2010). Providing a variety of experiences demands multiple ways of knowing and an even playing ground in the classroom (Freire, 1973/1994). With this in mind, communities of learning need to raise children's awareness, Freire's conscientization, about the similarities between their engagement in singing games performance and learning. This exploration of singing games in the literacy curriculum is more than identifying, understanding or addressing power, inequalities or injustices in learning contexts. It is also about the capacity to create active learning contexts, filled with questions, discussions, creative expression, and real examples of meaningful learning.

Play lore in literacy education is responsive and meaningful work. Culturally responsive teaching provides a diverse knowledge base, model caring to learning communities, which define respectful intercultural communication, and active learning (Gay, 2002). Improving communication, a fundamental aspect of socialization, supports the development of literacy. Arts play or singing games in performance is a socialization context (Addo, 2012). Rather than children standing idly, like receiving information in a typical classroom, they perform or comment on the singing games. It is meaningful because they own these play experiences and, therefore, have the cultural competence to question and make a meaningful contribution to the performance. Critical theorists (Giroux, 2000; Greene, 1986) would argue for teaching and learning that supports the active learning environment which exposes, discussed and solved social injustices because this is culturally relevant. Ladson-Billings (1995, 2009) sees academic success, cultural competence, and critical consciousness as resting on culturally relevant pedagogy. Critical consciousness develops when Freire (1973/1994) conscientization is nurtured. A lack of examination of the beliefs and assumptions about cultural diversity (one based on experience and constructed understanding rather than rigorous research) limits teacher's understanding and skills for engaging all students (Carlos, 2005). Bransford, Darling-Hammond, and LePage (2005) in their introduction to the seminal text *Preparing Teachers for a Changing World* have written "teachers must be aware of the many ways in which student learning can unfold in the context of development, learning, differences, language and cultural influences and individual temperaments, interest and approaches to learning" (p. 1). The multiple dimensions of the profession are daunting to even to the most experienced teacher.

Concerned with approaches to learning, Wlodkowski (2003) argues for a motivational framework for culturally responsive teaching. His four areas for consideration captures several of the dimensions articulated in Bransford et al. (2005), (a) establishing inclusion through respectful class-room relationships, (b) developing attitudes through relevance and choice, (c) enhancing meaning with rigorous learning experiences which include learner's perspectives, and (d) engendering competence with resources learner value. Performance strategies that help students to make connec-tions to literature and the content of literature in singing games situate this framework. Offering multiple modes of learning the singing game performance establishes inclusion and supports a curriculum that includes the learner's perspective. Thus, Okpewho's (1990) performance centered approach to the study of African arts, adds an additional dimension to the Wlodkwoski's motivational framework. Studying play lore students need to evaluate the social construction of the game in its arts fused dimensions. The poetry of singing games is according to Anyidoho (1991) a dramatic presentation, the fusion of poetry, music and action and includes, dance, mime and gesture. Critical pedagogy and culturally responsive teaching within a performance-centered approach frame this inquiry.

The Language of Play Lore

Singing games range from word plays with movement, jump rope games, and hand clapping games in circles and lines, and musical drama. Early literature on singing games from African cultures addresses the verbal and cultural meanings of texts (Abarry, 1989; Addo, 1995; Egblewogbe, 1975; Johnston, 1987; Offei, 1991; Ogede, 1994; Ohene, 1990). Egblewobge

(1975) focused on textual meaning in Ewe game songs, and Johnston wrote from the perspectives of Shangana-Tsonga children's music. Shangana-Tsonga people live in Northern Transvaal and Mozambique. Abarry (1989) wrote about the role Ga children of Ghana's game songs play in their moral, social and emotional development thus focusing on cultural meanings for analysis. Also, writing about Ga children's play songs, Offei (1991), like Abarry, views singing games performance as a means of inculcating socializing patterns for adult life. Ohene (1990) was more interested in game classification based on movement structure rather than language. Addo (1995) wrote about linguistic expressions as underlying the shared values and conceptions of people and, therefore, representing cultural ideas. Likewise, Ogede (1994) begins to explicate the aesthetic in the language of Igede children's play songs, addressing word, sound play, and poetry as symbolic reflections on life and social environment in the rural setting. Hailing from the Benue State of Nigeria, the Igede celebrate seasonal events like the New Yam festival and other life circle events celebrated throughout Africa. Children's musical play reflects the organization of music among the Igede encouraging solidarity, creativity and communal approval (Nicholls, 1988).

Language in the African aesthetic is central to understanding performance events (Addo, 1995); thus it is imperative to address that the language of singing games in performance. Ngugi (1986) argues that languages serve both communication and culture. Even though the cultural dimensions of language in singing games from African cultures increasingly gains attention in the scholarly literatures, its meaning in communication features strongly over possibilities in literacy education. Indeed when children play games, they communicate in patterns through language and gesture. These communication patterns may be in a structured form creating literary expressions, figures of speech or may be loosely presented, fluid responses to the flow of the game. I have written elsewhere that in play or games "each gesture, recitation, declamation, lyric, and instrumental rendition communicates information to both the participants and the audience" (Addo, 1995, p. 89). Even though communication event grows with and within each performance, the chapter presents the selected singing games selected for analysis as one event, each representing a culmination of several events.

Orature in Play Lore

Literature is artistically developed writing that uses language to capture the individual and collective experiences of people in places and spaces. Orature is more than oral literature because it foregrounds the indigenous language, reflects history, social fabric, collective, audience-informed performance and thus facilitates communication (Hawley, 2001). In a lecture to *study abroad students in Ghana*, Kwadwo Opoku-Agyemang (2010) spoke of three forms of orature: (a) short prose narratives that include proverbs and riddles, (b) oral poetry, including hymns, dirges, praise poetry, and poetry of abuse, and (c) drum language. He cited Chinua Achebe's (1958) *Things Fall Apart* as the first example of written oral literature, thus uses an inclusive approach to defining orature as all forms of narrative. Orature includes both written and oral forms. Singing games or play lore are orature with a distinctive character. Whether sung or chanted, the performance of singing games begins with a personal and collective initiative to engage in the game, and the ability to demonstrate a variety of literary ideas (character, setting, plot, problem/solution, language use, movement, themes, illustrations, genres) while making sense of and contributing to cultural expressions. Dube (2003) presents a summary on Ndebele children's oral literature and classifies them into lullabies, nursery rhymes and games, riddles, folktales, songs, jokes, tongue twisters, material arts, and games and nick names. Nyoni and Nyoni (2013) view singing games as examples of indigenous knowledge found in orature. The shifts between oral forms and writing make singing games and play lore a viable approach for studying literature.

Singing games like literature have recurring patterns that are rhythmic, and present unique dispositions. According to Ngugi (1986) when these repeated patterns build knowledge. In this chapter, my interest lies in the literacy knowledge developed in the performance of singing games. Whether or not children are aware of these constructions is not the focus of the chapter, but rather it is my intention to draw readers' attention to the wealth of language arts information that exists in the play lore for literacy education.

Interestingly, play lore exhibits the same features of communications arts as intergenerational, interdisciplinary, and consistently evolving. In the performance of African singing games among children, these dimensions are quite obvious. An analysis of singing games reveals that its language aspects, like other African literary texts, cannot be meaningfully discussed without the acknowledgement of its interconnection with embodied movement (dance, mime, and gesture), sonic (music) and visual arts (costume and scenery) (Nzewi, 2003). Interestingly, there is a parallel between Anyidoho's (1991) articulation of poetry performance and the performance of singing games. Like poetry in performance, singing games integrate artistic forms, audience, and the artist to provide a unifying experience. Children bring singing games to life in the dramatic chanting of the text similar to a poet's dramatic reading, and reinforce the verbal text of singing games with body language and paralinguistic devices. Also, because singing games occur in time, place and space, there are analytical implications of these intersections with children's interactions, providing a deeper layer of understanding of the singing game literature. For literary understanding to occur, children need to read, write, move, and listen to literature as well as critically reflect on techniques and language devices used to send a message. In the classroom, children will use singing games to illustrate and develop an awareness of how they creatively and playfully produce culturally relevant literature.

A performance analysis, therefore, best captures the interdependent elements and interdisciplinary aspects of language expression in singing games performance offering several applications for literature education. Literature enhances communication and socialization and these critical aspects of literacy development are the ultimate aim of schooling. Communication in singing games demands the ability to think, experience, explore, remember, collaborate, imagine, and participate on a wide range of topics and styles. Meaningful communication demands frequency or repetition, facility, depth-of-thought and creativity. Socialization through the performance of singing games includes the ability to demonstrate solidarity, supports inclusion, encourages exploration, cooperation, and cultural interlocution and the acknowledgement of gender roles with respect to African cultures (Addo, 1995, 1997). Used loosely, references to Ghanaian cultures are examples of African cultures. Questions explored include: How do Ghanaian singing games provide a context for studying African literature? What aspects of literature are evident in the textual content of Ghanaian singing games? What do singing games performances communicate?

In what follows, I will first present an analysis of three singing games and pay attention to language arts and literature content, context, and communication in performance. Space will not permit me to analyze the range of singing games as contexts studying African literature and literacy education. After each analysis of the three selected games, I will provide some pedagogical implications for using each singing game in literacy education. Then, I will close the chapter with a discussion of themes, skills development in the recreation and performance of these games offer insights for and support literacy instruction.

Range of Ghanaian Singing Games and Contexts for Studying African Literature

Singing games include short dialogues presented in call and response, monologues, descriptive passages, appellations, nick names, titles, proverbs, praise poetry, unedited prose, riddles, lullabies, tongue twisters, jokes, songs, and material arts. The three singing games selected are a monologue, "an appellations/title" play lore (Wɔfre me),   me short dialogues in call and response (Hena Na ɔkuto), and a legend in a descriptive passage (Robert). The Akan dominate my choices because, in addition to speaking Twi, I have conducted my research in Akan speaking areas and have only recently began to branch out into other areas of the country. Akan peoples speak Bia and Akan, live mostly in Southern Ghana. Including non-Akan, the Akan languages are spoken by 44% of Ghanaians making Akan the most spoken local languages in the country (Asante & Akyea, 2013). Considering the range of singing games will provide a picture of the developmental nature of language acquisition within play and language use as literature. The notations provided are only approximations to show the melo-rhythms (Nzewi, 1997) and slow of the singing game. Western notation does not accurately capture the rhythmic nuances of music from non-Western cultures.

Monologue-Titles (Wɔfre me)

Wɔfre me (Clap clap clap clap)

I am called (Clap clap clap clap)

Wɔfre me Clap clap clap clap)

I am called (Clap clap clap clap)

Wɔfre me Irene Osan'dɛɛ

I am called Irene because ...

"I" fata me.

"I" Suits me

Context, Content, and Communication

This is a chant and circle game in where each child tells his or her name as well as the first letter of the name. This game is about empathy and respect for each child in the circle and a central aspect of education. It is also about welcoming children into a new classroom and identity formation. What is interesting about this game is the collective syncopated clapping punctuates the call to play. All children chant the first phrase while clapping and one child, after another, moves into the circle dancing and clapping along, and introduces herself or himself.

Repetition of text characterizes this oral poetry in performance. The child repeats his or her name to convey the importance of knowing her name. The repeated rhythmic patterns the children clap give the poetry flow and movement. Much like drum language in oral literature, the repeated clapping in between short phrases send a message (Yankah, 1982). In performance, the child in the center needs to speak within the macros structure of the meter provided.

Beyond the repetition of phrases, we observe singing games as a starting point in the conversation about self here, illustrating Anyidoho's principle of continuity (Wilkinson, 1988). The children repeat the first letter of each name reinforcing the conversation about self.

Pedagogical Implications

Language arts are fundamental to all communication and therefore, include the learning of social mores. In this singing game, the children learn to present themselves in the community of players. Much like the community of learners in the classroom, the child needs to negotiate the classroom dynamics and, therefore, communication with peers and teaching staff is central.

This game will serve well as part of morning greeting. Not only does it reinforces and affirms each child, but also, reminds children on a fundamental aspect of language learning—sounds that begin their names. Playing the monologue will also remove the "drill" in some pedagogical practices. The teacher may choose to ask the children to identify the last letter in their names while they play the game. Creating games with phonemes, the smallest unit of linguistic sounds, teachers will be developing linguistic vocabulary during play. Phonemes are similar to a musical note or tones the children make during play as well as a gesture in play.

Present in *Wɔfre me* are the vowels: /e/, /a/, /ɔ /, /e/, in addition to all the vowels, in the child' name. Although /ɔ /, pronounced "door," "all," or "jaw," /e/ "air," "there" or "where" are not present in written English as vowels, the sounds are in most words. While playing the game, the teacher may choose to have children say the vowel sound presented on a card or visual aid. Vocabulary may be built with word families- rhyming words with the text of the singing game.

The rhythmic clapping allows the child in the center of the circle the opportunity to think about the letter beginning his or her name. Moving into the circle the rest of the children predict the responses of the child in the center creating what Van Berkum (2008) and his colleagues call an event related potential (ERP). These occur when the brain senses a stimulus, often a word or tone, and adjusts to make sense of a whole sentence. The value of singing games in general is that the movement of the child into the center is a cue for responding in playful communication to game demands. Playing this game builds fluency (the speed, accuracy, rate, phrasing of expression) as well as comprehension (using elaboration, fluency, flexibility, and originality to demonstrate an understanding of the language context).

Short Dialogues in Call and Response (Hena Na ɔkuto)

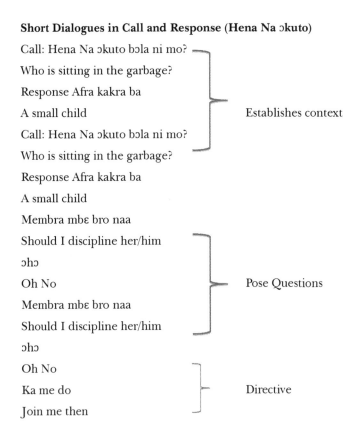

Call: Hena Na ɔkuto bɔla ni mo?

Who is sitting in the garbage?

Response Afra kakra ba

A small child

Call: Hena Na ɔkuto bɔla ni mo?

Who is sitting in the garbage?

Response Afra kakra ba

A small child   Establishes context

Membra mbɛ bro naa

Should I discipline her/him

ɔhɔ

Oh No   Pose Questions

Membra mbɛ bro naa

Should I discipline her/him

ɔhɔ

Oh No

Ka me do   Directive

Join me then

Context, Content, and Communication

Another circle game with a child is sitting in the middle of a circle, surrounded by children clapping while yet another child runs around of the outside of the periphery of the circle. There are several symbolic referents in this singing game. The circle represents a calamity—garbage or uncomfortable situation. One child runs outside the periphery of the circle asking questions about who is in the circle. The rest of the children answer her questions. She directs a selected child to join her in the run around the circle. By the end of the game, all the children as running around the circle, and following the leader.

Another example of oral poetry with repetition of short dialogues to keeps the play moving. In this performance, the children clap, a steady beat throughout the performance of short phrases. Here, the phrases include complete questions, short single word, or idea answers to direct commands. In the performance of this singing game, the children not only respond to questions but also have to respond to a movement directive.

Interestingly, a metric feel established with whole body movements, sung text and simultaneous handclapping points further to the continuity that exists within the performance and through the performance of the game. The child's command is simple and direct- *"join me!"*

Pedagogical Implications

Short dialogues provide opportunities for children to create their own sentences in context. The ongoing clapping in the performance of *Hena Na ɔkuto* is a scaffold for fluency in language development. An analysis of the short dialogue reveals that there are different parts to this singing game. The first repeated question ("Who is in the circle?") and answer ("A small child!") establishes the context of the play. The children may in small groups create a new context for playing a new version of *Hena Na ɔkuto*.

The next repeated question invites some suggestions from the rest of the children. Once in the play context, the children may think about what they would like to ask. This develops the children's ability to think about questions as well as provide answers to the question. Commeyras and Summer (1998) found that grade two children are eager to pose questions about what they need to know and understand about literature. In the same way, given a context for play, children will be willing to pose questions about the dialogue topics they choose. The teacher may assemble all the scenarios and questions the children pose, have the children play the same circle game with the new dialogue and end with the same directive as the game. Commeyras and Summer found that children listen more to each other, another important part of communication and were willing to discuss the questions they had created.

Using this singing game as a point of beginning (Anyidoho, 1991) and departure, children's level of participation in language exercises, as well as their understanding of language context and content will increase. The social aspects of the play, the circle structure, transferred to a small group, student oral participation in thinking about questions will reduce fear and support language learning.

Legends in Descriptive Passages (Robert),

Robert (2x) Papapa (clapping 2x)

Robert Mensa gokipa nɔma wae

[Robert mɛnsa gokipa nɔma waɪ]

'Robert Mensa was the goalkeeper with jersey number one'

Aka n-na-nsa na ɔ-a-kɔ aburokyire

[aka nansa na wakɔ aburotɕire]

'Three days before he was to travel overseas.'

Kwasea bi te hɔ ɔ-m-pɛ n'asɛm

[kwæsɪa bi tɪ hɔ ɔmpɛ nasɛm]

'Some foolish person who did not like him,'

Ɔ-a-kɔ-fa pentoa de a-wɔ ne mfe

[wakɔfa pɪntʊa dɪ awɔ nɪ ŋfɪ]

'He took a bottle and pierced through his ribs with it.'

Adeɛ kye a, ne yere awo

[adɪɛ tɕɪ a nɪ jɪrɪ awʊ]

'The next day his wife was delivered'

Ne ba no de sɛn, Kofi Anto

[nɪ ba nʊ dɪ sɛɪ Kofi Anto]

'What is the name of the child? Kofi Anto.'

Kofi Anto ɔ-a-n-to ne maame

[kofi antʋ wantʋ nɪ maamɪ]

'Kofi Anto did not see his mother.'

Kofi Anto ɔ-a-n-to ne papa

[kofi antʋ wantʋ nɪ papa]

'Kofi Anto did not see his father.'

Amina tumu gyengyen (chorus)

[amina tumu ʤeŋʤeŋ]

Tu gyengyen tu gyengyen tu gyengyen (chorus 2x)

[tu ʤeŋʤeŋ tu ʤeŋʤeŋ tu ʤeŋʤeŋ]

Robert Mensah

Children in Ghana

Context, Content, and Communication

A handclapping game with song, whole body movement and simultaneous vocables, this game, played in pairs, is popular throughout Ghana. This short prose narrative is a legend about a cultural icon, Robert Mensah, Ghana's premier goalkeeper in the 1970s. He died at age 32 from stab wounds from a bottle to his stomach after a bar brawl. The rest of the story, his wife expecting a child, and the sadness that comes with growing up without a father is present in the text. Cornett (1999) argues that literature addresses the critical questions and this lore address tragedy, violence, fame, grief, and parenting. Soccer is one of the most prominent sports in Ghana.

The thorough-composed contemplation on the loss of a great footballer, the children add their voices to the tragedy all Ghanaians shared. The hand clapping pattern is repetitive through the first eight lines of text. When the children introduce some alliteration for similar to drum language (ʤeŋʤeŋ), they create rhythmic patterns that complement a back and forth hopping whole body movement.

Figure 2.1: Back and forth movement and hand clapping.

There is a play on the naming of his son "Kofi Anto" meaning, "Kofi did not meet.." and there is with a pause referring back to his father. The facts about whether or not Robert Mensah's wife was expecting a child is yet to be verified.

Pedagogical Implications

The repetition of final consonant and the accented syllable in the expression "gyengyen" imitates the sound of drums in Ghanaian culture. The percussive aspects of the phrase give children opportunities to exploring with the starting sound /gy/ and closing sound /n/. Also, the familiar tune helps with reading flow and the children make create a new story to go with the melody.

For topics, children could create a time line of the history of soccer in the United States. Also the U.S. national team has met Ghana on a couple of occasion for the Fédération Internationale de Football Associa-tion (FIFA) cup. This could be the spin off subject for a short essay.

Children may analyze the development of the story in this singing game. The performance introduces the main character—Robert Mensah from the onset, and the sequence of event that followed make for a com-pelling narrative. A proficient student of literature needs to be able to identify basic literary elementary like, setting, plot, problem, and solution and character. Because this singing game carries with it a moral, it is vital for the children to explore relationships within the story. Also discussing their varying points of view on the problem and solutions will lead to dis-cussions of their near-to-home topics. They may then organize their self-selected topics into a sequential structure for story telling.

THE LITERACY CURRICULUM

Children develop their own distinct language patterns in play, and these may not on the surface reflect the formal language of schooling, and in Ghana these are beset with influences from home, peers, colonial language restrictions the church and simply social life. Children will have a glimpse into the life and language of Ghanaian children when they play, analyze, and use these games to create new games and become aware of the many possibilities with language learning.

Independence represents an enabling historical event that has im-pacted language learning in Ghana. The language of Ghana is evolving. An analysis of Ghanaian English reveals the nuances in language use that reflect Ghanaian constructions or the indigenous languages. Reviewing the shifts in language learning and the shifting collective and individual identities in the school setting might provide some pointers for literacy education. All these make literacy education a daunting task, yet, some ideas emerge from the analysis of these singing games.

  a. Dramatic reading of singing games texts—role playing
     A dramatic reading of the singing game text, particularly "Wɔfre me" and "Hena Na ɔkuto Bɔla ni mo?" (Who is sitting in the gar-bage?) is excellent for role playing exercises. By the end of grade four, children in the U.S. are to be able to identify and describe the components of the communication process. These singing games have a speaker/ and a receiver or listener.
  b. Addressing embodied arts,
     All the singing games embody arts including social aspects of learn-ing as well as encouraging visual imagery for interdisciplinary think-ing. Children develop motor sensory, auditory-listening, speech and

language, singing, literacy, creative skills while playing with play lore.

c. Exploring polarity for time—place

Comparing and contrasting similar games in North American will provide opportunities for exploring time and place. Several historical and social events inform children's play lore in North America and Ghana alike. These play lore may serve as a catalyst for social and historical criticism as well and literary analysis.

d. Literature

The themes that emerge are numerous. Inclusiveness in "*Wɔfre me*" and "*Hena Na ɔkuto Bɔla ni mo?*" (Who is sitting in the garbage?) suggests finding ways to coexist, unity, respecting difference. Also, pervasive in these play lore is the subject of community building - etiquette, respect, personal space, gender roles, family roles. The representation, sociopolitical, and historical realities come through clearly in the tragedy "Robert Mensah."

Here are some some examples of developing fact-finding teams on topics of interest, role-playing events, finding literature on events, creating new poetry, support studying various concepts in literature:

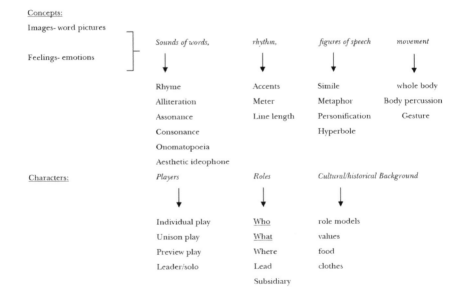

Concepts:				
Images- word pictures				
	Sounds of words,	*rhythm,*	*figures of speech*	*movement*
Feelings- emotions	↓	↓	↓	↓
	Rhyme	Accents	Simile	whole body
	Alliteration	Meter	Metaphor	Body percussion
	Assonance	Line length	Personification	Gesture
	Consonance		Hyperbole	
	Onomatopoeia			
	Aesthetic ideophone			
Characters:	*Players*	*Roles*	*Cultural/historical Background*	
	↓	↓	↓	
	Individual play	Who	role models	
	Unison play	What	values	
	Preview play	Where	food	
	Leader/solo	Lead	clothes	
		Subsidiary		

CONCLUSION

Singing games reflect communication. In this chapter, I demonstrated with six singing games the developmental and recurring communication patterns that are useful for literacy education. Additionally, the performance analysis shows the melo-rhythmic aspects of communication arts give the singing game performance flow and the child the structure for language expression. Repetition of phrases, figures of speech, tongue twisters, riddles, and dialogues all performance with movement and song, are intergenerational, interdisciplinary and consistently evolving. Singing games contribute to the body of African oral literature and support child-centered, culturally relevant literacy development, and suggests a pedagogical process for making this possible.

REFERENCES

Abarry, A. (1989). The role of play songs in the moral, social and emotional development of African children. *Research in African Literatures, 20*(2), 202-216.

Achebe, C. (1958). *Things fall apart*. New York, NY: Anchor Books.

Addo, A. O. (1995). Ghanaian children's music cultures: video ethnography of selected singing games. Doctoral dissertation, University of British Columbia, Canada, *Dissertation Abstracts International* 57/03, AACNN05909.

Addo, A. O. (1996). A multimedia analysis of selected Ghanaian children's play songs. *Bulletin of the Council for Research in Music Education, 129*, 1-28.

Addo, A. O. (1997). Children's idiomatic expressions of cultural knowledge. *International Journal of Music Education, 30*, 15-25.

Addo, A. (1998). Melody, language and the development of singing in the curriculum. *British Journal of Music Education, 15*(2), 139-148.

Addo, A. O. (2012). African education through the arts. In O. N. Ukpokodu & P. Ukpokodu (Eds.), *Contemporary voices from the margin: African educators on African and American education* (pp. 29-66). Charlotte, NC: Information Age Publishing.

Adzenyah, A., Maraire, J., & Tucker, J. (1997). *Let your voice be heard* (10th anniversary ed.). Danbury, CT: World Music Press.

Amoaku, K. (1991). *African songs and rhythms for children*. Mainz, Germany: Schott.

Anyidoho, K. (1991). Poetry as dramatic performance: The Ghana experience. *Research in African Literature, 22*(2), 41-55.

Asante, C., & Akyea, G. M. (2013). From the horse's own mouth: Gender perception in some Akan and Ewe proverbs. *ABIBISEM: Journal of African Culture and Civilization, 4*, 31-49.

Bransford, J., Darling-Hammond, L., & LePage, P. (2005). Introduction. In L. Darling-Hammond & J. Bransford (Eds.), *Preparing teachers for a changing world: What teachers should learn and be able to do* (pp. 1-39). San Francisco, CA: Jossey-Bass.

Burns, C. D. (2009). *The relevance of African American singing games to Xhosa children in South Africa: A qualitative study* (Doctoral dissertation). Montana State University Bozeman, Montana.

Campbell, P. S. (1994). Multiculturalism and the raising of music teachers for the twenty-first century. *Journal of Music Teacher Education*, *3*(2), 21-29.

Campbell, P. S., Williamson, S. & Perron, P. (1996). *Traditional songs of singing cultures: A world sampler*. International Society for Music Education. Warner Brothers.

Carlos, K. F. (2005). *We need a bigger harvest: The case for culturally relevant pedagogy in general music education* (PhD Dissertation). University of Illinois, Urbana-Champagne.

Chikodzi, I., & Nyota, S. (2010). The interplay of culture and mathematics: The rural Shona classroom. *The Journal of Pan African Studies*, *3*(10), 4-15.

Chikovore, J., Makusha, T., Muzvidziwa, I., & Richter, L. (2012). Children's learning in the diverse sociocultural context of South Africa. *Childhood Education*, *88*(5), 304-308.

Commeyras , M., & Summer, G. (1998). literature questions children want to discuss: what teachers and students learned in a second-grade classroom. *The Elementary School Journal*, *99*(2), 129-152

Cornett, C. E. (1999). *The arts as meaning makers: Integrating literature and the arts throughout the curriculum*. Upper Saddle River, NJ: Merrill Prentice-Hall,

Darling-Hammond, L., Bransford, J., LePage, P., Hammerness, K., & Duffy, H. (Eds.). (2005). *Preparing teachers for a changing world: What teachers should learn and be able to do*. San Francisco, CA: Jossey-Bass.

Diarassouba, S. (2007). *Establishment of Literacy Standards for an Oral Language: The Case of Nafara Discourse Patterns, Côte D'ivoire, West Africa* (Doctoral dissertation). Florida State University, Tallahassee, Florida.

Dube, C. (2003). Children's folklore: Ndebele. In P. M. Peek & K. Yankah, (Eds.), *African folklore: An encyclopedia* (pp. 129-134). New York, NY: Routledge.

Egblewogbe, E. Y. (1975). *Games and songs as educational media*. Accra, Ghana: Ghana Publishing.

Freire, P (1994). *Pedagogy of the oppressed* (Rev. Ed.). (Myra Bergman Ramos. Trans.). New York, NY: Continuum. (Original work published 1973)

Gay, G. (2002) Preparing for culturally responsive teaching. *Journal of Teacher Education*, *53*(2), 106-116.

Giroux, H. (2000). *Impure acts: The practical politics of cultural studies*. New York, NY: Routledge.

Greene, M. (1986). In search of a critical pedagogy. *Harvard Educational Review*, *56*(4), 427-442.

Hake, R. (1998). Interactive-engagement versus traditional methods: A six thousand Student survey of mechanics test data for introductory physics courses. *American Journal of Physics, 66,* 64-74.

Harrop-Allin, S. (2011). The implications of South African children's multimodal musical games for music education. *Leading Music Education International Conference*.

Harwood, E. (1998). Music learning in context: A playground tale. *Research Studies in Music Education*, *11*(1), 52-60.

Hawley, J. C. (2001). *Encyclopedia of postcolonial studies*. Westport, CT: Greenwood Publishing Group.

Ikwubuzo, I (2012). Stylistic features of Igbo Riddles. In J. K. S Makokha, J. O. Ogone, & R. West Pavlov (Eds.), *Style in African literature: Essays on literary stylistics and narrative styles* (pp. 191-234.). Amsterdam and New York: Rodopi.

Johnston, T. F. (1987). Children's music of the Shangana-Tsonga. *African Music, 6*(4), 126-143.

Kwami, R. (1999) *African songs for school and community*. Mainz, Germany: Schott.

Kubitsky, I. (1998). Ewe children's music from Ghana, West Africa, in the classroom. *Masters Abstracts International, 36*(05), 1214. (UMI No. 1389656)

Ladson-Billings, G. (1995). Toward a theory of culturally relevant pedagogy. *American Educational Research Journal, 32*(3), 465-491

Ladson-Billings, G. (2009). *The dream keepers: Successful teachers of African American children*. San Francisco, CA: John Wiley and Sons.

Lyoka, P. A. (2007). Questioning the role of children's indigenous games of Africa on the development of fundamental movement skills: A preliminary review. *European Early Childhood Education Research Journal, 15*(3), 343-364.

Mans, M, Dzansi-McPalm, M., & Agak, H. O. (2003). Play in musical arts pedagogy. In A Herbst, M. Nzewi, & K. Agawu (Eds.), *Africa-sensitive musical arts education* (pp. 195-214). Pretoria, South Africa: Unisa Press.

Mapara, J. (2009). Indigenous knowledge systems in Zimbabwe: Juxtaposing postcolonial theory. *The Journal of Pan African Studies, 3*(1), 139-155.

Marfo, K., & Biersteker, L. (2011). Exploring culture, play, and early childhood education practice in African contexts. In S. Rogers (Ed.), *Rethinking play pedagogy in early childhood education: Contexts, concepts and cultures* (pp. 73-85). London, England: Routledge.

Mbusi, N. P. (2012). *An investigation into the use of traditional Xhosa dance to teach mathematics: A case study in a Grade 7 class* (Master's thesis). Grahamstown, Eastern Cape, South Africa: Rhodes University.

Moore, R. S. (2002). Influence of multicultural singing games on primary school children's attentiveness and song preferences in music classes. *International Journal of Music Education, 39*(1), 31-39

Mwonga, S. C. J., & Wanyama, M. N. (2012). An assessment of the availability of resources to facilitate early childhood music and movement curriculum implementation in Eldoret municipality, Kenya. *Journal of Emerging Trends in Educational Research and Policy Studies (JETERAPS), 3*(5), 624-630.

Nicholls, R. W. (1988). Ensemble music of the Igede. *The Black Perspective in Music*, 191-212.

Ngugi, wa Thiong'o. (1986). *Decolonising the mind: The politics of language in African literature*. London, England: Martin's Press.

Nyoni, T., & Nyoni, M. (2013). The form and content of children's poetry and games on a kaleidoscopic cultural terrain. *Theory and Practice in Language Studies, 3*(2), 233-243.

Nyota, S., & Mapara, J. (2008). Shona traditional children's games and play: Songs as indigenous ways of knowing. *The Journal of Pan African Studies, 2*(4), 189-202.

Nzewi, M. (1997). *African Music: theoretical content and creative continuum.* Oldershausen, Germany. Institut für Didatik Popular Musik.

Nzewi, M. (2003). Acquiring Knowledge of the music arts in traditional society. In A. Herbst, M. Nzewi, & K. Agawu (Eds.), *Musical arts in Africa: Theory, practice and education* (pp. 13-37). Unisa, South Africa: Unisa Press.

Offei, G. O. (1991). *Ga children's songs* (Unpublished long essay). Diploma in African Music. University of Ghana, Legon.

Ohene, O. (1990). *Fun and Games for Children.* Accra, Ghana: Educational Press and Manufacturers.

Okpewho, I. (1990). The primacy of performance in oral Discourse. *Research in African Literature* (Review Essay), *21*(4), 121-128.

Opoku-Agyemang, K. (2010, June). *Folktales.* Lecture for the May 2010 Experiencing the Creative Arts in Ghana Global Seminar, University of Minnesota, Minneapolis and Saint Paul, Minnesota.

Ogede, O. S. (1994). Oral performance as instruction: Aesthetic strategies in children's play songs from a Nigerian community. *Children's Literature Association Quarterly, 19*(3), 113-117.

Russell, J., & Zembylas, M. (2007). Arts Integration in the Curriculum: A Review of Research and Implications for Teaching and Learning. In L. Bresler (Ed.), *International Handbook of Research in Arts Education* (pp. 287-302). The Netherlands: Springer.

Serwadda, M. (1987) *Songs and stories from Uganda.* Danbury, CT: World Music Press.

Tatira, B., Mutambara, L., & Chagwiza, C. J. (2012). The Balobedu cultural activities and plays pertinent to primary school mathematics learning. *International Education Studies, 5*(1), 78-85.

Titon, J. T. (Ed.). (1996). *Worlds of music: An introduction to music of the World's Peoples.* New York, NY: Schirmer Books.

Van Berkum, J. J. A. (2008). Understanding sentences in context: What brain waves can tell us. *Current Directions in Psychological Science, 17*(6), 376-380. doi:10.1111/j.1467-8721.2008.00609.x

Wiggins, D. G. (2007). Pre-K music and the emergent reader: Promoting literacy in a music-enhanced environment. *Early Childhood Education Journal, 35*(1), 55-64.

Wilkinson, J. (1988). Kofi Anyidoho. An Ewe Poet between Tradition and Change. *Africa*, 543-573.

Wink, J. (2010). *Critical pedagogy: Notes from the Real World* (4th ed.). London, England: Pearson.

Wlodkowski, R. J., & Ginsberg, M. B. (1995), *Diversity and motivation: Culturally responsive teaching.* San Francisco, CA: Jossey-Bass.

Wlodkowski, R. J. (2003). Fostering motivation in professional development programs. *New Directions for Adult and Continuing Education, 98*, 39-48.

Yankah, K. (1982). Voicing and drumming the poetry of praise: A case for aural literature. In K. Anyidoho, A. M. Porter, D. Racine, & J. Spleth (Eds.), *Interdisciplinary dimensions of african literature* (pp. 139-156) Washington, DC: Three Continents Press.

CHAPTER 3

CELEBRATING AFRICAN ORAL LITERATURE THROUGH POETRY

Barbara A. Ward and Deanna Day

The rhythmic sounds of hip hop beats pulse through the classroom air-waves, and several students who had been previously slumping in their seats sit up with dawning looks of puzzlement, curiosity, and interest suf-fusing their faces. As the poems in *Hip Hop Speaks to Children: A Celebration of Poetry with a Beat* (Giovanni, 2008) are spoken with hip hop beats playing in the background, students in an elementary education literacy methods class are starting to redefine poetry. "This is definitely not my mother's poetry or my old English teacher's poetry," said Jenn. This is poetry "that puts a new spin on what I know and think of poetry and how it is defined. I think it will do the same thing for my own students, and open up their minds, hearts, and ears" to poetry's possibilities.

"This poetry isn't like anything else I've ever heard," said Taylor. "I like how these poems were more lively and interactive. Kids would have fun listening to these poems."

Jon-Henry agreed, finding himself surprised to be enjoying poetry while tapping out beats on his desk. "I actually really enjoyed the poems," he said. "They were lively and fun, and I didn't worry too much about what they meant. I just got caught up in the music and the beats in the words being spoken."

Lindsey, too, said that the music's beats drew her in. "I looked around the room while the music was playing, and everyone was either dancing in place or sitting up straight and paying attention. If it resonated with me, it will resonate with my students. I will use this book [*Hip Hop Speaks to Children*] and look for more like it."

In many respects the reactions of these college students to reading and hearing African American poetry isn't all that surprising; nor should it be news that poetry would be an important part of African American oral literature. After all, the griots in West Africa were the individuals responsible for maintaining an oral record of their people's history through music, storytelling, and poetry. It's fitting that today's hip hop could rekindle interest in the spoken, rhythmic beats of poetry.

There is little doubt that hearing poems read aloud helps children cultivate an appreciation for sound and language or that poetry's rhythm and rhyme delight children of every age. Poetry also helps us see differently, validating individual human experiences and leading to self-understanding and understanding of those around us (Perfect, 1999). Heard's (1999) reminder that reading poetry to children begins with teachers and librarians translates into reading poems as a part of the daily literacy routine in the classroom, something heretofore unfamiliar to the preservice students who listened to the CD accompanying *Hip Hop Speaks to Children*. Sami, for instance, became enchanted with the poetic lines she heard and was surprised that this poetry was much more informal than the poetry she is accustomed to reading. "My elementary and high school teachers never even read poetry to us so this was a totally new experience," she said. "Who knew that poetry didn't have to be boring?"

Kelsey agreed, saying that she "liked that some of the poems were funny. I was laughing as I listened to several of the poems. I never really thought about being able to laugh while listening to poetry." Kelsey's reaction makes sense, though. Often, it seems that poetry becomes associated with only weighty issues and symbolism the further up the grade ladder students travel, and the nursery rhymes and funny lines they once enjoyed seem lost in the mists of time, left behind in elementary school. Perhaps that's because poetry is given such weightiness in later grades, and students are taught to focus on symbolism and rhyme patterns rather than just savoring the words being uttered.

Tireless poetry proponents Sylvia Vardell and Janet Wong (2012, 2013), editors of *The Poetry Friday Anthology for Middle School* and *The Poetry Friday Anthology, K-5 Edition* would agree wholeheartedly. Poetry should be an integral, intentional part of today's language arts classrooms, and teachers should read it aloud or involve their students in poetry read alouds. In their two books, Vardell and Wong include several suggestions for props and performance tips for novice poetry teachers.

Today's teachers should consider making poetry a fundamental, integral part of their literacy curriculum. Poetry can enable students to play with words, learn figurative language, and even practice their speaking skills, and it can be seamlessly woven into classrooms on a daily or weekly basis. Teachers may even justify its inclusion by pointing to how it supports the Common Core State Standards. It is helpful to ask ourselves how often we read aloud a poem to our students and whether children enjoy poetry in our classroom. As teachers, we need to rethink our purposes in sharing poetry, especially poems from different cultures. In doing so, we can provide authentic reading and writing engagements during writing workshop to enhance our students' appreciation for poetry. Like most literature, poetry functions in a way that most textbooks don't. It

> educates the heart as well as the head. It offers pleasure and enjoyment, as well as insights into what it means to be a decent human being in a society, benefits that will last far longer than the facts that can be tested easily on standardized tests. (Bishop, 2007, p. xiv)

This chapter investigates the benefits of poetry, particularly poetry written by African Americans, and delineates some ways that any teacher can bring poetry to life in a literacy classroom. As is the case of most African American literature for children, current African American children's poetry "functions both as an artistic expression intended to illuminate and sometimes entertain and as literature with a purpose" (Bishop, 2007, p. xiv). We begin with a review of the existing literature and then share how we infuse poetry into the classroom.

Review of Literature

Distinguished poet and recipient of the NCTE Excellence in Poetry for Children Award in 2006 Nikki Grimes, explains that, "Poetry is natural for children. It's part of their lives! From the ABCs to Mother Goose to patty cake to jump rope rhymes, poetry is already a part of their lives, so you're just building on that foundation. "It's already there" (Vardell & Oxley, 2007, p. 284).

Thus, poetry is perfect for chanting, singing and reading aloud since it easily captures children's ears, imaginations, and souls. Heard and Laminack (2008) concur that children are natural poets because they find wonder in ordinary things, are bursting with curiosity and have boundless feelings and emotions. Children essentially speak poetry all day long.

Many teachers and researchers have written about how poetry helps build literacy skills in children and young adolescents. Immersing students in poetry by making it a part of our daily literacy can help children become readers and writers (Calkins, 2003; Heard & Laminack, 2008). Furthermore, the sounds, words and imagery in poetry inspire an interest and enjoyment in reading (Strange & Wyatt, 1999). Poetry should be woven throughout the whole school year in elementary, middle and high school. In addition, teachers need to provide poems and poetry anthologies that reflect the many cultures of their students. Every child should have the experience of finding himself or herself in the lines of a poem. Please see Appendix A for a list of African American poets and anthologies at the end of the chapter.

Reading Poetry

The predictable language, rhythm, and rhyme in poetry make children eager participants in oral and choral readings. Oftentimes, when children hear a poem read aloud a couple of times, they become familiar with the words, catch onto the pattern and are able to read the poem back with little effort. Heard and Laminack (2008) remind teachers to a read a poem aloud to students before asking them to read the poem since their voices provide a "training wheels" transition and support that help children read the poem independently. After hearing a poem read aloud by a teacher, students have some idea about how it might be read, and will read it better than they would have otherwise.

Reading and sharing African American poetry in our classrooms is critical. American children of all races and ethnicities can expand their worldview as they become acquainted with Black music, Black history, Black achievers and Black poetry (Bishop, 2007). Through poetry, teachers can acknowledge the experiences, perspectives, struggles, and triumphs of African Americans (Brooks & McNair, 2008). Reading aloud African American poems such as *Honey, I love* (Greenfield, 1978) and *In Our Family* (Adoff, 1982) affirms the worth and beauty of Black children (Bishop, 2007). Because so many African American poets draw inspiration from family dynamics, readers may find the work of modern writers such as Hope Anita Smith to be particularly touching and relevant. Smith's three poetic works (*The Way a Door Closes*, 2003; *Keeping the Night Watch*, 2008; and *Mother Poems*, 2009) provide book-length testimony of the pain caused when a father walks out on his family or the hole left by the death of a mother. Culturally responsive pedagogy maintains the importance of using multicultural literature, including the genre of poetry, from the multitude of cultures represented in our world in our classrooms. The recent multicultural curricular reform movement strongly urges that teachers include in their classroom reading selections the literature of groups that have been underrepresented or ignored in the past. Thus, as scholar Bishop (2007) suggests,

> African American children's literature can be affirming for children who have historically not found affirmation in classroom materials. It can also connect with other children of color whose life experiences in this society are tainted by the poison of racism and often marked by struggle. Reading such literature has the potential to help all students understand who we are today as a society and how we might become a better society tomorrow. (p. xiv)

Reading poetry aloud during the elementary years can help teach and reinforce print concepts such as left to right progression, spaces between words, letter and sound correspondence and punctuation (Heard & Laminack, 2008). Since poems are full of unusual or surprising vocabulary and word patterns, they are influential in building language and word awareness. Furthermore, choral reading, paying attention to rhythm, cadence and pacing, build reading fluency (Faver, 2008). Parr and Campbell (2006) note that awareness of rhyme, rhythm, and alliteration alongside phonemic awareness distinguishes effective readers from those at risk.

Heard (1999) suggests that all teachers be poetry collectors, identifying poems that speak to them in some way. Teachers need to be on the lookout for poetry that will appeal to their students' interests and cultural experiences. Shanklin (2009) proposes finding compelling poetry to balance the classic poetry that often appears in textbooks. Having a range of poetry available will help give more choices. Students can be invited to bring in their own favorite pop culture songs or raps to share too. Classrooms should have poetry books and anthologies available for choice reading, poems displayed on chart paper and quotes by poets on the walls. As teachers and students read poetry they can begin to discuss what a poem is, what a poem looks like, what makes up a poem, what a poem can be about and the shape and space of a poem (Ridolfi, 1997).

Reading and performing poetry provides numerous opportunities for children to practice, with pleasure, the essential skills of literacy—phonemic awareness, phonics, fluency, vocabulary, and comprehension (Stanley, 2004). Children at every grade level enjoy performing a poem—either for a classmate, small group, entire class or community. Faver (2008) discovered that performing poetry dramatically, either for the daily school announcements, poetry tour (performing room-to-room) and poetry cafés (at the close of a grading period, open mike poetry night), built fluency, comprehension, self-confidence, and made reading fun. Trousdale, Bach, and Willis (2010) learned that performing small-group poems in middle school helped students share and listen to others and find their own individual interpretation of the poems.

Children find poetry easier to read than stories or books because poems are shorter in length. Poems usually only have a few words on a line and are surrounded by plenty of white space and repetition, making them seem less threatening for readers who are struggling or lack enthusiasm for reading (Cullinan, Scala, & Schroder, 1995). For older students, verse novels are ideal because their appearance makes them approachable. Students new to novels in verse may be hesitant initially, but the short length, condensed language and writing form usually changes their reluctance to enthusiasm. Many teachers have found that stories in verse foster a love of poetry and reading in intermediate and young adolescents (Campbell, 2004; Isaacs, 2003).

Perfect (1999) cautions teachers to spend more time celebrating the delights of wordplay and the rhythm and beats and less time interpreting poetry with children and adolescents since tearing apart of a poem to find meaning or overanalyzing a poem wrings the joy out of poetry. Rosenblatt's (1938) transactional theory reminds us to aesthetically read and experience a poem first. Teachers need to create a classroom where students feel safe to share their thoughts, feelings, and connections about a poem. Later, students can explore, discuss, and find the meaning in a poem. One way to broaden students' understanding of a poem is to complete think-and-feel-alouds. Eva-Wood (2008) adapted Oster's (2001) think-aloud strategy and had her students verbalize their feelings and thinking as they read poetry. She found that this helped students gain confidence in their interpretations of texts along with an increased awareness of the metacognitive tools they used to help them read.

Sekeres and Gregg (2007) added a little poetry to their literacy routines and helped struggling readers. Gregg's students read at various reading levels, so she used poetry as a common literacy experience to help meld the entire class into a working whole. The class participated in echo reading, choral reading, repeated reading of favorite poems, poetry performances and when students were hooked on poetry—lessons on rhythm, rhyme, alliteration, imagery symbolism, and so forth. In another study, Stange and Wyant (2008) realized that poetry improved literacy and student behavior. After reading aloud poems associated with character education there was less lying, cheating, tattling, making fun of others and bullying in the classroom.

Writing Poetry

Once children have been marinated in poetry they are ready to write poetry. Parr and Campbell (2006) found that reading poetry inspired students to write poetry. Routman (2001) suggests teaching poetry writing at the beginning of the school year because it is the best way to engage and celebrate all students—not just as writers, but as valued members of the classroom community. In addition, Routman (2000) contends the most powerful force for students is to see, hear and talk about poems by other kids because these poems deal with typical concerns and interests of children. Reading poems by peers helps children believe that poetry writing is doable and pleasurable.

Both Heard (1999) and Routman (2001) encourage students to write free verse poetry versus rhyming poetry. They note that when kids are released from the structure of rhyme they can express themselves much easier. Students will be able to play with language, space, and form. In addition, children of all ages need to see their teachers demonstrating how to write a poem because this will help them take a risk and write one too. If we ask our students to write on the spot, we need to do the same (Routman, 2000).

After students have watched their teacher write a poem they are ready to try writing a poem together whole group. Once this modeling has taken place, students are ready to independently write poems. Davis and Hill (2003) note that children need choice on topics and form—allowing them to write poetry any way they like. Students can write a poem about what they are thinking, what they like to do or what they know a lot about. This sustained writing time is usually 20 minutes or longer where the goal is to discover the joy of poetry. Later, teachers can help students revise and edit.

Some days students can be invited to write a particular kind of poem. For example, students can write in the style of another poet. Some teachers encourage students to find a poem that speaks to them and imitate that style of writing (Davis & Hill, 2003). Linaberger (2004) suggests these questions to help children write like another poet: What do you like about the poem? Is it the length of the lines? The subject matter? Borrow a line from the poem and write your own poem. Write your own poem in the same style or length.

There are multiple mini-lessons teachers can teach and discuss around poetry writing such as: selecting topics, writing with voice, choosing words and using line breaks. One of Gill's (2007) poetry mini-lessons includes showing that poets write poetry to capture their thoughts, feelings and experiences. She shares a couple of poems that show emotional experiences along with a poem that she has written. Next, she invites students to think about an experience—favorite time of day, favorite place, something beautiful they saw, or a feeling they had—and to write a poem to capture the images and feelings. Walter Dean Myers's (2009) story in rhyme, *Looking Like Me*, could lend itself very well to poetry writing so that students could write their own I AM poems or Who am I poems to celebrate their cultural heritage. Students could use Wordle or create digital podcasts or voice thread to publish and read aloud their own work after hearing exemplary and self-affirming lines such as these from Myers: "When you look in a mirror, / who do you see? / A boy? A girl? / A son? A daughter? / A runner? A dancer? / Whoever and whatever you see– / just put out your fist and give yourself an 'I am' BAM!" (n.p.).

Both Olshansky (1994) and Reilly (2008) invite students to engage in art and poetry workshop. Olshansky has students create textured paper such as bubble prints, marbleized paper, or sponge prints. Reilly has students converse through finger painting about a book they have read. Later, students use the art or textured papers to find and write a poem. These authors believe that the visual arts and kinesthetic components awaken student's imaginations and help them during the writing process. These visual art pieces also enhance the finished poems.

Other teachers are experimenting with poetry and technology. Curwood and Cowell (2011) implemented a digital poetry curriculum in high school. After students read, critiqued and wrote poetry, they used digital tools such as moviemaker and imovie to reinterpret the poems using multimodal elements. Students were engaged in multiliteracy learning by practicing linguistic, visual, aural, gestural and spatial skills, all essential for the 21st century. Bradley (2011) encouraged her students to use concise, vivid, and sensory-appealing language in Twitter poems. Students were limited to 140 characters or approximately three lines to write a poem and publish them on Twitter. Another teacher, Tarasiuk (2009), had her middle school students write and produce original free verse poetry podcasts. By incorporating technology and media students demonstrated their ability to interpret meaning and fostered appreciation of meaning making through their own words, music, and images.

Graves (1992) asserts that poetry should not be limited to reading and writing time, but should be used throughout the curriculum. Shanklin (2009) suggests incorporating poetry into units of study across disciplines so that students are exposed to poetry as a natural use of language. Poetry and social studies make perfect pairs when exploring several topics or time periods. For instance, students could learn about the importance of jazz and other forms of music significant to the nation's history with text set pairings of Arnold Adoff's (2011) rollicking *Roots and Blues: A Celebration* and Carol Boston Weatherford's (2008) biography *Before John Was a Jazz Giant: A Song of John Coltrane*, both of which would necessitate musical accompaniment. They could explore various aspects of the civil rights movement through exploration of several free verse titles written by Carole Boston Weatherford including *The Beatitudes: From Slavery to Civil Rights* (2009), *Birmingham, 1963* (2007) or her poetry title *Remember the Bridge: Poems of a People* (2002) as well as reading those titles against others dealing with segregation, integration, and Jim Crow laws such as Tony Abbott's *Lunch-Box Dream* (2011), Matt Faulkner's *A Taste of Colored Water* (2008) or Michael S. Bandy's *White Water* (2011). With all of these exemplar texts, students will learn to read and write poetry and to appreciate it as a genre as well as recognizing that poetry provides different perspectives on historical events and need not be read simply in isolation.

Infusing Poetry

There are many ways that poetry can be presented in a classroom. Teachers often focus on poetry during one particular month of the year, typically April, which is National Poetry Month, or during a poetry unit. But those approaches often marginalize poetry, making it seem to matter only during brief time periods. Far better is the approach suggested by Vardell and Wong, sharing a poem every day or during a poetry break or even designating one day each week as Poetry Friday. In the case of the preservice teachers at a large university in Washington State who listened to *Hip Hop Poetry* at the start of this chapter, the teacher typically began each class session with a poem that seemed to fit the season or mood or served as a mentor text for the kind of writing being modeled that week. Since children "live on what they feed upon" (Paterson, 2000, p. 5), she carefully considered and then selected poems and books that will "truly nourish them, that will enlarge their minds, that will prepare them to make wise decisions" (p. 5). Classroom mentor texts must be chosen carefully, and teachers at every grade level must be ever-mindful to find good poetry that represents various cultural groups. For instance, during their semester together, they read and recited poems from *Jazz* (Myers, 2008), *Sweethearts of Rhythm* (Nelson, 2009). *Joyful Noise: Poems for Two Voices* (Fleischman, 1988), *Toad by the Road: A Year in the Life of These Amazing Amphibians* (Ryder, 2007), *Hailstones and Halibut Bones: Adventures in Poetry and Color* (O'Neill, 1989), *BookSpeak: Poems about Books* (Salas, 2011), and the poem "Where I'm From" by George Ella Lyon (1999). The approach to the poetry varied from week to week; sometimes, the instructor simply read the lines and then had the students read along with her. Other times, they read the poems in two or three voice style or in rounds. Sometimes the words were simply savored with no comment at all, and at other points, students would volunteer their favorite golden poetry lines. They were already accustomed from their children's literature class to choosing lines or passages from their reading that had personal significance to them as they read or that resonated with them. The lines become golden since they are worth remembering, recording or sharing with others. They also provide a quick way to encourage students to participate in class.

The preservice teachers were introduced to hip hop poetry by listening to one poem at a time from the CD that accompanies the text of *Hip Hop Speaks to Children: A Celebration of Poetry with a Beat* (Giovanni, 2008). The collection contains poems by Nikki Giovanni ("The Girls in the Circle"), Calef Brown ("Funky Snowman"), Eloise Greenfield ("Oh, Words"), James Berry ("People Equal"), Charles R. Smith Jr. ("Allow Me to Introduce Myself"), Elizabeth Swados ("Me"), Oscar Brown Jr. ("Dat Dere"), Maya Angelou ("Harlem Hopscotch"), Gwendolyn Brooks ("We Real Cool"), Claude McKay ("If We Must Die"), all poems played in class for the students as well as their having copies of the poems to read alongside the vocal renditions. Among others, there are also poems by Tupac Shakur ("The Rose that Grew in Concrete) and Langston Hughes ("Harlem Night Song" & "Dream Variations").

The poems themselves and the accompanying CD seemed to open students' eyes and ears to the possibilities of poetry. Holly, for instance, found this form of poetry to be "different and exciting." For Kristin, the poems' lines were rather haunting. Although at first she said they "definitely have a different feel with rhythm," but a couple of days later, she noted how "haunting" some of them are, for instance, "We Real Cool" by Gwendolyn Brooks. "I didn't really get it the first time I heard it, and then I started thinking about all the things people do just to seem cool, you know, the risks people take that end up in a literal dead end," she said. "We might be 'real cool,' as the poet says, but we are also real dead. I can't stop thinking about that." Annie agreed, adding that often oral poetry "can sound monotonous, but this added expression and life" to the poems.

The students chose a couple of favorites "Funky Snowman" by Calef Brown and "Dat Dere" because of what Bree called "their funky nature" and the realistic images the poets painted with their words. "They made me laugh," she said. Almost every student remarked on the liveliness and energetic nature of the poems on the CD. Except for a handful of students, the reaction of the rest of the class can be summed up through Paige's words: "They could get any student more interested in poetry. Unlike many of the poems typically read in class, these lines can speak to my future students."

Brittney expressed delight in reading and hearing African American poetry because of the poems' cultural aspect. "I've never heard any poetry focused on the African-American culture during my years of schooling. Schools don't seem to teach it." Hearing these poems has prompted her to look for more poetry by African Americans and plan a unit on Langston

Hughes. Xisa echoed Brittney's sentiments, noting the "soulful feel" to them. "I felt like I was experiencing a culture, not just a poem," she said. Like Brittney and Xisa, Katie was excited at how well the poems spoke to her. "I guarantee that they will speak to children," she said. "There are so many hidden messages you can gain from them." As McNair (2008) suggests, examining literature such as hip-hop poems can help preservice teachers recognize "how issues of race are operative within the contexts of children's literature and education" (p. 21).

Since the students had copies of the poems being recited on the CD in front of them, they could follow along as the performers read. This led to several interesting reactions from some of the students. For instance, although Whitney enjoyed the performers' interpretation of the poems, she also was intrigued that "they sound so different than how I would read them." These reactions seem to support what researchers such as Bishop (2007) have found about African American poetry since it seems to affirm self-identity, express emotions, and validate "the everyday lives of children whose physical images and life experiences have been consistently devalued by omissions from the literature available to them in schools and libraries" (p. 103). In whatever form, whether it be a chapter book, a picture book or poetry, multicultural literature expands students' knowledge of the world around them, allowing them to see themselves through the experiences of others but also encouraging themselves to see others more clearly.

Michael concurred with Whitney, adding that "listening to the different poetic interpretations made me wish that I had already memorized the lyrics, no, the poems, so I could sing along for everyone."

The class eventually discussed the differences between reading a poem silently and hearing a poem read aloud. "It's really a lot like acting," explained Michael. "As you read, you become the person or inhabit the poem."

While Catie liked hearing the interpretations of the poems because of their variety, she realized that she prefers to read poems silently to herself and then decide for herself what they mean.

Sometimes, hearing the poems read on the CD, I couldn't think of any other possible way to interpret them or different ways for them to mean something, The 'People Equal' poem is a great case in point. Now that I've heard it, I can't get the performer's performance out of my head. In some ways, the performing locks in the meaning. It's like when you watch the movie of a book before reading the book. You simply cannot make your own movie after seeing another movie of the book.

Some students such as Amy found the poems interesting but "a little too much for me. They were too hard for me to follow." Kristen and Trish agreed, with Kristen saying that she "could not get over the grammar and

the children's song nature of it. I don't think I understood many of these."
Although Trish recognizes that she needs to set aside her own biases, she
admitted that "the lack of grammar was bugging me. I couldn't get past
that to enjoy the poems." Despite Trish's concern about grammatical
correctness, most of the selected poems had at least one fan among
the student audience, who make poetry much more enjoyable than the
students had considered it before hearing the poems. It isn't just college
students who become excited about the possibilities of sharing African
American oral traditions through poetry. A group of eighth graders in
Tallulah, Louisiana also realized that poetry can effectively capture the
sights, sounds, tastes, and smells of their daily lives and special occasions
when they read Nikki Giovanni's "Knoxville, Tennessee" and used it as a
pattern on which to base their own personal "Tallulah, Louisiana" poems.

Giovanni's poem evokes a sense of time and place and focuses on the
sensuous pleasures of food associated with time spent with family members, and the eighth graders quickly picked up on the pattern and themes
in her poem while emulating them in their own. For instance, Bridney
wrote, "I always like summer best / You can eat fresh mustard greens /
From my granddaddy's garden / And fried okra, / Chicken, / And fish,
shrimps, / And mashed potatoes / Macaroni, / And a homemade cake / Or
pie at my aunt's house / And listen to blues music / Out in the back yard /
Or even go to restaurants / With my family members /And go dressed nice
all the time." LaVonda's poem also contained descriptive details about
food. She wrote, "fried chicken you can smell / Your grandmother cooking
miles away/ While sitting outside / listening to R&B / while relaxing with /
Friends and family / Summer is a season that / I will always love." After she
wrote her poem, she sat pensively for a moment, and then revealed with a
laugh, "I think I'm making myself hungry."

While Kemberly, too, focused on the pleasures of fresh summer produce, she paid attention to Giovanni's final lines and tried to evoke a similar feeling with her poem. She wrote,

> I always like summer best / You can eat fresh greens out the can / And okra
> fresh from the garden / And shrimp out the bag / And pizza from the store /
> And lots of barbecue ribs / And grapes and strawberries / fresh out the box/
> And vanilla ice cream just out / The freezer / And listen to the R&B music /
> Outside with family / And going to church on Sundays / With your grandpar-
> ents / And swimming with friends / But mostly being warm, / not only when
> going to bed / or falling sleep.

Even though these students all read three to four levels below their assigned
grade level, none of them had any problems writing a poem fashioned
after Giovanni's. Clearly, home and food and the positive associations
their favorite dishes had for them were easy topics from which to draw

poetic inspiration. Their positive reactions to listening to Giovanni's verses and then crafting their own were their first indication that poetry could actually be fun to read and write and that it could provide a means of self-expression. Coincidentally, it is two African American poets, Nikki Grimes and Nikki Giovanni, whose work often speaks most powerfully to today's students. The two poets once toured the college circuit together sharing their adult poetry. Nikki Grimes was sure she would always write for adults until her first children's book was published, and she found her writing niche.

Both Nikki Grimes and Nikki Giovanni are extraordinary poets. Their love of language, words and poetic artistry appeal to all ages, from children to adults. The themes about which they write are universal—from personal stories, integrating their cultures, to poems that celebrate the wonders of the world around them as well as those that challenge the status quo. Both writers' work shows evolution of their craft and a keen sense of history. Perhaps it wouldn't be too outlandish to designate them as American griots, enthusiastic recorders of the important but often ignored moments that matter and those that give life meaning.

NIKKI GRIMES

Nikki Grimes is one of the most productive and creative African American poets for children. Her body of work includes: *What Is Goodbye* (2004), *Dark Sons* (2005) and *Bronx Masquerade* (2001) the Coretta Scott King Author Award novel. In 2006 she received the National Council of Teachers of English Excellence in Poetry Award. Grimes writes with honesty about life issues such as race, culture, place, and society. The characters in her poems are struggling to find their way in uncertain situations, which make them believable and easily relatable.

Grimes was born in Harlem, New York, on October 20, 1950. One of her parents was an alcoholic and the other was a gambler so she grew up in and out of foster homes. She thinks back on this time as happy because she found the library where books became her survival tool. She began writing poetry when she was six years old as a foster child. She loved words and language and was fascinated with word meanings and word games. In 1977 her debut novel was published *Growin'* (1977). Her first book of poetry was *Something on my Mind* (1978). She has since published more than 50 titles. Grimes writes more than poetry. In addition, she has written easy-readers, biographies, historical fiction, and alphabet books.

One of her most memorable poetry collections is *Meet Danitra Brown* (1994). Grimes (2004) says she tried to write a story about two best friends and it just wasn't coming out right. She began with a pair of character sketches where each critical element then became an individual poem. Slowly the friendship is revealed, poem-by-poem. Grimes has written more anthologies about these characters: *Danitra Brown Leaves Town* (2002) and *Danitra Brown, Class Clown* (2005).

As a child Grimes often felt invisible between the pages of a book because so few featured characters who looked like her. Her face, voice and life were missing from the literature she encountered. Today she writes for readers who've had a similar experience, whether they have been marginalized for reasons of race, culture, or a different form of otherness (Grimes, 2005). She states, "I write to give them a voice, to place them in the center of the action, to give them validation, affirmation. I write to say 'I see you. And yes, your story matters'" (p. 23).

Grimes is convinced that poetry can break down racial barriers, shatter cultural stereotypes and forge community She explains, "The safest way to learn about another culture is between the pages of a book. And no matter the culture, we're all alike beneath the skin. Good books show that" (McBroom, 2011, p. 42). Grimes (2005) advocates that teachers share poetry from unfamiliar cultures to help their students think differently. She believes the most important common denominator is the human heart.

When asked why she writes, Grimes (2005) answered, "I write to build bridges. I write to heal. I write to encourage. I write to inspire. I write to affirm. I write to inform" (p. 22). Grimes writes 6 days a week in the morning. She has notepads everywhere, in her car, and in her purse so that when a word comes to mind she begins writing (Vardell & Oxley, 2007). To Grimes poetry is a literature of brushstrokes, "The poet uses a few choice words, placed just so, to paint a picture, evoke an emotion, or capture a moment in time" (Hopkins, 2005, p. 70). To find out more about Grimes visit her website: www.nikkigrimes.com

NIKKI GIOVANNI

Born in Knoxville, Nikki Giovanni is one of the best-known African American poets who reached prominence during the late 1960s and early 1970s. Her unique and insightful poetry testifies to her own evolving awareness and experiences: from child to young woman, from naive college freshman to seasoned civil rights activist, from daughter to mother. Frequently anthologized, Giovanni's poetry expresses strong racial pride and respect for family. Her informal style makes her work accessible to both adults and children. In addition to collections such as *Re: Creation (1970), Love Poems (1997),* and *The Collected Poems of Nikki Giovanni (2003),*

Giovanni has published several works of nonfiction, children's literature and recordings, including the Emmy-award nominated *The Nikki Giovanni Poetry Collection* (2004). A frequent lecturer and reader, Giovanni has taught at Rutgers University, Ohio State University, and Virginia Tech. Tennessee in 1943, Giovanni captured the attention of others during the late 1960s and 1970s when she wrote poetry that captured the rebellious nature of those times. Known for her outspokenness, in her writing and in lectures, she is steadfastly committed to civil rights and equality. Her writing tends to focus on individuals and the ability each one of us has to make a difference in ourselves and in the lives of others. Her upbringing, growing up in all-Black suburb of Cincinnati, Ohio and spending the summers with her sister in Knoxville with their grandparents in Knoxville had a large influence on her and on her writing. She attended her grandfather's alma mater, Fisk University, from which she graduated with honors. After graduating, she attended both the University of Pennsylvania and Columbia University. She published her first book of poetry, *Black Feeling Black Talk*, in 1968, and within the next year published a second book. Early in her career she was dubbed the "Princess of Black Poetry," and over the course of more than three decades of publishing and lecturing she has come to be called both a "National Treasure" and, most recently, one of Oprah Winfrey's 25 "Living Legends." Many of Giovanni's books have received honors and awards. Her autobiography, *Gemini*, was a finalist for the National Book Award. Several of her books, including *Hip Hop Speaks to Children: A Celebration of Poetry with a Beat* were honored with NAACP Image Awards. Giovanni's spoken word recordings have also achieved widespread recognition and honors. Her album "Truth Is On Its Way," on which she reads her poetry against a background of gospel music, was a top 100 album and received the Best Spoken Word Album given by the National Association of Radio and Television Announcers. Her Nikki Giovanni Poetry Collection, on which she reads and talks about her poetry, was one of five finalists for a Grammy Award.

Giovanni has received numerous honors and awards throughout her career. The recipient of some 25 honorary degrees, she has been named Woman of the Year by *Mademoiselle* Magazine, *The Ladies Home Journal*, and *Ebony* Magazine. Giovanni was the first recipient of the Rosa L. Parks Woman of Courage Award, and she has also been awarded the Langston Hughes Medal for poetry. The author of some 30 books for both adults and children, Nikki Giovanni is a University Distinguished Professor at Virginia Tech in Blacksburg, Virginia. Readers can learn more about her at her website at http://www.nikki-giovanni.com/

APPENDIX A

Recommended Poetry Books by African American Poets

Adoff, A. (2011). *Roots and blues: A celebration.* New York, NY: Clarion.

Adoff, A. (2001). *Daring dog and captain cat.* New York, NY: Simon & Schuster.

Adoff, A. (2000). *The basket counts.* New York, NY: Simon and Schuster.

Adoff, A. (2000). *The return of Rex Ethel.* San Diego, CA: Harcourt.

Adoff, A. (2000). *Touch the poem.* New York, NY: Scholastic.

Adoff, A. (1997). *I am the darker brother: An anthology of modern poems by African Americans.* New York, NY: Simon and Schuster.

Adoff, A. (1997). *Love letters.* New York, NY: Scholastic.

Adoff, A. (1995). *Outside inside poems.* New York, NY: HarperCollins/Lothrop, Lee & Shepard.

Adoff, A. (1995). *Slow dance heart break blues.* New York, NY: Lothrop, Lee & Shepard.

Adoff, A. (1995). *Street music: City poems.* New York, NY: HarperCollins

Adoff, A. (1991). *In for winter, out for spring.* San Diego, CA: Harcourt Brace Jovanovich.

Adoff, A. (1989). *Chocolate dreams.* New York, NY: Lothrop, Lee & Shepard.

Adoff, A. (1986). *Birds: Poems.* New York, NY: Lippincott.

Adoff, A. (1986). *Sports pages.* New York, NY: J.B. Lippincott.

Adoff, A. (1985). *The cabbages are chasing the rabbits.* San Diego, CA: Harcourt Brace Jovanovich.

Adoff, A. (1982). *All the colors of the race: Poems.* New York, NY: Lothrop, Lee & Shepard.

Adoff, A. (1981). *Today we are brother and sister.* New York, NY: Lothrop, Lee & Shepard.

Adoff, A. (1980). *Friend dog.* New York: Lippincott.

Adoff, A. (1979). *Eats.* New York, NY: HarperCollins/Lothrop, Lee & Shepard.

Adoff, A. (1979). *Greens: Poems.* New York, NY: HarperCollins/Lothrop, Lee and Shepard

Adoff, A. (1979). *I am the running girl.* New York, NY: Harper & Row.

Adoff, A. (1978). *Under the early morning trees.* New York, NY: Dutton.

Adoff, A. (1978). *Where Wild Willie.* New York, NY: Harper & Row.

Adoff, A. (1977). *Tornado! Poems.* New York, NY: Delacorte.

Adoff, A. (1976). *Big sister tells me that I am black.* New York, NY: Holt, Rinehart &Winston.

Adoff, A. (1975). *Make a circle, keep us in: Poems for a good day.* New York, NY: Delacorte.

Adoff, A. (1973). *Black is brown is tan.* New York, NY: Harper & Row.

Giovanni, N. (2008). *The grasshopper's song.* Somerville, MA: Candlewick.

Giovanni, N. (2008). *Lincoln and Douglass: An American friendship.* New York, NY: Henry & Holt.

Giovanni, N. (2008). *Hip hop speaks to children.* Chicago, IL: Sourcebooks Jabberwocky.

Giovanni, N. (2005). *Rosa.* New York, NY: Henry & Holt Company.

Giovanni, N. (2004). *The girls in the circle (Just for you!)*. New York, NY: Scholastic.

Giovanni, N. (1996). *The genie in a jar.* New York, NY: Henry & Holt.

Giovanni, N. (1996). *The sun I so quiet.* New York, NY: Henry & Holt.

Giovanni, N. (1994). *Knoxville, Tennessee.* New York, NY: Scholastic.

Giovanni, N. (1980). *Vacation time: Poems for children.* New York, NY: William Morrow.

Giovanni, N. (1973). *Ego-tripping and other poems for young people.* Chicago, IL: Lawrence Hill.

Giovanni, N. (1971). *Spin a soft black song: Poems for children.* New York, NY: Farrar, Straus & Giroux.

Greenfield, E. (2010). *The great migration: Journey to the north.* New York, NY: Amistad.

Greenfield, E. (2009). *Brothers and sisters: Family poems.* New York, NY: HarperCollins

Greenfield, E. (2006). *The friendly four.* New York: Amistad.

Greenfield, E. (2006). *When the horses ride by: Children in times of war.* New York: Lee & Low.

Greenfield, E. (2003). *In the land of words: New and selected poems.* New York, NY: Amistad.

Greenfield, E. (2001). *I can draw a weeposaur and other dinosaurs.* New York, NY: HarperCollins.

Greenfield, E. (1998). *Angels: An African American treasury.* New York, NY: Jump Sun.

Greenfield, E. (1998). *For the love of the game: Michael Jordan and me.* New York, NY: HarperCollins

Greenfield, E. (1996). *Night on a neighborhood street.* New York, NY: Puffin

Greenfield, E. (1995). *On my horse.* New York, NY: Harperfestival.

Greenfield, E. (1993). *Daydreamers.* New York, NY: Puffin.

Greenfield, E. (1993). *Nathaniel talking.* London: Writers and Readers

Greenfield, E. (1991). *Under the Sunday tree.* New York, NY: HarperCollins

Greenfield, E. (1978). *Honey, I love and other poems.* New York, NY: Crowell.

Grimes, N. (2013). *Words with wings.* Honesdale, PA: Boyds Mills Press/Wordsong.

Grimes, N. (2011). *Planet middle school.* New York, NY: Bloomsbury.

Grimes, N. (2007). *Oh, brother.* New York, NY: Greenwillow.

Grimes, N. (2007). *When gorilla goes walking.* London: Orchard.

Grimes, N. (2006). *Thanks a million.* New York, NY: Greenwillow.

Grimes, N. (2005). *At Jerusalem's gate: Poems of Easter.* Grand Rapids, MI: Eerdmans.

Grimes, N. (2005). *Danitra Brown, class clown.* New York, NY: Amistad.

Grimes, N. (2005). *It's raining laughter.* Honesdale, PA: Wordsong.

Grimes, N. (2004). *Tai chi morning: Snapshots of China.* Peru, IL: Cricket.

Grimes, N. (2004). *What is goodbye?* New York, NY: Hyperion.

Grimes, N. (2004). *When daddy prays.* Grand Rapids, MI: Eerdmans.

Grimes, N. (2002). *Dreams by day, dreams by night: An anthology of poems and photographs.* New York, NY: Mondo.

Grimes, N. (2002). *My man blue.* New York, NY: Puffin.

Grimes, N. (2002). *Under the Christmas tree.* New York, NY: HarperCollins.

Grimes, N. (2001). *A pocketful of poems.* New York, NY: Clarion.

Grimes, N. (2001). *Danitra Brown leaves town.* New York, NY: Amistad.

Grimes, N. (2001). *Stepping out with grandma Mac.* London: Orchard.

Grimes, N. (2000). *Is it far to Zanzibar? Poems about Tanzania.* New York, NY: HarperCollins.

Grimes, N. (2000). *Shoe magic.* New York, NY: Scholastic.

Grimes, N. (1999). *Aneesa Lee and the weaver's gift.* New York, NY: HarperCollins.

Grimes, N. (1999). *At break of day.* Grand Rapids, MI: Eerdmans.

Grimes, N. (1999). *Hopscotch love: A family treasury of love poems.* New York, NY: HarperCollins.

Grimes, N. (1998). *A dime a dozen.* New York, NY: Dial.

Grimes, N. (1997). *Meet Danitra Brown.* New York, NY: HarperCollins.

Grimes, N. (1996). *Come Sunday.* Grand Rapids, MI: Eerdmans.

Grimes, N. (1994). *From a child's heart.* East Orange, NJ: Just Us.

Hughes, L. (2013). *Lullaby (For a black mother).* New York, NY: Harcourt.

Hughes, L. (2012). I, too, am America (Bryan Collier, Illus.). New York, NY: Simon & Schuster.

Hughes, L. (2009). *The Negro speaks of rivers.* New York, NY: Hyperion.

Hughes, L. (2005). *Let America be America again.* New York, NY: George Braziller.

Hughes, L. (1998). *Carol of the brown king: Nativity poem.* New York, NY: Atheneum.

Hughes, L. (1997). *The sweet and sour animal book.* New York, NY: Oxford University.

Hughes, L. (1995). *The book of rhythms.* New York, NY: Oxford University.

Hughes, L. (1945). *The weary blues.* New York, NY: Knopf.

Hughes, L. (1932). *The dream keeper and other poems.* New York, NY: Knopf.

Johnson, A. (1998). *The other side: Shorter poems.* New York, NY: Orchard Books.

Myers, W. D. (2011). *We are America: A tribute from the heart.* New York, NY: Collins.

Myers, W. D. (2009). *Looking like me* (Christopher Myers, Illus.) New York, NY: Egmont.

Myers, W. D. (2008). *Jazz.* New York, NY: Holiday House.

Myers, W. D. (2007). *Blues journey.* New York, NY: Holiday House.

Myers, W. D. (2000). *Angel to angel: A mother's gift of love.* Madison, WI: Demco Media.

Myers, W. D. (1997). *Glorious angels: A celebration of children.* New York, NY: HarperCollins.

Myers, W. D. (1997). *Harlem.* New York, NY: Scholastic.

Myers, W. D. (1996). *Brown angels: An album of pictures and verse.* New York, NY: HarperCollins.

Nelson, M. (2012). *Faster than light: New and selected poems, 1996-2011.* Baton Rouge, LA: Louisiana State University Press.

Nelson, M. (2009). *Sweethearts of rhythm* (Jerry Pinkney, Illus.). New York, NY: Dial Books.

Nelson, M. (2008). The freedom business: Including a narrative of the life & adventures of Venture, a native of Africa (Deborah Muirhead, Illus.), Honesdale, PA: Boyds Mills Press/Front Street.

Nelson, M. (2005). *A wreath for Emmett Till* (Philippe Lardie, Illus.) .New York, NY: Houghton Mifflin Books for Children.

Nelson, M. (2004). *Fortune's bones: The manumission requiem.* Honesdale, PA: Boyds Mills Press/Front Street.

Nelson, M. (2001). *Carver: A life in poems.* Honesdale, PA: Boyds Mills Press/Front Street.

Shange, N. (2012). *Freedom's a-callin me.* New York, NY: Amistad.

Shange, N. (2009). *We troubled the waters.* New York, NY: Amistad.

Shange, N. (2004). *Ellington was not a street.* New York, NY: Simon & Schuster.

Smith, H. A. (2009). *Mother poems.* New York, NY: Henry Holt & Company.

Smith, H. A. (2008). *Keeping the night watch.* (E. B. Lewis Illus.). E. B. Lewis. New York, NY: Henry Holt.

Smith, H. A. (2003). *The way a door closes.* (S. W. Evans, Illus.). New York, NY: Henry Holt.

Thomas, J. C. (2012). *In the land of milk and honey.* New York, NY: Amistad.

Thomas, J. C. (2008). *The blacker the berry.* New York, NY: Amistad.

Thomas, J. C. (2007). *Shouting!* New York, NY: Jump At the Sun.

Thomas, J. C. (2002). *Crowning glory.* New York, NY: Joanna.

Thomas, J. C. (2001). *A mother's heart, A daughter's love: Poems for us to share.* New York, NY: Joanna Cotler.

Thomas, J. C. (2001). *Joy!* New York, NY: Jump At the Sun.

Thomas, J. C. (2000). *Hush songs.* New York, NY: Jump at the Sun.

Thomas, J. C. (2000). *I have heard of a land.* New York: HarperCollins.

Thomas, J. C. (1997). *Gingerbread days.* New York, NY: Harper Trophy.

Thomas, J. C. (1995). *Brown honey in broomwheat tea.* New York, NY: HarperCollins.

Weatherford, C. B. (2009). *The Beatitudes: From slavery to civil rights* (Illus. by Tim Ladwig). Grand Rapids, MI: Eerdmans Books for Young Readers.

Weatherford, C. B. (2008). *Becoming Billie Holiday* (Illus. by Floyd Cooper). Honesdale, PA: Boyds Mills Press/Wordsong.

Weatherford, C. B. (2008). *Before John was a jazz giant: A song of John Coltrane* (Illus by Sean Qualls). New York, NY: Henry Holt.

Weatherford, C. B. (2007). *Birmingham, 1963.* Honesdale, PA: Boyds Mills Press/ Wordsong.

Weatherford, C. B. (2002). *Remember the bridge: Poems of a people.* New York, NY: Philomel.

APPENDIX B

Suggested Poetry Websites

http://www.favoritepoem.org/index.html is a site dedicated to celebrating and documenting poetry's role in American's lives. There is an interactive gallery with favorite poems and videos, including resources for teachers.

http://www.loc.gov/teachers/classroommaterials/ presentationsandactivities/activities/history/ this Library of Congress cite shows that poetry tells us about history. Students can analyze historical poems and create new poems. Resources for teachers included.

http://www.poets.org/page.php/prmID/370 from the academy of American poets teachers can sign up for a poem-a-day and gain many resources. During Black history month there are featured poems by African American poets with many related poems.

http://www.readingrockets.org/calendar/poetry/ is a popular literacy cite with videos of acclaimed poets, the importance of learning through poetry with links to websites, lists of poetry books and many resources. There is information about movements such as jazz poetry, Negritude and slam poetry. Featured videos

http://www.poetryfoundation.org/children/ contains poems, the best poetry books and resources. Each month the current children's poet laureate chooses one poetry book to highlight. In addition, there are resources for teaching African American poetry.

http://www.poetry4kids.com includes rhyming dictionary, poetry games, poetry contests, news and surveys, discussion forums and poetry resources for teachers.

http://www.perfectpoems.com is a poetry collection site for beginning reading and writing of words.

http://www.colegiobolivar.edu.co/library/primary_poetry.htm thousands of poems and poets and available including lesson plans for teachers.

http://www.poetryteachers.com is a site completely for teachers with how to teach poetry, activities and scripts for poetry theatre.

http://teenink.com/Poetry/ contains poetry written by teens organized by themes and issues. Students can vote for their favorite poems, discuss poems and submit poems for other kids to read.

REFERENCES

Abbott, T. (2011). *Lunch-Box dream*. New York, NY: Farrar, Straus & Giroux.

Adoff, A. (1982). *All the colors of the race* (Illus. by J. Steptoe). New York, NY: Beech Tree/William Morrow.

Adoff, A. (2011). *Roots and blues: A celebration*. New York, NY: Clarion.

Bandy, M. S. (2011). *White water* (Illus. by Eric Stein). Somerville, MA: Candlewick Press.

Bishop, R. S. (2007). *Free within ourselves: The development of African American children's literature*. Westport, CT: Greenwood Press.

Bradley, K. (2011). Twitter poem in-class writing exercise. *English in Two-Year College, 39*(2), 195.

Brooks, W. M., & McNair, J. C. (Eds.). (2008). *Embracing, evaluating, and examining African American children's & young adult literature.* Lanham, MD: Scarecrow Press.

Calkins, L. M. (2003). *Units of study for primary writing: A yearlong curriculum.* Portsmouth, NH: FirstHand/ Heinemann.

Campbell, P. (2004). The sand in the oyster: Vetting the verse novel. *The Horn Book Magazine, 80*(5), 611-616.

Cullinan, B., Scala, M.C., & Schroder, V.C. (1995). *Three voices: an invitation to poetry across the curriculum.* York, ME: Stenhouse.

Curwood, J. S., & Cowell, L.L.H. (2011). iPoetry: Creating space for new literacies in the English curriculum. *Journal of Adolescent & Adult Literacy, 55*(2), 110-120.

Davis, J., & Hill, S. (2003). *The no-nonsense guide to teaching writing: Strategies, structures, and solutions.* Portsmouth, NH: Heinemann.

Eva-Wood, A.L. (2008). Does feeling come first? How poetry can help readers broaden their understanding of metacognition. *Journal of Adolescent & Adult Literacy, 51*(7), 564-576.

Faulkner, M. (2008). *A taste of colored water.* New York, NY: Simon & Schuster Books for Young Readers.

Faver, S. (2008). Repeated reading of poetry can enhance reading fluency. *The Reading Teacher, 62*(4), 350-352.

Fleischman, P. (1988). *Joyful noise: Poems for two voices.* New York, NY: HarperCollins.

Giovanni, N. (2008) *Hip hop speaks to children.* Chicago, IL: Sourcebooks Jabberwocky.

Greenfield, E. (1978). *Honey, I love and other love poems.* Illus. by D. & L. Dillon. New York, NY: Harper Collins. Gill, S. R. (2007). The forgotten genre of children's poetry. *The Reading Teacher, 60*(7), 622-625.

Grimes, N. (1977). *Growin'.* New York, NY: Dial.

Grimes, N. (1978). *Something on my mind.* New York, NY: Dial.

Graves, D. (1992). *Explore poetry.* Portsmouth, NH: Heinemann.

Grimes, N. (1994). *Meet Danitra Brown.* New York, NY: Lothrop, Lee & Shepard.

Grimes, N. (2000). The power of poetry. *Book links, 9*(4), 36.

Grimes, N. (2001). *Bronx masquerade.* New York, NY: Dial

Grimes, N. (2002). *Danitra Brown leaves town.* New York, NY: HarperCollins.

Grimes, N. (2004). *What is goodbye?* New York, NY: Hyperion.

Grimes, N. (2004). Spotlight on Nikki Grimes: Where do poems come from? A CLA workshop presentation. *Journal of Children's Literature, 30*(1), 7-12.

Grimes, N. (2005). The common denominator. *English Journal, 94*(3), 22-24.

Grimes, N. (2005). *Danitra Brown, class clown.* New York, NY: HarperCollins.

Grimes, N. (2005). *Dark sons.* New York, NY: Hyperion.

Heard, G., & Laminack, L. (2008). *Reading and writing poetry across the year, grades K-2.* Portsmouth, NH: FirstHand/ Heinemann.

Heard, G. (1999). *Awakening the heart: Exploring poetry in the elementary and middle school.* Portsmouth, NH: Heinemann.

Hopkins, L. B. (2005). Nikki Grimes. *Teaching K-8, 36*(2), 70.

Isaacs, K. T. (2003). Stories in verse. *Book Links, 12*(5), 10-14.

Linaberger, M. (2004). Poetry top 10: A foolproof formula for teaching poetry. *The Reading Teacher, 58*(4), 366-372.

Lyon, G. E. (1999). *Where I'm from: Where poems come from.* Photos by B. Hoskins. Spring, TX: Absey.

McBroom, K. (2011). Author profile: Writing as service: a profile of Nikki Grimes. *Library Media Connection, 29*(4), 40-42.

Myers, W. D. (2009). *Looking like me* (Illus. by Christopher Myers). New York, NY: Egmont.

Nelson, M. (2009). *Sweethearts of rhythm* (Illus. by Jerry Pinkney). New York, NY: Dial Books.

Olshansky, B. (1994). Making writing a work of art: Image-making within the writing process. *Language Arts, 71*, 350-356.

O'Neill, M. (1989). *Hailstones and halibut bones: Adventures in color* (Illus. by J. Wallner). New York, NY: Doubleday Books for Young Readers.

Oster, L. (2001). Using the think-aloud for reading instruction. *The Reading Teacher, 55*(1), 64-69.

Parr, M., & Campbell, T. (2006). Poets in practice. *The Reading Teacher, 60*(1), 36-46.

Paterson, K. (2000). Asking the question. *New Advocate, 12*(1), 1-15.

Perfect, K. A. (1999). Rhyme and reason: Poetry for the heart and head. *The Reading Teacher, 52*(7), 728-737.

Reilly, M. A. (2008). Finding the right words: Art conversations and poetry. *Language Arts, 86*(2), 99-107.

Ridolfi, K. (1997). Secret places. *Voices from the Middle, 4*(1), 38-42.

Rosenblatt, L. (1938). *Literature as exploration.* New York, NY: Modern Language Association.

Routman, R. (2001). Everyone succeeds with poetry writing. *Instructor, 111*(1), 26-30.

Routman, R. (2000). *Kids' poems: Teaching third & fourth graders to love writing poetry.* New York, NY: Scholastic.

Ryder, J. (2007). *Toad by the road: A year in the life of these amazing amphibians* (Illus. by Maggie Kneen). New York, NY: Henry Holt.

Salas, L. P. (2011). *BookSpeak: Poems about books.* Illus. by J. Bisaillon. New York, NY: Houghton Mifflin Harcourt/Clarion.

Sekeres, D. C., & Gregg, M. (2007). Poetry in third grade: Getting started. *The Reading Teacher, 60*(5), 466-475.

Shanklin, N. (2009). Exploring poetry: How does a middle school teacher begin? *Voices from the Middle, 16*(3), 46-47.

Smith, H. A. (2003). *The way a door closes* (Illus. by S. W. Evans). New York, NY Henry Holt.

Smith, H. A. (2008). *Keeping the night watch* (Illus. by E. B. Lewis). New York, NY: Henry Holt.

Smith, H. A. (2009). *Mother poems.* New York, NY: Henry Holt.

Stange, T. V., & Wyant, S.L. (2008). Poetry proves to be positive in the primary grades. *Reading Horizons, 48*(3), 201-214.

Stange, T.V., & Wyant, S.L. (1999). Aren't we going to write today? Using parody in grade 3. *Reading Horizons, 39*(3), 159-173.

Stanley, N. (2004). A celebration of words. *Teaching Pre K-8, 34*(7), 56-57.

Tarasiuk, T. (2009). Extreme poetry: Making meaning through words, images, and music. *Voices from the Middle, 16*(3), 50-51.

Trousdale, A., J., & Willis, E. (2010). "One question leads to another": The value of talk in the choral reading of poetry. *Voices from the Middle, 18*(2), 46-54.

Vardell, S. M., & Oxley, P. (2007). An interview with poet Nikki Grimes. *Language Arts, 84*(3), 281-285.

Vardell, S., & Wong, J. (2012). *The poetry Friday anthology K-5 Edition*. Princeton, NJ: Pomelo Books.

Vardell, S., & Wong, J. (2013). *The poetry Friday anthology for middle school*. Princeton, NJ: Pomelo Books.

Weatherford, C. B. (2002). *Remember the bridge: Poems of a people*. New York, NY: Philomel.

Weatherford, C. B. (2007). *Birmingham, 1963*. Honesdale, PA: Boyds Mills Press/ Wordsong.

Weatherford, C. B. (2008). *Before John was a jazz giant: A song of John Coltrane* (Illus. by Sean Qualls). New York, NY: Henry Holt.

Weatherford, C. B. (2009). *The Beatitudes: From slavery to civil rights* (Illus. by Tim Ladwig). Grand Rapids, MI: Eerdmans Books for Young Readers.

CHAPTER 4

RECOGNIZING AFRICAN MUSIC AS A POWERFUL PEDAGOGICAL TOOL IN CLASSROOM SETTINGS

Theresa Tuwor

Introduction

African music is made up of the language, the customs, and values of the society. Each culture has its own distinctive styles which reveal much about a people and their way of life. This chapter proposes that African music be integrated in the classroom as a teaching tool because it has the tendency to improve learning and also move away from the traditional Western teaching strategies. Apart from that, there are various reasons for integrating music as a teaching and learning tool in the classroom. In this chapter, the author discusses the characteristics, functions, and theories of African music that support the integration of African music in the classroom.

Naturally, music stirs emotions, relieves tension, focuses the mind, reduces mental fatigue, and releases good feeling. In the classroom, it

African Traditional and Oral Literature as Pedagogical Tools in Contest Area Classrooms: K-12, pages 65–77
Copyright © 2014 by Information Age Publishing
All rights of reproduction in any form reserved.

enhances creativity and boosts learning—the main goals of teaching and learning. Innovatively, using African music in the classroom will enhance learning and retaining new concepts. Historically, people in all human cultures have recognized and purposefully used the powerful effects of music in their daily lives. There are different forms of music—friendship, work, dance, love, and so forth (Gefter & Marshall, 2008). It is seen as a very important aspect in communication and entertainment in most cultures as well as a natural teaching tool. As Brew (2006) points out, music is found in every culture and is used as means of expression. It is a means of delivering message; used as a medium of poetry; serves as a form of entertainment, and can be treasured for its aesthetic values. Guth (n.d.) also claims that children who are fortunate enough to be exposed to weekly music lessons or general music classes reap many benefits. She explains further that it is an evident outlet for creativity and self-expression.

African Music

Graham (1988) states that, "in Africa, music is perhaps the main manifestation of culture in its broadest sense" (p. 4). Aning (1973) posits that traditional African music may be defined as that music which is associated with indigenous African institutions of the precolonial era. African music is basically the music of the indigenous peoples of Africa. Music and dance are terms that are usually used to denote musical practices of African people. This explains that ancient African society did not separate their everyday life activities from their music and other cultural experience.

It is widely observed that African traditional music has undergone changes throughout the centuries. What is termed African traditional music today is probably very different from African music in former times. For example, Nidel (2005) states that "high Life music is in part indebted to the instruments brought by the sailors, soldiers, and missionaries of colonization in West Africa" (p. 35). So the individual musician, his style and creativity played an important role in the composition. In view of the role of African music and learning, Tchebwa (2005) states that African music is a path through which knowledge is transmitted. According to him, there are fivefold of the purposes of African music:

1. Educational: Music is used to teach traditional tales, word and thinking games (proverbs, charades, etc.). It is also used during initiation periods to teach African values.
2. Liturgical: It is a tool to communicate to the ancestors, the values and songs devoted to the divinities, to the protecting spirits, (prayer, chants, magic incantations, etc).

3. Playful: Music is generally used for entertainment, for instance, at social gatherings, such as weddings and celebration of special achievements etc.
4. Functional: It is important during all ritual actions in life such as music for drinking, fishing, making palm wine, splitting wood, etc.
5. Cathartric: Music is used to support and attack mystical power from the world beyond, as a form of intercessor and catalyst of social violence under reign of the gods, the protecting spirits, etc.

Characteristics of African Music

One of the characteristics of African music is its emphasis on rhythm as well as a percussive concept of music performance. Aning (1973) states that African musical rhythms may be played in solo, vocal, cradle songs, folk stories, children's play, drum language. The author further explains that there are other multilineal organized rhythms. These are found in accompanied solo and choral music, unaccompanied choral music, and instrumental ensemble music. Another characteristic feature is the way melodies are organized. Different African people use different kinds of scales, while some build their melodies upon varieties of the pentatonic scales; others built on hexatonic scales; while others also construct their songs on the heptatonic levels (Aning, 1973). Much of traditional African music is also associated with dance, which adds to the multidimensional effect of the musical presentation. Apart from that, African music also has high degrees of amplitude which may be due to the fact that African music is generally performed outdoors.

Types of African Music

African traditional music is a vital part of everyday life. It is a part of most social activities such as religious ceremonies, festivals, social rituals, birth, death, and so forth. It is believed among Africans that music serves as a link with the spirit world. Among Africans, music is highly functional in ethnic life, crossing every life activity, in hunting and in political activities. Music is ultimately tied to the things that are most important to the welfare of individual and the community as well.

During colonial times, European instruments such as saxophones, trumpets, and guitars were adopted by many African musicians; their sounds are integrated into the traditional patterns. Music varies across the African continent. In Africa, each ethnic group of Southern African descent has very simple songs. East Africans specialize in music played on xylophones. West Coast ethnic groups have made the art of drum playing a highly developed skill.

Africa is a large and diverse continent, and therefore the music of Africa is diverse in nature as it is largely influenced by the different cultures and geographical locations. The instruments are made according to the accessibility of raw materials in a geographic area and sometimes the language sounds of specific groups. For instance, the people located in forest regions seem to have music that is dominated by instruments made of wood. The process of preserving music through oral traditions has propelled African communities to be creative, as each of their songs can be modified to suit a particular occasion. Different instruments and vocal traditions have been transferred and adapted by different African societies as a result of this preservation process (Tchebwa, 2005).

Below are some of the characteristics of the different types of music in different regions of the continent:

East Africa: Eastern music has a unique drumming style, Islamic influence, and the absence of "hot rhythm." This region also known as the Swahili region has cultural affinities from the traditions such as the Bantu, Ethiopic and Nilotic. Music in the region includes melodies of *nanga* zither or the *nyati* lyre. This is also where urban and rural poetry as well as sacred powers are drummed out of the mighty *ingoma* and the *rwoga* drums of the Tutsi and Hutu ethnic groups. Kenya is also home to the musical genre known as Ogopa which has become very influential in eastern Africa (Rocheleau, 2009; Tchebwa, 2005).

Central Africa: Music in this region places greater emphasis on percussion instruments. The region has sound from its citharas, *sanza,* pluriarcs and the *lokole* drums. Their music conveys an ancient past that goes back to proto-Bantu times. The musical traditions in the region are in tune with ancestral ways of life, either sitting or nomadic, practice by pastoral or crop-growing people. These are shared between traditions of Nilotic, Bantu or the Ethiopian cultures (Rocheleau, 2009; Tchebwa, 2005).

West Africa: In this region emphasis is placed on percussion instruments in their musical rhythms. This region is abundant with diversity of Sahelian music full of courtly poetry. The lyrics of West African music mostly revolve around issues of everyday human lived experiences (Rocheleau, 2009; Tchebwa, 2005).

North Africa: Oriental and Arabic music, which are related to the Arabic language and its accents have had great influence in this region. In addition, the Ottoman influence in the north part of the continent has reinforced modal music. Northern African nations have become home to a type of music known as *Rai* which is popular in Algeria. *Rai* traditionally serves as a form of folk music for significant entertainment at various social settings (Rocheleau, 2009; Tchebwa, 2005).

Functions of African Music

Rocheleau (2009) explains that the social function of music has varying cultural meanings to different people across the continent of Africa. Understanding the many genres of music that spread across the diverse regions of this continent is crucial in determining the role of music in African society. The utilitarian value of music in Africa lies in its association to lived experiences. These experiences relate to all social functions including births, discussing politics, economic life, and to the accompaniment of everyday experiences. African music links the living to the ancestors and future children (Rocheleau, 2009). In terms of its aesthetic value Africa music is culturally constructed. People's values, preferences, and tastes are strongly linked to cultural factors, such as economics, gender, history, age, and family. In African societies, music is seen as inseparable from human existence. It carries long traditions and values that are associated with the people and represents part of their identity.

Theoretical Framework

Theoretically, music is said to be helpful to learners in understanding their cultures. Postcolonial theory is one of the theories that can explain the need for African music in the classroom. This theory explains the effect of cultural legacy of colonialism on third world countries (Browne Smye, & Varcoe, 2005). It is a postmodern intellectual discourse that analyses the cultural legacy of colonialism (Loomba, 1998). The main goal of postcolonialism is combating the remaining effects of colonialism on cultures. For this reason, African music has the ability to provide the child mental freedom and also help students learn the content areas across the curriculum as related to the cultural settings (Loomba, 1998).

Cannella and Viruru (2004) also advocate for teaching techniques and practices that would treat everyone equally and result in "social justice and freedom for all" (p. 123). Harris (2002) explains that music is an enjoyable way to provide the base of prior knowledge that is so critical to learning. For instance, after singing songs in Spanish, an English-speaking child will recognize words as he studies Spanish language and culture that increases the child's ability and interest. (http://www.songsforteaching.com/rationale.htm).

During the periods of European colonization, the culture of Africa was no longer embraced for all that it had to present. Amuah (1997) claims that the negative attitude of the missionaries toward African culture affected the promotion of traditional African music, this hostile attitude resulted in the condemnation of all aspects of African culture as devilish. African music could not be promoted in the schools because it was considered the music of the devil. However, the important role of African music in everyday life and even in political popular music did not die with the attainment of independence in many African countries.

Although there was a negative result for African music and culture outside of the continent, within the continent music continued to grow through colonization and migration. Apart from that, postindependence circumstances also helped shape the African music of today (Rocheleau, 2009). It served as a way to hold onto the culture and to inspire hope for the future, as well as helped to calm the frustrations many faced under European. Using African music as an instructional tool in the classroom would reintroduce African culture into the school curriculum because African music has cross-cultural influences through trade and cross-border trade (Rocheleau, 2009).

According to Huber, Kline, Bakken, and Clark (1997), what is needed for students to get the most out of learning in American education is culturally sensitive and responsible pedagogy. They explain further that culturally responsible pedagogy subsumes all diversities to ensure sensitivity to and responsibility for all learners. The method of teaching and the curriculum should be mindful of where the learner is. African students just as their colleagues in America and all over the world need curriculum and teaching strategies that resonate with their cultural setting. African traditional education involves the use of folk music, storytelling, and proverbs, for this reason, African music would follow the traditional trend of teaching and learning as well as play effect role in teaching African children in the classroom. For effective teaching and learning there should be no conflicts between home and school culture. Apart from that, teachers have to be responsive to cultural issues. "Much of what happens in the classrooms is incongruous and 'out of sync' with what happens in the home and community and community experiences" (p. 132).

According to Goodwin (1997), as teacher educators are looking out for how to effectively introduce multicultural practices in their curricula, African music should not be left out in this process. It should integrated as culturally responsive pedagogue, which will also serve as means of presenting sociopolitical studies, African history, and social change content to children. These strategies are being used in the teacher education program to equip student-teachers for the diverse nature of their classroom. For the classroom to meet the demand of preparing children cultural-knowledge for the globalized society African music will not only be important teaching tool, but be an instrument for socialization. Ehrensal, Crawford, Cast, Elluccii, and Gregory (2005) state that

> the metaphor of the melting pot left it to the schools to educate students from many cultures through a common language, a common history, and common goals, principles, and values. The schools bore the burden of producing the social and cultural integration required to create "real Americans." (p. 70)

Other theories that explain the importance of integrating African music in the classroom are critical race theory (CRT) and critical pedagogy. These theories examine society and culture, how racial power is maintained over time, and in particular, how law may play a role in this process. According to Delgado and Stefancic (2001), critical race theory which is focused on studying and transforming the relationship among race, racism, and power, not only tries to understand our social situation, but to change it; it sets out not only to ascertain how society organizes itself along racial lines and hierarchies, but to transform it for the better. It is also explains that CTR is any attempt to (re)engage excluded learners with the curriculum, teaching and assessment, must be aware of culture and ethnicity (p. 2). CRT functioned as a discourse on schooling and inequality that has developed in tandem with theories of race and pedagogical practice in ways that reflect the context of African American education (Jennings & Lynn (2005). The effect of using African music as a teaching tool in the classroom could bridge gap of cultural insensitiveness in the classroom.

Reasons for Using African Music in the Classroom

Music has always been a way for children to remember stories and learn about the world around them. The increased focus on academic curriculum standards often makes it more challenging to integrate music into classroom lessons. With a little creative planning, music can actually serve as a method to teach some units in the curriculum. To this effect Quintanar-Sarellana (1997) argues that pedagogical methods and learning material should be culturally relevant specific. He also emphasizes the need to incorporate the student's background in the educational process. In the same vein, Dillard (1997) also explains that "centering the pedagogy and practices of education involves including and situating pedagogy and practice authentically in relation to one's own culture and background experiences" (p. 92). This supports the idea why African music should be integral of the African child's classroom.

Harris (2002) states that teachers are encouraged to use auditory, visual, kinesthetic, and tactile modes to supplement the learning experience. While music is obviously an auditory activity, the kinesthetic, visual, and tactile modalities can be activated via clapping, dancing, and instrument playing. Research suggests that the more senses we use, the deeper and broader the degree of learning. Gardner's research on multiple intelligences supports this idea. He describes how people demonstrate different skills and talents while trying to learn. In this context, music is viewed as a multisensory approach to enhance learning and retention of academic skills (Lazar, n.d.). Therefore, classrooms must provide different approaches to meet an individual student's areas of strength in order to be the most successful (Gardner, 1985). African music resonates with the use of more senses because most traditional and modern African music are companied by clapping and dancing. These factors make African music stands as a good and effective instructional tool.

According to Stover (n.d.), music researchers continue to find correlations between music and the development of the human brain. The author says the International Foundation for Music Research argues that music plays a crucial role in the development of school-aged children. In Edwards, Bayless and Ramsey's (n.d.) work, they outline six reasons why the importance of music and movement activities should not be underestimated. Below are some relevant reasons:

1. Mental capacity and intellect. Mathematical concepts can be developed as children sing counting songs because children can form connection between music and the development of mathematical thinking.
2. Development of creativity. Children can use improvised materials to create music. For example, they can use a stick can be transformed into a horn, a box can become a drum, or a broom can become a dance partner. Children make up songs or give new words to old songs for pure enjoyment as well as create an invented world that stimulates a child's creativity.

Most African music is accompanied by dance so it can be used to make lessons active and interactive as students can dance or move the rhythm of the music. In Edwards et al. (n.d.) work they mention that music can develop creativity in the students. This is clear evidence that African music will help learners and teachers to be creative in terms of creating improvised instruments to perform music in the classroom.

According to Nompula (2011), researchers also agree that songs teach children manners and correct social behavior. Through games and indigenous African music, children not only learn the language but also how to behave. Apart from that, children are encouraged to respect and cooperate with the leader, participate in musical performances since they learn to listen, which in turn develops respect for and a supportive spirit in working with the leaders in society.

Amuah (1997) claims that the knowledge, understanding and skills needed for an optimum experience of African music are critical to the growth of the child into a fully-fledged Ghanaian and for that matter African who is knowledgeable of the practices of his/her cultural heritage. It will lead to cultural awakening in the students, as the student sing African songs they will learn new language and structural patterns and also reinforce African identity

- Strengthens creativity in students because they will have the chance to create instruments using materials from their direct culture environment that will make the learners experience and relate to the music they perform
- To help prevent the collapse of African indigenous music. Amuah (1997) states that the educational system has the responsibility to avoid Africa's rich musical heritage from being totally hidden. In this case the students do not only learn the content of a lesson but also the music and its contextual meaning.
- Memorization of longer word strings will be facilitated. Children will noticeably increase their vocabulary bank. These word structures can include a range of sociolinguistic situations appropriate to the age and needs of the pupils such as greetings, idioms, requests and any language items necessary for basic classroom functions and routines (p. 10).

Harris (2002) asserts that music can be used to stimulate interest in subjects across the curriculum and also provide an introduction to lesson. According to him, as one's base of prior knowledge grows, interest and learning become easier, and a positive sequence is established. When introducing a lesson on African, an African-related music would be good to provide an entry to the lesson or topic. The increased focus on academic curriculum standards often makes it more challenging to integrate music into classroom lessons. With a little creative planning, music can actually serve as the method to teach selected lesson or units of the curriculum. In this context, music is viewed as a multisensory approach to improve learning and retention of academic skills. Using music to introduce an exercise is a great way to activate vocabulary and get students thinking in the right direction.

Sample Activities of Using Music as a Teaching Tool

Below are sample activities of using African music in the classroom

Learning Activity One: A Musical and Artistic Experience

This activity is an introduction to one aspect of African culture which combines listening, music and artistic response.

1. Have your students listen to the interactive Swahili folktale on— website Swahili 4 kids: http://swahili4kids.com/lyricsandtext.html
2. After the students have heard the folktales ask them to draw a picture based on it.
3. While they draw, play music from the following websites—African Arts and Music: http://www.pbs.org/wnet/africa/tools/music/activities. html
http://www.theholidayspot.com/kwanzaa/kwanzaa_music.htm
http://www.humansong s.com/artists htm
http://www.african-drumbeat.co.uk/

Using music to teach social studies: Songs of African countries and their capitals

Songs about Presidents of African countries

Above are examples of songs that can be adopted from this website to serve as prdagogical tool: http://www.songsforteaching.com/socialstudiessongs. htm

Acron Naturalist: The Acron Naturalist website has a list of environmental topics teachers and students can adopt a popular song—http://www. acornnaturalists.com/store/MusicSamples.aspx

Lazar (n.d.) lists some strategies of integrating music in the classroom for which African music will be good as instructional tool. Below are examples:

- Play music from various eras when teaching African history. Play songs that represent a historical event and have students discuss relevance of the lyrics. For example a popular song for liberation struggle in South Africa by Amandla, the Cultural Troupe of the National Congress Liberation Movement (Mlama, n.d.).

Ayakinggikaza	They tremble
Agangigikaza ayesabamagwala	They shiver

Athi Kungcono sibuyelemuva   The cowards have cold feet
Qiniselani nani maghawe   They say it is better to retreat
Sekuseduze Lapho syakhona   Steel yourselves
                                    Intensify the struggle you
                                    brave ones
                                    Our destination is close
                                    (our victory is certain)

CONCLUSION

This chapter set out to discuss the importance of integrating African music in the classroom. African music, like other forms of music used in the classroom, can play vital roles in teaching. African music has different characteristic features that can be used to teach abstract concepts. It draws on African history, behavior, stories, values, beliefs, and so forth. Apart from making teachers move away from the Westerns methods of teaching, African music enriches the classroom with traditional cultural practices.

Internet Resources

http://www.songsforteaching.com/   http://intelli-tunes.com/
http://gs.fanshawec.ca/tlwm/   www.SongsForTeaching.com

REFERENCES

Acorn Naturalists. (n.d.). Retrieved from http://www.acornnaturalists.com/store/MusicSamples.aspx

Amuah R. I. (1997). African music education in Ghanaian teacher training colleges: Past, present and future. *The African Music Education, 9*, 1- 23.

Aning, B. A. (1973). Varieties of African music and musical yypes. *The Black Perspective in Music, 1*(1), 16-23.

African Arts and Music. (n.d.). Retrieved from http://www.pbs.org/wnet/africa/tools/music/activities.html

Africa—Teacher Tools: African Arts and Music Lesson Plans. (n.d.). Retrieved from PBS http://www.humansong s.com/artists.htm

Brew, N. (April, 2006). Importance of music education. Retrieved on December 2012 from http://www.studymode.com/essays/Importance-Music-Education-85678.html

Browne, A .J., Smye, V. L., & Varcoe, C. (2005). The relevance of postcolonial theoretical perspectives to research in aboriginal health. *Canadian Journal of Nursing Research, 37*(4), 16-37.

Cannella S. G., & Viruru, R. (2004). *Childhood and postcolonization: Power, education and contemporary practice.* London, England: Routledge Falmer.

Delgado, R., & Stefancic, J. (2001). *Critical race theory: An Introduction* (2nd ed.). Philadelphia, PA: Temple University Press.

Dillard, B. C. (1997). Placing student language, literacy, and culture at the center of teacher education reform. In J. E. King, E. R. Hollins, & C. Warren (Eds.), *Preparing Teachers for Cultural Diversity* (pp. 854-96). New York, NY: Teachers College Press.

Edwards, L. C. Bayless, K. M., & Ramsey, M. E. (n.d.). Four important reasons for including music in the classroom. Retrieved from http://www.education.com/reference/article/four-important-reasons-including-music/

Ehrensal, A. L. P. , Crawford, L. R., Castellucci, A. J., & Gregory, A. (2005). The Americas melting pot versus Chinese hot pot. In J. P. Shapiro & A. J. Stefkovich (Eds.), *Ethical leadership and decision making in education: Applying theoretical perspective to complex dilemmas* (2nd ed., pp, 70-81). Mahwah, NJ: Lawrence Erlbaum Associates.

Gardner, H. (1985). *Frame of mind: The theory of multiple intelligences.* New York, NY. Basic Books.

Gefter, A., & Marshall, M. (2008). The six forms of music. Retrieved from http://www.newscientist.com/article/dn14603-the-six-forms-of-music.html

Goodwin, A. L. (1997). Historical and contemporary perspectives on multicultural teacher education: Past lessons and new directions. In E. J. King, E. R. Hollins, & C. Warren (Ed.), *Preparing teachers for cultural diversity* (pp. 5-22). New York, NY: Teachers College Press.

Guth, P. (n.d.) Importance of music education. Retrieved on http://education.more4kids.info/23/the-importance-of-music-education/

Graham, R. (1988). *The Da Capo guide to contemporary African music.* New York, NY: DaCapo Press.

Harris, S. R. (2002). Song as a tool for content area learning. Retrieved from http://www.acesandeighths.com/hip_hop.html

Huber, T., Kline, F. M. F., Bakken, L., & Clark, F. L. (1997). Transforming teacher education: Including culturally responsible, pedagogy (pp.129-145). In E. J. King, E. R. Hollins, & C. Warren (Ed.), *Preparing teachers for cultural diversity* (pp. 129-145). New York, NY: Teachers College Press.

Jennings E. M., & Lynn, M. (2005). The house that race built: Critical pedagogy, African-American education, and the re-conceptualization of a critical race pedagogy. *Educational Foundations, 19,* 3-4

Jensen, E. (2002). Implementing music in the classroom. Retrieved from http://www.songsforteaching.com/ericjensen/1.htm

Lazar, M. (n.d.) Interactive strategies for using music in the academic curriculum. from http://www.songsforteaching.com/lazar/interactivestrategies.htm

Loomba, A. (1998). *Colonialism-postcolonialism. The new critical idiom.* New York, London: Routledge.

Mlama, O. P. (n.d.). Tanzania's cultural policy and its implications for the contribution of the arts to socialist development. Retrieved from http://archive.lib.msu.edu/DMC/African%20Journals/pdfs/Utafiti/vol7no1/aejp007001003.pdf

Nidel, O. R. (2005). *World music: The basics*. New York, NY: Routledge.

Nompula, Y. (2011). Volorising the voice of the marginalized: Exploring the value of music in African education. *South African Journal of Education, 31*, 396-380.

Rocheleau, M. (2009). Functions of African music. Retrieved from http://voices.yahoo.com/social-function-african-music-3403568.html?cat=37

Stover, J. (n.d.). More music in the classroom.... Why? Making the case for music as an educational tool. Retrieved from http://www.songsforteaching.com/makingthecaseformusicintheclassroom/research.php

Swahili 4 kids. (n.d.). http://swahili4kids.com/lyricsandtext.html

Quintanar-Sarellana, R. (1997). Culturally relevant teacher preparation and teachers' perceptions of language and culture of linguistic minority students. In E. J. King, E. R. Hollins, & C. Warren (Ed.), *Preparing teachers for cultural diversity* (pp. 40-52). New York, NY: Teachers College Press.

Tchebwa, M. (2005). *African music: New challenges, New vocations*. Sagrafic, Barcelona: UNESCO.

Using music to teach social studies. (n.d.). Retrieved from http://www.songsforteaching.com/socialstudiessongs.htm

CHAPTER 5

BRINGING LITERACY TO LIFE

Constructing Lessons Through Artifacts, Books, and Drama

Kimetta R. Hairston and Josephine Wilson

INTRODUCTION

The use of literacy as a tool to promote students' interest and construct lessons through creative artifacts, drama, and writing is engaging and effective in both elementary and higher education classroom settings. This chapter explores the lives of two educators who used social-constructivist strategies to impact the lives of their students.

Constructivism encourages students to construct their own knowledge while participating in individual and collaborative activities and assignments. Berk (2010) explains that, "Although constructivist approaches vary, many are grounded in Piaget's theory, which views children as active agents who reflect on and coordinate their own thoughts rather than absorbing those of others" (p. 248). This approach connects with cooperative learning, where students work in small groups and use personal experiences and self-reflections to achieve learning outcomes.

African Traditional and Oral Literature as Pedagogical Tools in Contest Area Classrooms: K-12, pages 79–94
Copyright © 2014 by Information Age Publishing

They become immersed in social-constructivist learning environments (Bodrova & Leong, 2007; Palincsar, 2003). Social-constructivist learning environments allow students to collaborate and participate in a wide range of challenging assignments and activities with teachers and peers to comprehend information and reach a common goal. Berk (2010) stated that "As children acquire knowledge and strategies from working together, they become competent, contributing members of their classroom community and advance in cognitive and social development" (p. 248). As they engage in cooperative learning experiences they interact around a variety of themes that result in powerful learning.

Hairston and Wilson present similar themes that emerge through separate experiences with their students through dramatic presentations and self-reflections. Both authors present constructivist teaching resources and strategies on how to use literacy to bring life to stories. In addition, students role play to present information. As McMaster (1998) believed, role playing and drama are invaluable teaching methods that support literacy development. Shared themes and strategies in this chapter detail cultural connections to literary works. Resources such as autobiographies, biographies, children's literature, sample lessons and artifacts; that can be used in classroom settings, are depicted throughout.

ACT ONE—A TEACHER'S DRAMATIC TALE

"I Believe"—Constructing Literacy Awareness Through Drama

During Hairston's first-year teaching experience, she transformed a biographical reading assignment of famous humanitarians and leaders into a unit of study that eventually evolved into the dramatic stage play, "I Believe." Her fifth grade students performed the play in May of 2000, and the news of the production was a success across the school district ("NN Public and Private Schools," 2000).

Imagine if you will, a moment in time in which the words of some of history's most inspirational and motivational leaders are brought to life by the very generation that embodied their dreams and aspirations. What began as a literacy assignment, quickly evolved into a moment that touched all who watched from the audience and who participated in the play. The production left every soul freed, liberated, and with a new founded belief in the future generation who celebrated Black History Month and the Civil Rights Movement.

Deasy (2002) reports that literacy in the form of detailed understanding of texts, appears to give power to playwrights and elevate children's reading and social skills within a classroom setting. By the end of the unit, the fifth grade students advanced two to three grade levels in reading, were eager to write, and made cultural connections that were expressed through social interactions and presentations in the classroom. The interactions converted negative attitudes toward reading into positive and motivating attitudes toward learning. The following shares Hairston's journey toward the production of "I Believe." Also included, are current reflections from some of the fifth grade students and the school's music teacher.

ACT ONE—SCENE ONE

From Biography to Children's Literature to Creative Autobiography

In a public school in Eastern, Virginia, a fifth grade language arts/social studies class were engaged and excited about learning how to read and write about humanitarians and leaders from diverse cultures and ethnic backgrounds. Language arts and social studies were combined in an initiative from the school district to integrate reading and writing throughout the social studies curriculum. This effort was to increase scores on the Virginia Standards of Learning Test (Virginia Department of Education [VOED], 2000). "Social studies demands not only basic skills such as recall of details, sequence of events, and recognition of main ideas, but also a higher level of critical thinking" (Education Research Service [ERS], 2004, pp. 79-80). The Virginia Standards of Learning social study objectives, allowed Hairston the opportunity to create activities and lessons through reading and research. ERS (2004) suggests that when these types of integrations occur, students become motivated and begin to have positive attitudes and higher achievement levels in reading. In this particular experience, the positive attitudes and high levels of achievement demonstrated by the students exceeded the teacher's expectations.

The class consisted of 21 students ranging from ages 10-12; 11 males and 10 females; 12 African Americans, 7 Caucasians, and 2 Asians. Almost half of the students were bused in from local downtown housing project areas, and the others were from the surrounding local community. Some were from military families that had recently transferred to the area, while others had lived in this part of Virginia all of their lives. The reading levels in the class ranged from Primer Reader to above grade level. For this particular assignment, the fifth grade students were immersed in books of their choice, ranging from K-9 grade reading levels. The unit of study was conducted from mid-November through February. The following themes emerged throughout the unit: cultural connections, liberation, ownership, and the love for learning.

Constructing Thematic Assignments

The first assignment was to use research tools to construct a biography about famous humanitarians and leaders from any time period. Some of the choices included: Martin Luther King, Jr., Rosa Parks, John F. Kennedy, Malcolm X, Maya Angelou, Mahatma Gandhi, Albert Einstein, Sojourner Truth, Queen Lydia Liliuokalani, Joan of Arc, Nelson Mandela, President Jimmy Carter, Michael Jordan, Oprah Winfrey, and Jackie Robinson (see Appendix). In addition, students had to locate a children's literacy book/story that complimented the biography of the person they were researching (see Appendix). The students also had the choice of using other sources to find information such as the school librarian, webpages and Internet articles, plays and films, and books on tape. The criteria for the assignment needed to include the following information: the humanitarian and leader's name, date of birth, parents and siblings, a hometown description, ethnic background, five to eight childhood facts, five to eight cultural facts, why the individual was considered a humanitarian and leader, five to eight facts about how the person impacted Civil Rights, three to five conflicts and/or controversies the person faced in their adult lives, five to eight photos or illustrations, and a reflection on why the student chose this person. Finally, the student could add any additional information they wanted to the biographical sketch of the person.

In the second assignment, students were given the following quote by Oliver Wendell Holmes (1829): "What lies behind us and what lies before us are tiny matters compared to what lies within us." The students had to respond to the quote in two ways: What does the quote mean to you, and what do you think the quote meant or means to your famous humanitarian and leader? During this phase, students began to make cultural connections to the assignment. A 10-year old African American male reflected and wrote:

> This quote means that you should never give up. I am researching Dr. King and if part of his dream had not come true, I wouldn't be sitting here today. He did not stay in the past but looked ahead and found solutions for problems that he may have never imagined. In the 1960's, Blacks couldn't go to restaurants and eat. Now my grandmother owns her own restaurant called Polly's. The quote means no matter what obstacles get in your way, the future can and does hold possibilities and long as you believe that you can achieve your dream.

The amount of enthusiasm, creativity, and commitment to the two as-signments became pleasantly overwhelming. The students were illustrat-ing the love for learning. For example, the students began talking about "their" humanitarian and leader as if they knew them personally. They were encouraged to keep a daily reflection journal. A 10-year old Korean female wrote in her journal:

> I am learning so much about Rosa Parks and her work with Dr. King, she was a very strong woman who I can now say I admire. I am not considered Black or White, but I am considered a different color. If part of [King's] dream wasn't accomplished people would be treating me differently. I am so happy to be learning about humanitarians, it is so exciting that I wake up ready to come to school each day just to see what I will find out next!

Over a course a month, the teacher collected reflections, letters, daily assignments, journals, and reading logs to assess the students' research, writing, and reading comprehension levels. In addition, mini-lessons were conducted throughout the unit whenever the teacher needed to clarify and/ or reinforce terms and other information for the students. The students were bringing the "characters" from the books to life.

As the days went on, the fifth grade class began to work collaboratively and took ownership over assignments, in order to complete tasks and create new activities and lesson ideas. Often during lunch, they were "caught reading" by the principal and other teachers, and received positive behavior stars for the class chart posted in the cafeteria. Some students were going home and talking to their parents and grandparents, some of whom had experienced the Civil Rights Movement first hand. Parents were calling in and sending notes to the teacher expressing "thank you" and "how excited it was to see their children engaged and learning. One parent shared, "I have never witnessed my child so excited about learning. Thank you!"

Even with all of the assignments, collaborations, and sharing, the stu-dents wanted more.

ACT ONE—SCENE TWO

From Autobiographies and Artifacts to Role Play and Speeches

By January, the unit was taking on a life of its own. The students asked if they could write an autobiography of their famous person. The teacher had to step back and think about this request because an autobiography is a story that is written or told by the person it is about. She did a mini-lesson, in which the students had to compare autobiographies to biographies. Next students were assigned the task of locating their famous humanitarian and leader's autobiography. If one did not exist, they still had to locate or read another autobiography in order to understand the style of writing and what was included in the literary work (Appendix C). Once again, Hairston wanted to make sure that the students understood the components of an autobiography. This did not deter the students, they wanted to "become" the famous humanitarian/leader and write an autobiography. They felt a sense of liberation with the connections that they had made with their historian/leader. So Hairston constructed a "creative autobiography" assignment.

Liberated…. The "Creative Autobiography"

The "creative autobiography" allowed the fifth graders to write person's story as if they were them. Students completed assignments in which they took on the characteristics of the humanitarian and leader. Social study objectives aligned with the tasks (VODE, 2000). For example, the students had to do more in-depth research on the time period that the humanitarian and leader came from and create artifacts that included a timeline of events, personal effects the person may have used, and clothing. Student also had to identify three to five famous quotes and/or speeches; study photos and documentaries, then students would present the information to the class.

The final "planned" assignment was the class presentation in which the student would role play and dress up as their humanitarian and leader. This assignment included reciting a portion of the autobiography the student wrote, and ending with a portion of an authentic poem, quote, or speech by the humanitarian and leader. The days leading up to the class presentations were engaging, as students worked hard on memorizing the speeches or poems, finalizing their costumes, and practicing the overall production of the role playing presentation. Parents, school administrators, the music and art teachers, the school librarian, and Kindergarten classes were invited to attend the classroom presentations.

The RSVP responses to attend the event were so large, that the class presentations had to be moved to the school cafeteria. The presentations were videotaped and the students impressed everyone by the knowledge that was exploding out of the dramatic role playing of their humanitarian and leader. The school's music teacher reminisced recently stating:

> There are truly no words that will adequately express what I experienced that day. To be given the opportunity see students work come to life and see

them engrossed in their work is an educator's dream. The excitement on their faces was priceless as they shared their findings from research and took on the role of their humanitarian.

After the event, students expressed emotions of happiness and pride. However, when they returned to the classroom, there was an overwhelming sadness in the air. They realized for the first time, that this was the final day of the unit. They pleaded with Hairston to think of something so that it would not end. Motivated by the dedication, hard work, and their expressions for the love of learning, Hairston decided to construct one more assignment for the unit.

ACT ONE—SCENE THREE

From Classroom Assignments to Dramatic Production

With the assistance of her fifth grade class and the school's music teacher, Hairston integrated the students' "creative autobiographies," speeches, and poems and wrote the script for the play, "I Believe." The final draft of the play was complete just in time for Black History Month. Also during this time, the students were busy rehearsing the play and continuing to work on class assignments. The play needed a dramatic ending, and the students suggested a song that they were singing during music class. Hairston decided to include the song along with symbolic Civil Rights photos and signs from the past in order to relay the message and determination of equality and justice for all. Working in and responding to drama involves the manipulation and interpretation of a bewildering array of iconic, didactical and symbolic signs, some of which are visual and some of which are audible (Kempe, 2001). So, the music teacher collaborated with Hairston and the finale ended with an explosion of music.

The play truly revealed cultural connections, liberation, ownership, and the love for learning through the music, playwright, and student performances. In a recent conversation with the music teacher, she reminisced about the event and said:

As the music specialist/teacher, I jumped at the opportunity to share with my students how creative writing and song lyrics are synonymous with each other. During the planning process of the play, I came across a song from a music publication called *Music K8* magazine that I knew would serve a poignant finale to this experience. *Music K8* had released a song in honor of the late Dr. Martin Luther King Jr. entitled, "Free At Last." The lyrics to this song are written in the form of students talking to Dr. King and letting him know, and I quote, "We heard what you said. You spoke out with wisdom.

Your message was spread." The song ends with a dramatic combination of harmony and dynamics as the singers quote Dr. King's "I Have a Dream" speech using the words, "Free at Last" and once again literacy comes to life. There was not a dry eye in the building, as the students echoed, "Thank God Almighty, we are free, free at last!" It was truly a moment to remember.

"I Believe"—The Plot

Judge N.B. and a group of uncaring and peer pressured "nonbelievers" control a local community. They spend hours each day passing new laws that constantly represent inequality and injustice for all. Being negative and mean is their fuel. Their goal in life is to make everyone doubt that Dr. Martin Luther King Jr.'s dream ever affected current issues on Civil Rights that his dream will ever become a reality.

One day, a group of Believers decide to hold a sit-in in front of Judge N.B.'s courthouse. They pave the courthouse stairs with signs that read, "I Believe" and they shout the phrase at the top of their lungs. The judge becomes outraged, and she and her followers decide to come outside and confront the nonviolent student sit-in. As they approach the crowd, they realize that there are more Believers in the town than they could have ever imagined. There is a brief confrontation between some of the nonbeliev-ers and the crowd, and then one brave believer stands up and says, "Judge N.B., I believe in Dr. King's dream. I think that it is alive and in all of us today. That is why we sit here in a nonviolent manner. We want justice and equality for everyone in this community. I believe in Dr. King's dream so much that if we all just close our eyes, he will appear. If that happens, will you and the nonbelievers believe?" Judge N.B. and the nonbelievers can-not control their laughter. The judge asks, "How can someone believing in equality and justice and a dream really bring back Dr. Martin Luther King, Jr.?"

The crowd once again in unison chant, "I believe! I believe! I believe!" Then, magically from the crowd, appears Rosa Parks, Jackie Robinson, Joan of Arc, Malcolm X, and others from the past and they say that they believe in Dr. King's dream. Next Maya Angelou, Michael Jordan, Oprah Winfrey, and President Jimmy Carter join the sit-in and express that they believe. Then, the crowd becomes silent, because all of a sudden and standing at the podium appears Dr. Martin Luther King, Jr. He gives a speech of how those who had paved the way for him allowed him to be the man he was at this moment. He ends with quotes from his famous, "I have a dream" speech. Afterwards every protester begins singing the song, "Free At Last." As the song echoes through the crowd gradually one by one the nonbelievers leave Judge N.B.'s side and become believers. By the end of the song the judge is standing alone. Tears in her eyes, she removes her dark sun glasses, falls to her knees, and shouts—"I Believe!" The crowd applauds.

ACT ONE—SCENE FOUR

In Her Words: Hairston's Constructive Reflection on Lifelong Lessons

Over the months of the unit, planned activities lessons were reconstructed to meet the needs of the students in Hairston's class. It was evident that students appreciated the unit and gained knowledge in research, social studies, writing, and literacy development. However, the climax was the role play class presentations that exposed the cultural, emotional, and social connections and interactions that motivated the students to share their learning with others. Drama can be a major contribution in the development of literacy because it provides a collaboration in which experiences and ideas are shared and the interpretations of words are celebrated (Kempe, 2001). In this experience, a unit was successful because of the student's love for learning and the cultural, emotional, and personal connections that they made through literature and drama.

This experience motivated Hairston to continue to teach as a constructivist and integrate diversity and multiculturalism throughout curriculum and instruction practices for current and future educators. She continues to teach preservice teachers and educators in higher education the strategies and tools she used as a classroom teacher. Currently, Hairston remains in contact with 7 of the 21 fifth grade students and the music teacher.

ACT TWO—SCENE ONE

From Practice to Teacher Candidates Dramatic Reflections of Literacy

During the 2008 Fall Semester, teacher candidates were enrolled in a historically black college or university (HBCU) in central Maryland. They took Wilson's Methods of Teaching Reading and Methods of Teaching Social Studies courses in Early Childhood or Elementary Education. Wilson planned and developed lessons for students during Phase I of their yearlong internship experience. Phase I teacher candidates were enrolled in five methods courses while spending 2 days in a professional development school (PDS) site off campus under the supervision of a mentor teacher and university supervisor who provided teacher candidates support and evaluated their teaching performance on a regular basis. Teacher candidates bridged the content knowledge and theory taught in their methods classes with practical application in their PDS settings. Wilson's courses instruction took in a classroom out at one of the PDS sites.

Bringing Books to Life

Teacher candidates had as one assignment, "Bringing Books to Life" which required them to plan and develop a developmentally appropriate lesson incorporating a familiar children's picture book in which their students would dramatize the book. Among the objectives of the lesson were to create a literacy experience that provided students the opportunity to express creativity, cultural connections, liberation, ownership, and the love for learning. Research has supported positive uses of children's picture books in developing literacy experiences for young children (McGee & Schickedanz, 2007; Schickedanz & Casbergue, 2009). The interns in this developmental phase of the assignment, planned, developed materials, and dramatized a children's book with the help of supportive peers as participants in the implementation of the activity. The children's books selected by the teacher candidates took into consideration the interests of the students in their classrooms (Appendix 3).

Teacher candidates were informed what constituted effective teaching in the delivery of literacy instruction for student learning. In other words, effective teaching required more than having knowledge of subject matter and pedagogical skills. According to Banks et al. (2005):

> Teachers' attitudes, and expectations, as well as their knowledge of how to incorporate the cultures, experiences, and needs of their students into their teaching, significantly influence what students learn and the quality of their learning opportunities. (p. 243)

According to Vygotsky's (1978) sociocultural theoretical perspective, learning is socially constructed and mediated. Peers, parents as well as teachers can play a vital part in promoting learning through shared activities. Research also supports the notion of socially-constructed learning in the lives of young children (Bodrova & Leong, 2007). The Bringing Books to Life assignment provided the teacher candidates an opportunity to plan meaningful literacy lessons that required the participation of their peers in thinking about literary content.

Teacher candidates needed practice in planning for diverse learners. They wanted to know how to incorporate literary content that would give students' opportunities to dramatize or reenact children's picture books that capitalized on the students' strengths and needs. Teacher candidates wanted to learn to become effective and culturally responsive educators. In addition to wanting to provide their students with meaningful and engaging literacy experiences, teacher candidates wanted to know ways in which to connect with students, the school and their own culture (Molls & Gonzalez, 2004). The teaching assignment allowed teacher candidate to connect with their own cultures while designing this literary experience for their students. They were actively engaged with their peers and constructed additional ideas and artifacts to enhance the dramatic presentation of the picture books dramatized.

ACT TWO—SCENE TWO

Lesson Plans in Action—Artifacts and Dramatic Presentations

At the start of each semester, teacher interns were required to complete a "Time Capsule," which is an open-ended questionnaire that elicits their response about goals they set for themselves at the beginning of the semester and what they hoped to learn about reading and writing instruction during the semester. The overwhelming response to what teacher candidates hoped to learn about reading and writing instruction was that they hoped to discover ways of making reading more enjoyable for their students while improving their literary knowledge.

Thematic Reflections

Teacher candidates recognized their need to connect with their students in order to make learning meaningful. Most importantly, the teacher candidates expressed a "love for learning."

Some of the comments made by the teacher candidates were: One student said, "I want to be able to learn techniques that I can use to teach students the joy of reading so they can learn about different things." Another student added, "I hope to get to know all the students in my classroom and to provide each one the needed tools to be turned on to reading and writing."

While teacher candidates realized that they needed to make learning experiences relevant and enjoyable for their students they were not certain of the techniques needed to make this happen. In order for them to understand and plan for the diverse learning needs of their students they first had to discover picture books that could relate to their own experiences. They thought of ways to engage their peers in their presentation of the books selected. This experience of working cooperatively with their peers helped them to express their cultural beliefs through their literary connection with picture books.

Amy expressed to her peers that she experienced a cultural connections as she planned the Book-to-Life assignment. She stated that when she chose the book, *The Quilt* (1994) by Ann Jonas, it brought back so many memories of her childhood days when her own grandmother made quilts for her family in Russia. She displayed a dress she had as a toddler and other garments her mother saved as they migrated to the United States. Amy's Book-to-Life presentation related to her own experiences as a child in another country. She stated that she realizes the importance of including parents in the planning of children's literacy experiences.

Jackie's dramatization of *The Enormous Carrot* (1988) by Vladimir Vagin required the support of her peers linking arms together to pull up the enormous carrot. She shared that this book reminded her of days she spent on her family farm and the hard work during planting and harvesting seasons. She told the class that the hard work she endured made her a stronger person and she learned to preserve when faced with tough situations. Her reflection on the experience gave her a sense of "empowerment."

The teacher interns used dramatization of the picture books they selected to relate to their own cultural experiences which in some cases were liberating experiences. Lauren's portrayal of the "Cat in the Hat" by Dr. Seuss provided her peers with the red and white striped hat as she engaged them repetitious scenes from the book. She recalled those days when her mother read the same book to her and the thrill she experienced in dramatizing the book as a child. The words were very familiar to her because this was one of her favorites from childhood. It was books like Dr. Seuss which fostered her creativity and enjoyment in reading.

As a result of this exercise, the teacher candidates embraced their own cultural and literary experiences and realized that the picture books they chose to dramatize might have a similar impact on students in their classrooms. In planning for literacy instruction they were becoming familiar with the background, cultural experiences and interests of their classroom students.

ACT TWO—SCENE THREE

In Her Words: Wilson's Constructive Reflection on Lifelong Lessons

In preparing teacher candidates for a career in the teaching profession, it is my desire to provide them with many opportunities to "craft the art of their trade" by first seeing themselves as lifelong learners. The tools that teacher candidates acquire to become effective, culturally responsive educators come from equipping them to become academic scholars, knowledgeable about students, themselves and the subject matter they teach. Teacher candidates should be provided many opportunities to reflect on their practice of teaching as well as reflect will practicing teaching. The process of reflection and practice should be continuous throughout their careers as educators.

ACT THREE—SCENE ONE

From Continuity of Learning to Thematic Reflections

A conversation between two colleagues who were reflecting on memorable classroom experiences where their students were engaged in learning, evolved into a discussion about constructing lessons from literary works into dramatic presentations. Dramatic activities have been found to be crucial to literacy development because children are involved in reading and writing as a holistic and meaningful communication process (McNamee, McLane, Cooper, & Kerwin, 1985). Moreover, Hairston and Wilson found that although they were in two different learning environments, similarities, such as using effective constructivist modeling and teaching strategies to bring life to literature; uncovered similar themes. Cultural connections existed throughout both experiences.

Cultural connections that arose during teaching evolved from culturally responsive pedagogy (Hairston, 2006). Teachers who use effective teaching benefit all students, highlight student achievement trends, and include information; such as personal experiences and respectful responses that accommodate diverse groups, can expect cultural connections to occur in their classrooms (Banks et al., 2005). Hairston and Wilson modeled culturally responsive teaching practices, and the evidence was illustrated through the students' reflections and final products. These practice allowed students to become liberated in their thought processes and dramatic presentations.

Liberation in literacy developed when critical thinking and personal reflections took over the students' desire to learn. Freire (2000) explained that by creating teaching techniques that encourage experiential knowledge of personal experiences, critical thinking and praxis, progresses to a state of liberation. The expression of liberation for both the fifth grade students and the preservice teachers arose when they presented their artifacts, and role played the characters from the literary works. Student took ownership over the learning experience.

Ownership in literacy comes about when students are given choices in their learning. As Dr. Hairston and Dr. Wilson presented lessons to their students, they allowed their students to add details, objectives, and learning outcomes in order to give them ownership of their tasks.

> Students gain ownership by being able to choose the books that interest or intrigue them, by writing on their own thoughts, feelings and reflections; not by reading only what is presented to them in a textbook or by filling in predetermined answers on a worksheet. (Phillipich, 2008, p. 6)

When a student takes over the ownership of an assignment or project, there is an emotional display for the love of learning.

The love for learning is probably the most purposeful theme that emerged from Hairston and Wilson's classroom experiences. They both modeled with enthusiasm; collaboration, commitment, and creativity in their teaching styles, and these components transferred to their students. According to Bandura (1986), modeling is a vital part of helping students learn the process of constructing meaning and it assist them in learning various strategies and skills in the classroom. The love for learning was expressed through the students' dramatic presentations, written reflections, and verbal expressions.

Bringing literacy to life and constructing lessons through artifacts, books, and drama has imprinted memories in the hearts and minds of Hairston and Wilson. Their journeys in reaching and teaching students through education are continuous life endeavors that they possess. They believe that, "The function of education is to teach one to think intensively and to think critically.... Intelligence plus character—that is the goal of true education" (Dr. Martin Luther King, Jr., n.d).

APPENDIX: SELECTED CHILDREN'S WEBSITES

http://www.goodreads.com/shelf/show/biographies-for-young-children

1000 Biographies http://carolemarshbookstore.net/index.php?main_page=index&cPath=8

Black History http://carolemarshbookstore.net/index.php?main_page=index

Biographies of Famous African Americans http://carolemarshbookstore.net/index

The Best Biographies for Kids http://1000biographies.com/

REFERENCES

Bandura, A. (1986). *Psychological modeling: Conflicting theories*. Chicago, IL: Aldine-Atherton.

Banks, J. A., Cookson, P., Gay, G., Hawley, W., Irvine, J. J., Nieto, S., Schofield, J. W., & Stephan, W. G. (2005). *Diversity within unity: Essential principles for teaching and learning in a multicultural society*. Seattle, WA: Center for Multicultural Education at the University of Washington.

Berk, L. E. *(2010). Exploring lifespan development* (3rd ed.). Boston, MA: Allyn & Bacon.

Bodrova, E., & Leong, D. J. (2007). *Tools of the mind: The Vygotskian approach to early childhood education* (2nd ed.). Upper Saddle River, NJ: Merrill/Prentice Hall.

Deasy, R. J. (Ed.). (2002). *Critical links: Learning in the arts and student academic and social development*. Washington, DC: Arts Education Partnership.

Education Research Service (2004). *Reading at the Middle and High School Levels: Building Active Readers Across the Curriculum* (3rd ed.). Arlington, VA: Education Research Service.

Freire, P. (2000). *Pedagogy of the oppressed* (30th anniversary edition). Bloomsbury Academic; 30th Anniversary edition, September 1, 2000.

Hairston, K. R. (2006). The culture learning process in higher education: An internal cultural experience to enhance curriculum development and student relationships in the classroom. *The Pennsylvania Association of Colleges and Educators Journal* (PACTE), *5*(1), 14-21.

Kempe, A. (2001). Drama as a framework for the development of literacy. Retrieved from http://www.nfer.ac.uk/nfer/PRE_PDF_Files/01_25_10.pdf

King, M. L. K., Jr. (n.d.). Quote. Retrieved from http://www.dictionary-quotes.com/the-function-of-education-is-to-teach-one-to-think-intensively-and-to-think-critically-intelligence-plus-character-that-is-the-goal-of-true-education-martin-luther-king-jr/

McGee, L. M., & Schickedanz, J. (2007). Repeated interactive read-alouds in preschool and kindergarten. Retrieved from www.readingrockets.org

McMaster, J. C. (1998). "Doing" literature: Using drama to build literacy. *The Reading Teacher, 51*(7), 574-584.

Moll, L. C., & Gonzalez, N, (2004). Engaging Life: A funds of knowledge approach to multicultural education. In J. A. Banks & C. A. Banks (Eds.), *Handbook of research on multicultural education* (2nd ed.) San Francisco, CA: Jossey-Bass.

Holmes, O. W. (1829). Quotes.net. Retrieved from http://www.quotes.net/quote/4004

Jonas, A. (1994). *The Quilt.* NY: Greenwillow Books.

McNamee, G. D., McLane, J. B., Cooper, P. M., & Kerwin, S. M. (1985). Cognition and affect in early literacy development. *Early Childhood Development and Care, 20,* 229-244.

NN public and private schools end Black History Month defining Civil Rights. (2000, March 2-March 8,). *The Hampton Roads Voice,* p. 9.

Palincsar, A. S. (2003). Advancing a theoretical model of learning and instruction. In B. J. Zimmerman (Ed.), *Educational psychology: A century of contributions* (pp. 459-475), Mahwah, NJ: Erlbaum.

Phillipich, S. (2008). *Ownership of literacy: Motivating students through choice* (Unpublished paper). Curriculum and Instruction in Literacy, 560 Professor Marsha Baisch February 26, 2008. Retrieved from stacyphillipich1.efoliomn.com

Schickedanz, J. A., & Casbergue, R. M. (2009). *Writing in preschool learning to orchestrate meaning and marks.* Newark, DE: International Reading Association.

Vagin, V. (1988). *The enormous carrot.* New York, NY: Scholastic.

Virginia Department of Education. (2000). Virginia Standards of Learning 2000. Retrieved from http://www.doe.virginia.gov/testing/sol/released_tests/2000/released_tests2000.shtml

Vygotsky, L. (1978). *Mind in society: The development of higher psychological processes* (14th ed.) M. Cole, V. John-Steiner, S. Scribner, & E. Souberman, (Eds.). Cambridge, MA: Harvard University Press.

CHAPTER 6

UNDERSTANDING THE INFLUENCES OF AFRICAN CULTURAL NAMING PATTERNS ON THE IDENTITY AND PERSONALITY DEVELOPMENT OF IMMIGRANT CHILDREN OF AFRICAN DESCENT IN NORTH AMERICA

Michael Baffoe

Introduction

In today's Western societies when people are more and more likely to interact and work with members of other cultures, a new educational priority is fast emerging, namely the need for educators to provide students with the skills and knowledge that will enable them to communicate effectively across different cultures. Teachers are in an excellent position

African Traditional and Oral Literature as Pedagogical Tools in Contest Area Classrooms: K-12, pages 95–109
Copyright © 2014 by Information Age Publishing

to play a large role in this endeavor. However, more often than not, the importance of culture is relegated to the background of classroom teaching and learning.

This chapter sets up the background and the context of cultural understanding of the naming ceremonies and naming patterns in African cultural systems and shows how these have major impact on the identity and personality development of children of African descent. The thrust of this work is to explore the significance of personal names to cultural identity and the various ways in which cultural identity contributes to pedagogy in North American classroom settings. Personal names are vital aspects of cultural identity. Shakespeare was right when he asked: "What's in a name?" That which we call rose by any other name would smell as sweet. We may have loved or hated our names as children but we were not totally indifferent to it. Every society has a naming system, and all these systems have certain common elements. Throughout the world, each child is assigned a sound or series of sounds that will be his or her name. Because that name is a part of the language of the child's parents, it immediately identifies the child as belonging to a particular society. So our names identify us both as individuals and as members of a group (Anderson, 1979).

This chapter seeks to explore the background and the context of the naming ceremonies and naming patterns in African cultural systems and shows how these have major impact on the identity and personality development of children of African descent in the diaspora especially in North America. It starts by exploring the significance of personal names to cultural identity of Africans. Next it provides an overview of the naming patterns in selected African societies on the continent providing examples of selected names and their significance. The methodology used and the theoretical framework that guided the study are then presented followed by a discussion of the findings from the study and suggestions for further exploration into this area. The findings from the study are then discussed followed by concluding remarks on the implications of this study for pedagogy in North American classroom settings.

It is important to provide an overview on the definitions of *identity* which is defined as a feeling, inter-subjectively shared by individuals in a given group that is based on a sense of common origin, common beliefs and values, common goals, and a sense of shared destiny (Suarez-Orozco, Suarez-Orozco, & Doucet, 2004). *Identity* has two components: *Personal Identity*, which refers to how one views himself/herself (determination and choice), is influenced to a large extent by the dominant ideologies. There is also *Social Identity* which refers to how the society/world around us views us. How society views us have a great influence on how we view and see ourselves.

Ethnic Identity

The issue of ethnic identity is an important one for all persons in the diaspora particularly those of African descent because it establishes the psychological reference points and ability to cope with the discrimination and prejudice to which children of color are subjected in Western societies, especially in North America. Nagel (1994) points out that individuals and groups attempt to address the problematics of ethnic boundaries and meaning through the construction of identity and culture. The construction of ethnic identity and culture is the result of both structure and agency, a dialectic that is played out by ethnic groups and the larger society. Nagel further argues that although ethnicity is the product of actions undertaken by ethnic groups as they shape and reshape their self-definition and culture, ethnicity is also constructed by external social, economic, and political processes and actors.

This constructionist view of identity also posits that through the actions and designations of ethnic groups, their antagonists, political authorities, and economic interest groups, ethnic boundaries are erected dividing some populations and unifying others (Barth, 1969; Moerman, 1974). Ethnicity is thus constructed out of the material of language, religion, culture, appearance, ancestry, or regionality. The location and meaning of particular ethnic boundaries undergo continuous negotiation, revision and revitalization both by ethnic group members themselves as well as by outside players, observers or authorities (Nagel, 1994).

The argument here is that cultural identity derived from any route within the realm of culturally-relevant practices including naming patterns, lays a solid and natural foundation for all aspects of identity that we later take on in life. Just as a name has various aspects, such as the social, political, spiritual, professional, and cultural, all of which work in unison to impact and be impacted by cultural identity, so does overall identity, personal or collective (Lassiter, 1979).

Research Questions

1. The following questions were posed for this study:
2. What role does personal name play in shaping or regaining cultural identity?
3. Does culturally-relevant name enhance or hinder the achievement of cultural identities?
4. Is reclaiming of cultural identity through the bearing of culturally-relevant names a necessary adjunct to decolonization?

5. Of what significance are culturally-relevant naming systems and names to Africans in the diaspora especially in North American societies?

6. What is the significance and impact of these culturally-relevant names to youth of African descent in North American classroom settings?

Methodology

The study was done through conversations and interviews with a large number of Africans (on the continent), with a number of African immigrants in the diaspora, and some North Americans of African descent in a number of locations in Canada and the United States. Participants were asked questions on the meanings of their specific names, both first names, and surnames and their significance. Some questions centered on the issue of whether the respondents had ever changed their names, from African to Western colonized names and vice versa. Emphasis was also placed on questions centering around the names of the children of the study participants in the diaspora, whether the parents followed the naming practices and patterns as obtained on the continent and why. They were then asked to explain the significance and meanings of the names that they gave to their children. The next group of participants were youth of African descent living in North America. Questions centered on what they make of their names, the pride or otherwise they carry or attach to their African names and how those names affect their identities and personality development in North American society.

Theoretical Framework

The study draws its theoretical foundation and strength from the body of literature on critical race theory and its tenet of counter-storytelling, ethnic identity construction and post-colonial theory. Critical race theory (CRT) serves an important role through its use of counter-storytelling and narratives of racially marginalized students in predominantly urban school setting (Delgado, 1989). In addition, as Leonard (2008) articulates, CRT aligns with culturally relevant pedagogy; both concepts encourage "intentional behavior by a teacher to use gestures, language, history, literature, and other cultural aspects of a particular race, ethnic or gender group to engage students belonging to that group in authentic student-centered learning" (p. 8). McDonald (2003) points out that CRT explicitly focuses on social inequalities arising through race and racism. The impact that colonization and Christianity have had on African cultures can be viewed within the lens of both critical race theory and postcolonial theory. First, critical race theory works to name and discusses the daily realities of racism and expose how racism continues to advantage Whites (in this instance the missionaries and colonizers) and disadvantage people of color (in this Africans and people of Africa descent [Dei, 1998]). Second, CRT legitimates and promotes the voices of people of color by using storytelling to integrate experiential knowledge drawn from a shared history as "the other" into critiques of dominant social orders (Ladson-Billings, 1998). For the participants in this study, Africans and people of African descent, struggling to maintain or reclaim a critical part of their cultural system, especially in the diaspora which Ladson-Billings (2000) calls, the "experience of a racialised identity" (p. 262), this aspect of critical race theory is very pertinent.

Postcolonial theory, according to Ghandi (1968), is a postmodern intellectual discourse that consists of reactions to, and analysis of, cultural legacies of colonialism. It is also referred to as the cultural, intellectual, political, and literary movement of the 20th and 21st centuries that is characterized by the representation and analysis of the historical experiences and subjectivity of the victims, individuals and nations of colonial power (Browne Smye, & Varcoe, 2005; Macey, 2000). Furthermore, postcolonialism is marked by its resistance to colonialism and by the attempt to understand the historical and other conditions of its emergence as well as its lasting consequences (Macey, 2000).

Postcolonial theoretical perspectives can contribute to understanding how continuities from the past shape the present context of issues and events affecting former colonial subjects (Browne et al., 2005). Christianity is a legacy of colonialism, and it is pertinent to examine its lingering practice among Africans, both on the continent and as immigrants in the diaspora, more than half a century after the end of colonial rule in Africa (Baffoe, 2013).

Significance of African Names

In many parts of Africa, a child's naming day is a festive occasion that usually occurs a week or so after the birth. Girls are named sooner than boys in some places, but only by a day or two. An older person bestows the name, first by whispering it to the baby, because a newborn should know his or her name before anyone else does, then by announcing the name to everyone attending the ceremony. In Africa, personal names have meanings, often very powerful and significant, which affect personality, identity development, hinder or enhance life chances and initiatives (Masolo, 1995).

Naming traditions in Africa depend on the region, but can include double first and last names and factor in emotions around birth and pregnancy. In Africa, as in the rest of the world, the birth of a child is an event of great joy and significance. Much importance is attached to the naming of the child. The hopes of the parents, current events of importance and celestial events that may have attended the birth are all given consideration in naming the child. It is believed that the name chosen will exert an influence for better or for worse on the life of the child and on the family as well. Most names from Africa therefore refer to the details surrounding a child's birth, such as the season, day of the week, number of family members, or the emotional state of the family during birth (Gyekye, 1996; Madubuike, 1976).

Names are not just given in Africa. African names serve to establish a connection between them and the cultural backgrounds of specific ethnic groups. They are given in recognition of specific achievements or feats, or in recognition of the good deeds of a specific person after whom a child is named. These names provide powerful information about cultural affinity and more. They may be expressions of spirituality, philosophy of life, political or socioeconomic status as defined by a given ethnic cleavage (Gyekye, 1996). African names tell stories, convert ideas to stories and tell stories about different aspects of life. Some of these aspects may be the commemoration of unusual circumstances a particular family or community previously experienced or some world events that took place around the time of the birth of a particular child. Others may be the time, day, season, place of a child's birth, and even the child's looks at birth (Madubuike, 1976).

Outside the cultural environment of specific ethnic groups, names contribute in boosting and nurturing cultural pride and identity. They may also showcase a people's appreciation of their culture and their readiness to uphold, defend and live their culture with pride and dignity (Appiah, 1992). The following are some interesting examples of various naming patterns and their significance in various parts of Africa unearthed from the study.

Somali names relate to circumstances or events, such as the season during which a child is born. Example: *Roblai* (the one who brings rain); *Nadifa* (born between two seasons); *Jama* (one who brings people together); and *Diah* (born during full moon). Likewise, Sudanese also choose the names of famous people, the days of the week, and names based on the birth circumstances for their children. Examples are: *Konyi* (first born son); *Masala* (the great mother); and *Nyawela* which means *on a jou*rney (Madubuike, 1976).

The Watutsi in Rwanda also place emphasis on meaning of the names for children: *Bizimana* (only God knows); *Nkudinshuti* (I like friends); *Bamgababo* (there is a dispute in the family). The Abaluhya in Kenya also give infants names identifying the season s/he was born and another identifying the day s/he was born: *Nafula* (born during rainy season), *Jimiyu,* born in dry season) (Skhosana, 2002).

The Ndebele and Zezuru of Zimbabwe, like other African groups also name children one week after birth with names relating to meaningful circumstances or events. Examples are: *Tapera* (the enemy has all but wiped us out); *Makata* which means *liberty is to be found at the top of a steep mountain* (Skhosana, 2002).

In Chad as well as in the Central African Republic names commonly reveal family members' special talents or occupations. Examples are *N'guississandje* (founder of a family of lions); *Tomalbaye* (strong courageous man). The naming system of the Basa of East Cameroon revolves around names referring to the psychological state of the parents before and during childbirth, and names speaking to the relationship between the family and the community. Examples are: *Pegwo* (disappointment); *Jurode* (faithful) and *Sohna* (anxiety) (Skhosana, 2002).

In Mali (West Africa), the Fulani have combinations of Muslim first names and other names referring to birth circumstances. Examples are: *Falala* (born into abundance); *Moro* (shameless); *Diengoudo* (the late comer); *Guedado* (wanted by no one). The Wolof of Senegal give names denoting the genealogical tree, so every Wolof child has a name referring to their past or to their ancestors ((Madubuike, 1976).

The Dagara of Burkina Faso not only decides on names as a community, but also works to make a name match the child's purpose. If the Dagara picks a name potentially construed as negative, the true purpose and intention are stated. Apart from giving children names signifying the days on which they were born, the Goun of Benin also give children names referring to circumstances surrounding the birth, and names expressing emotions such as joy or sorrow: Affoyon (welcome at the right time); Bidoun meaning *joy of birth* (Hodari, 2009).

The Akans of Ghana typically keep an infant indoors for seven days and names the child on the eighth day by which time the child is regarded as a "full human being." The first name the Akans give to a child is the *kra din,* or soul name. The day on which the child is born determines the *kra din.* For example a Sunday male born is names *Kwasi* or*Kwesi* while a female Sunday born is names *Esi*. A Friday male born is named *Kofi* while a female is named *Efua*. The Akans believe that the day of the week on which the child is born ultimately reveals which spiritual force guides and governs the child. The second name the Akans give to a child is a formal name known as *din pa* (literally means good name), which ties the child to their ancestral clan(s). That name is usually given by the father who names the baby after an individual he admires or his heroes he wishes to honour (Gyekye, 1997).

The naming pattern of the Yoruba of Southwestern Nigeria works on a three-name system. The first name is the personal name *(oruko)*; the second name is the praise name *(oriki)*, which reflects the hopes for the child while the third name connects the child to its family or community *(orile)*. Examples are: *Olu Gbenga* (God has elevated me); *Fumilayo* (one who gives me joy). The Igbo of Eastern Nigeria tend to name children based on observation, birth marks, or some other remarkable characteristics. Examples are: Ogbonna (image of his).... The Igbo also commonly name children for the market day on which they were born: *Nweke, Adafo,* or *Okorie* (Samaki, 2001).

Discussion/Analysis of Findings

Two major historical world forces, Christianity and colonization have contributed significantly in shattering the strong connection between personal names and African cultural affinity. The impact of these events, have ever since, contributed to the gradual erosion of this powerful aspect of African culture: naming and names. The combined efforts, policies and practices of the agents of Christianity, the forerunner to colonialism have caused a number of Africans and people of African descent to give up their culturally-relevant names in favour of foreign ones, usually termed as *Christian* names (Baffoe, 2002). They succeeded, to a large extent, in abrogating many religious, socioeconomic, and political traditions which were intimately intertwined with the people's naming practices. They attempted, and also succeeded in most cases to replace African traditions with European ones through coercing some Africans to accept Western values and beliefs which consequently disabled many desirable African traditional structures, including authentic African naming practices.

A third powerful historical force that has had a profound impact on African cultural names and naming practices was the Trans-Atlantic slave trade, the forceful uprooting of many Africans from their natural habitat and cultural roots to the Americas and Caribbean (Mazuri, 1986). This event which eroded the culture of its victims also mutilated African naming practices among them. Today, in the 21st century, over 600 years later, there are many Africans on the continent and in the diaspora who continue to carry foreign names whose meanings they do not know. Some of these names have no relevance to any link with the cultural background of their bearers.

It must be noted, however that there are some people of African descent and some on the African continent who still cherish these colonial and/or *Christian* names. There are some who do not and since the mid-1960s have made practical efforts to shed their colonial/Christian names to reclaim authentic African cultural names (Baffoe, 2002). They have done so and continue to do so with pride, dignity, and psychological healing in some instances. As part of the renewed struggles for individual cultural identities, many African parents and parents of African descent are now increasingly giving their children what they term as desirable, meaningful, culturally-relevant names. Some African adults who grew up with non-African names are changing them to authentic African ones.

Naming Practices Among Africans in the Diaspora

Unlike African Americans who were affected by the slave trade and got stripped off most of their cultural practices including naming patterns and its cultural ceremonies, African immigrants in the Diaspora cling tenaciously to most of their cultures with naming ceremonies being one of those (Masolo, 1995). The author visited many African communities in Canada and the United States and participated in a number of the cultural naming ceremonies. The enactment of these ceremonies mimick those that are performed "at home" (countries of origin) on the African continent. Diasporic Africans continue to name their children according to the traditions and patterns performed "at home."

Visits to naming ceremonies in some Nigerian, Ghanaian (West African) and Kenyan (East African) communities in Canada and the United States found community and family members performing child naming ceremonies before sunrise as pertains in their communities in Africa. They followed the traditional African naming practices of assigning the naming roles and responsibilities to the elders in their diasporic communities. Most of the respondents recounted their pride in holding on to their culturally-meaningful African names and/or continuing the cultural practice and tradition of naming their children born in the diaspora and giving them culturally-meaningful names.

Personality Development

An important aspect of personality affected by names is self-concept. Self-concept, according to Deluzain (n.d.) develops as children develop, and it is learned from the verbal and nonverbal messages that significant people in the children's lives send them. Parents are the most important message-senders, but as children mature and become more and more independent, the messages of teachers, classmates, and other people all contribute to their developing concepts of self. In the same way, a person's name has an impact on the process of building a self-concept because the name helps determine the messages other people send the child. Certain names are looked upon as undesirable while other names carry positive connotations. From the foregoing it can be discerned that all African cultural names carry powerful messages and connotations some of which can affect the self-concept and personality development of the child as he/she grows up.

Personality means characteristics and appearance of a person: pattern of thought, feeling, behavior, communication ability and physical features. The personality of a person takes its basic formation in the beginning period of a childhood. Friends, teachers and the environment of the school have their own positive or negative impact on the child (Garwood, 1976). Some of the youth respondents in this study pointed out how they feel ashamed sometimes of their African names which become the butt of jokes among their peers. Some of these take the form of jokes, teasing and even ridicule. These jokes, teasing or ridicule can make children self-conscious about their names. At worst, if these names carry serious jokes and ridicule, they can affect the self esteem of the child and undermine his/her healthy personality development. Murphy (1957) gave a dramatic example of a psychiatric case history of a young college student whose last name was "Stankey" but whose other student friends nicknamed "Stinky." His classmates held their noses whenever they were around him and he reacted by withdrawing from the group and becoming aloof and isolated. The young man blamed his father for his social problems by giving him that name.

The above example is dramatic and powerful enough to stand on its own without the added support of scientific research. However there are other research that point in the direction of the impact of names on self concept and personality development (Anderson, 1979; Garwood, 1976; Strumpfer, 1978). Imagine also what impact the name "Osama" or "bin Ladin" will have on children who have already been given these names. Such children will have very difficult times living in North American or Western societies at this time in history. If they live anywhere else they may never be able or be permitted to fly on an airplane due to the imposition of no-fly lists by countries and airlines on people bearing certain names who are rightly or wrongly viewed as potential terrorists.

There are some Ghanaian Akan names that also carry some heavy connotations and impact on those that bear them. For example there is a name called *diawuo* which means a killer or murderer; *antobam*, the one that did not meet his father. Such names have serious implications for their bearers as they grow up. Among the Luganda in Eastern Africa, the male name, *Gwandoya* means "met with misery." It is possible that someone bearing this name may blame the significance of the name on every misfortune that comes his way in life. Among the Luo in Kenya, the name *Awiti* means "thrown away" usually given to a child born prematurely who the parents fear may not survive (Skhosana, 2002). What about if the child survives and grows into adulthood bearing a name that means someone that is regarded as useless fit to be discarded or thrown away?

In Their Own Words: Narratives From Participants

Below are excerpts from the narratives of some of the study's participants that underscore the above assertions. From some parents on their pride in giving culturally-meaningful African names to their children in the diaspora:

> The name I bear was given to me by my father who named me after a great man in his clan. My name Nyansapo in the Ghanaian Akan language means bundle of wisdom. I have always considered myself full of wisdom. I have achieved quite a lot academically and in business. My friends regularly consult me for advice because they believe that I have wisdom. The fact that they consult me regularly make me believe that I possess some noticeable degree of wisdom. I therefore named my son who was born in Toronto after myself ... and by extension the great one after whom I was named. I believe my son will also grow up maybe wiser than me. (Respondent of Ghanaian origin, Toronto, Canada)

From another:

> My wife and I have been trying for more than ten years to have a baby without success. When we finally had one two years ago, he died only a day after birth. We prayed very hard to God to show mercy on us to have a baby that will grow up with us. So when we had our next baby who is now four years old, we immediately named her **Olu fumilayo** (God give me joy). When we had our next child, a boy, I regarded him as my crown, my jewel, my successor. I knew that God has abundantly blessed us, so I named him **Adegoke** meaning my crown has been exalted. (Respondent of Nigerian (Yoruba) origin, Montreal, Canada)

Narratives From Some Youth of Africa Descent

My first name is Busumuru. My father tells me that it means the Great One, the Mighty One. He says he named me after his grandfather who was one of the great pillars in his big family and clan in Africa. He said he hoped I would grow up to be a great person. Because of my belief in this name, I have tried to achieve only the best so far in my life to achieve the perceived greatness to honour the name of my great grandfather and I believe I will be great

I like my African name........ It gives me an attachment to my African roots and I feel very proud of it. Some of my Canadian Caucasian friends in school are even adopting African names when I explain to them that our names have meanings and significance to times, seasons and links to the great people in African history.

Implications for Pedagogy in North American Classroom Settings

Culture, and culturally-relevant items, including names are central to learning. Culture plays a role not only in communicating and receiving information, but also in shaping the thinking process of groups and individuals (Gay, 2000). Teaching, according to Gay (2003), is an increasingly cross-cultural phenomenon, in that teachers "are frequently not of the same race, ethnicity, class, and language dominance as their students" (p. 1). This therefore calls for the need for effective teacher preparation "which addresses the need for teachers to acknowledge students' diversity and incorporate their pluralistic backgrounds and experiences into the learning experiences and classroom environment" (Ladson-Billings, 2001). Weinstein, Curran, and Tomlinson-Clarke (2003) also underscore the need for teachers "to develop the knowledge, skills and predispositions to teach children from diverse racial, ethnic, language and social class backgrounds" (p. 270). Similarly, Hackett (2003) also emphasized the need for teachers to develop a "strong cultural identity so as to be responsible for teaching the whole child by teaching values, skills, knowledge for school success and participation in society, linking classroom teaching to out-of-school personal experiences and community situations" (p. 329).

There are some teachers who sometimes make fun of the cultural names of minority students. I remember an incidence in one of my university classes where a Caucasian instructor always pretended that she found the name of a student of Somalian origin difficult to pronounce. Some of the students resorted to making fun of the name of this student and that adversely affected his concentration and interest in that course. He eventually dropped that course. To counter such incidents and their negative effects on students' identity, personality development and academic achievement, Dingus (2003) cautions that "no student should have to sacrifice cultural heritage, ethnic identity, and social networks in order to obtain an education" (p. 99). In discussing factors contributing to students' success in classrooms, Boykin, Tyler, and Miller (2005) posit that students succeed when academic tasks include themes representative of their own culture.

Conclusion

This study took a look at the events, reasoning and logic behind naming systems and cultural names in Africa. It sought to look at the implications of such names for the personality development of people especially youth of African descent in North American societies and in classroom settings. From the results of this study and as shown from some of the narratives of the study's participants, it can be inferred that the importance and significance of culture cannot be overemphasized or downplayed. As most authors referenced above have emphasized, there is the need to acknowledge the cultural, racial, ethnic, and class differences that exist among people. Its implication is that students' cultural backgrounds which include their names are very relevant to their interpersonal relationships in school settings. When teachers create an environment which is based on caring and respect in which each student and his/her cultural background is valued, the result is that students become more motivated, learn and achieve more (Stipek, 2002).

In this age of globalization, if we are to understand ourselves and others, and if teachers will be effective in the delivery of their lessons to their students of diverse backgrounds, and as Asimeng-Boahene (2010) succinctly puts it, we need to teach "the inter-connectedness of human experiences by fostering alternative visions of reality that can be referenced by advancing the use of indigenous pedagogies, such as storytelling, proverbs, legends and myths" (p. 439). This is the reality of the modern global world and we should not stray from it and the challenges and opportunities that it presents.

REFERENCES

Anderson, C. P. (1979). *The Name Game*. New York. NY: Jove.
Appiah, K. A. (1992). *In my Father's House: Africa in the philosophy of culture*. Oxford, England: Oxford University Press.
Asimeng-Boahene, L. (2010). Counter-storytelling with African Proverbs: A vehicle for teaching social justice and global understanding in urban, U.S. schools. *Equity & Excellence in Education, 43*(4), 434-445.

Baffoe, M. (2013). Spiritual well-being and fulfilment, or exploitation by a few smart ones? The proliferation of Christian churches in West African immigrant communities in Canada. *Mediterranean Journal of Social Sciences, 4*(1).

Baffoe, M. (2002). *Demonizing African culture in the name of Christianity.* Montreal, QC: Black Studies Center.

Barth, F. (1969). *Ethnic groups and boundaries.* London, England: George Allen and Unwin,

Boykin, A., Tyler, K., & Miller, O. (2005). In search of cultural themes and their expressions in the dynamics of classroom life. *Urban Education, 40*(5), 521-549.

Browne, A. J., Smye, V. L., & Varcoe, C. (2005). The relevance of postcolonial theoretical perspectives to research in aboriginal health. *Canadian Journal of Nursing Research, 37*(4), 16-37.

Dei, G. J. S. (1998). Interrogating African development and the diasporan reality. *Journal of Black Studies, 29*(2), 141-153.

Delgado, R. (1989). Storytelling for opportunists and others. A plea for narrative. *Michigan Law Review, 87,* 2411-2441.

Deluzain, H. E. (n.d.). Behind the name. The etymology and history of first names. Retrieved from http://www.behindthename.com/articles/2.php

Dingus, J. (2003). Making and breaking ethnic masks. In G. Gay (Ed.), *Becoming multicultural educators: Personal journey toward professional agency* (pp. 91-116). San Francisco, CA: Jossey-Bass.

Garwood, S. G. (1976). First-name stereotypes as a factor in self-concept and school achievement. *Journal of Educational Psychology, 68,* 482-487.

Gay, G. (2000). *Culturally responsive teaching: Theory, research, and practice.* New York, NY: Teachers College Press.

Gay, G. (2003). Introduction: Planting seeds to harvest fruits. In G. Gay (Ed.), *Becoming multicultual educators: Personal journey toward professional agency* (pp. 1-16). San Francisco, CA: Jossey-Bass.

Ghandi, L. (1968). *Postcolonial theory: A critical introduction.* London: Oxford University Press.

Gyekye, K. (1996). *African cultural values: An introduction.* Philadelphia, PA: Sankofa.

Gyekye, K. (1997). *Tradition and modernity: Philosophical reflections on the African experience.* New York, NY: Oxford University Press.

Hackett, T. (2003). Teaching them through who they are. In G. Gay (Ed.), *Becoming multicultural educators: Personal journey toward professional agency* (pp. 315-340). San Francisco, CA: Jossey-Bass.

Highly qualified teachers for every child. (2006, August). Retrieved from http://www.ed.gov/nclb/methods/teachers/stateplanfacts.html

Hodari, A. J. (2009). *The African book of names: 5000+ common and uncommon names from the African continent.* Deerfield Beach, Fl: Health Communications.

Ladson-Billings, G. (1998). Just what is critical race theory and what's it doing in a nice field like education? *Qualitative Studies in Education, 11*(1), 7-24.

Ladson-Billings, G. (2000). Racialized discourses and ethnic epistemologies. In *Handbook of Qualitative Research* (pp. 257-277). Thousand Oaks, CA: Sage.

Ladson-Billings, G. (2001). *Crossing over to Canaan: The journey of new teachers in diverse classrooms.* San Francisco, CA: Jossey-Bass.

Lassiter, J. E. (1979, March). *Meta-anthropology, normative culture and the anthropology of development.* Paper presented at the 1979 annual meeting of the Northwest Anthropological Conference, Eugene, Oregon.

Leonard, J. (2008). *Culturally specific pedagogy in the mathematics classroom: Strategies for teachers and students.* New York, NY: Routledge.

Macey, D. (2000). *Dictionary of critical theory.* London, England: Penguin Books.

Madubuike, I. (1976). *A handbook of African names.* Washington: Three Continents.

Masolo, D. A. (1995). *African philosophy in search of identity.* Nairobi: East African Publishers.

Mazuri, A. A. (1986). *The Africans: A tripple heritage.* Toronto, Canada: Little, Brown.

McDonald, H. (2003). *Exploring possibilities through critical face theory: Exemplary pedagogical practices for Indigenous students.* Proceedings of the Joint AARE/NZARE Conference. 2003 Joint AARE/NZARE Conference, November 29-December 3, 2003, Auckland, NZL.

Moerman, M. (1974). Accomplishing ethnicity. In R. Turner (Ed.), *Ethnomethodology: Selected Readings* (pp. 54-68). Baltimore, MD: Penguin Education.

Murphy, W. F. (1957). A note on the significance of names. *Psychological Quarterly, 26,* 91-106.

Nagel J. (1994). Constructing ethnicity: creating and recreating ethnic identity and culture. *Social Problems, 41*(1), 152-176.

Skhosana, P. B. (2002). Names and practices among Southern Ndebele male persons. *Nomina Africana,* 1 & 2.

Strumpfer, D. J. W. (1978). The relationship between attitudes towards one's name and self-esteem. *Psychological Reports, 43,* 699-702.

Stipek, D. (2002). *Motivation to learn: Integrating theory and practice* (4th ed.). Boston, MA: Allyn and Bacon.

Suarez-Orozco, C., Suarez-Orozco, M. M., & Doucet, F. (2004). The academic engagement and achievement of Latino youth. In J. A. Banks & C. A. M. Banks (Eds.), *Handbook of Research on Multicultural Education* (2nd eds., pp. 420-437). San-Francisco, CA: Jossey-Bass.

Weinstein, C., Curran, M., & Tomlinson-Clarke, S. (2003). Culturally responsive classroom management: Awareness into action. *Theory Into Practice, 42*(3), 269-276.

CHAPTER 7

MIRROR OF A PEOPLE

The Pedagogical Value of African Proverbs as Cultural Resource Tools in Content Area in Social Studies Classrooms

Lewis Asimeng-Boahene

When thought is lost, it is proverbs that are used to search for it.

— African proverb.

Justice is like fire. If you cover it, it burns.

—African proverb.

A person is a person through persons.

—*Xhosa* (South Africa)
Proverb: *Umuntu ngumuntu ngabantu.*

A wise child is talked to in proverbs

(Asante, Ghana).

African Traditional and Oral Literature as Pedagogical Tools in Contest Area Classrooms: K-12, pages 111–128
Copyright © 2014 by Information Age Publishing

INTRODUCTION

Excellent and effective teaching demands a host of devices, techniques and strategies not only to achieve cross critical outcomes but because variety, itself, is a *sine qua non*. One pedagogical tool which perhaps is too seldom used is the indigenous knowledge system. However, cognizant of current speed and wave of globalization among nations in the 21st century, preparing children to function effectively as global citizens in the present-day complex but globally interconnected world will require not only teacher educators but also students who possess knowledge of histories, experiences, cultural practices, and epistemological and methodological assumptions of other parts of the world. The chapter offers African traditional oral communication through proverbs as a meaningful tool for teaching concepts of citizenship education, social justice, and critical thinking skills in a content area social studies classroom.

The changing demographic landscape of immigrant populations and other minorities in the last decade in the U.S and the speed and intensity of globalization as a process for the growing interconnectedness among nations in the 21st century calls for the necessity to highlight and situate the missing voices of linguistic minorities in the education landscape. Schools should be places of possibilities that foster responsible and dedicated world citizens who have the ability to engage in careful, reflective thoughts, viewed in various ways as requirements for social justice, critical thinking skills and responsible citizenship in a democratic society. The above four epigrams exemplify distinct and powerful appeal of African proverbs as valued resource for the revitalization of the mainstream pedagogical landscape as they are the embodiment of "the wisdom of many and the wit of one" (Cooper, 2004, p. 11).

The objective of this chapter is to open up a dialogic space to shed light on how to provide an alternative perspective for the mainstream idiosyncratic models of pedagogy for educators with inspiration and resources they need to investigate their own practices, uncover their own biases, and raise questions to foster revisions of existing pedagogical practices. It also contests the geopolitical framework of knowledge construction and the extent to which "non-African" and "African" epistemologies are both considered as valid sources of knowledge, identity formation, and sociohistorical power relations.

This chapter is divided into five sections, and readers will quickly sense their interconnectedness and overlap. I begin with a discussion of what African proverbs are about. Next, I address the theoretical frameworks, which support the use of African proverbs in promoting social justice, critical thinking, and citizenship education. I then discuss critical thinking, social justice, and citizenship education in social studies. The next discussion addresses the rationale of incorporating African proverbs into citizenship education, critical thinking, and social justice. The final part consists of suggestions/ideas/activities for using African proverbs as pedagogical tools for social justice, critical thinking, and citizenship education in a social studies class.

African Proverbs: The Warp and Woof of African Orature

As the priced personification of the wisdom of many, proverbs in general have a universal audience. They have been studied from a number of interdisciplinary, theoretical, and geographical perspectives (Asimeng-Boahene, 2009; Finnegan, 1970; Gyekye, 1996; Mieder, 2004). As the study of proverbs has voyaged across diverse geographical locations and scholarly perspectives, it has become a subject of passionate discussions concerning its epistemological conceptualization, theoretical boundaries, and methodological relevance (Andrzejewski, 1985; Appiah, Appiah, & Agyeman-Duah, 2007; Asimeng-Boahene & Marinak, 2010; Boateng, 1983; Duncan, 2005; Reagan, 2005). Throughout Africa, proverbs provide a highly abbreviated, often poetic window on human experience and on local understandings of the world. Thus, "African proverbs are in fact a finely-wrought form of expression where meanings are tightly interleaved, creating associations between apparently disparate realms of experience that throw new light on events and order perception" ("Participatory Management," 2000, p. 2).

Though the indigenous pedagogical tools of the various Africa oral literatures include fairy tales, legends, jokes, proverbs and riddles, among others, proverbs stand out from myriad contemporaries in terms of their utility value as tools for citizenship education, social justice, and critical thinking. In addition, their educative and communication powers take a broader picture of culture, politics, and histories (Boateng, 1983; Mieder, 2004). This assertion is forcefully argued by educationalist Carter G. Woodson (1933) when he accentuated the need for educators to use proverbs as well as folklore in their instructional methods so that the child could be familiar with "what his background is, what he is today, what his possibilities are, and how to begin with him as he is and make him a better individual of the kind that he is" (p. 151). This suggestion articulates eloquently the value of appreciating the need to see the world through the eyes of other cultures. No wonder then that the virtues and wisdom of African proverbs and their ability to influence social relations have been addressed for years in Africa (Abbam, 1994; Achebe, 1994;

Grant & Asimeng-Boahene, 2006). In spite of this, proverbs' potential value as pedagogical tool for modern thought and life is little recognized and therefore untapped and not well defined (Reagan, 2005).

However, notwithstanding this lack of intellectual visibility and utility in the Western academia, it should be pontificated that, as power of the tongue, pearls of wisdom, and the universal story of mankind, "one short proverb can provide the equivalent of pages of philosophical discussion" (Appiah et al., 2007, p. xii). Thus, African proverbs provide a window on the collective experiences, dreams, and values of a cultural group. Consequently, they serve as a "mirror of a people" as they reflect the beliefs, rituals, and songs of a group's cultural heritage (Cullinan & Galda, 1994). Hence, to Appiah et al. (2007), "The genius wit and the spirit of a nation are discovered by their proverbs" (p. xii). That is, proverbs also are used in various political, judicial, economic, social, and cultural contexts, both formal and informal platforms. African proverbs play a considerable role in traditional legal cases, where they are used by both sides in traditional courts in the solution of societal conflicts to present their arguments (Jones, 1995) and, if used judiciously, can win or settle disputes and conflicts among some ethnic groups in Africa.. It is said among the Akans that: "*Ano na yede wen etire*" literally, "the mouth is used to protect the head" (Asimeng-Boahene, 2009). Thus, to misuse proverbs can be reprehensible so Siqwana-Ndulo (1989) writes, "The proverb validates and augments a trend of argumentation, affirming to the discourse participants that the speaker's view point has the blessings of an unquestionable truism" (p. 22). In conclusion, I echo Appiah et al.'s statement that proverbs are a treasure beyond price, for they are in summation, "the verbal shrine for the soul of a nation" (p. xiv).

PROVERBS AS A CULTURAL RESOURCE TOOLS FOR CRITICAL THINKING, SOCIAL JUSTICE, AND CITIZENSHIP EDUCATION

Theoretical Framework

The major concepts that promote the use of the African proverbs as alternative paradigm of reality for enhancing the teaching of critical thinking skills, social justice and citizenship education take inspirations from critical race theory (CRT), critical literacy and culturally responsive pedagogy (CRP). They were chosen because they all anchor the lived experiences of diverse learners, support instructional outcomes, give hope to people normally ignored, provide voice for the voiceless, and challenge the totalizing hold of the mainstream pedagogy (Delgado, 1995; Freire & Macedo, 1987; Moll, Amanti, Neff, & Gonzalez, 1992; Waxman & Padron, 1995).

CRT is one of the reference points because it examines the system of education as part of a critique of societal inequality. It challenges the prevailing social and cultural assumptions regarding culture and intelligence, language and capability, through research, pedagogy, and praxis (Calmore, 1992). It is also committed to social justice and offers all welcoming response to racial, gender, and class oppression and attempts to link theory with practice, scholarship with teaching, and academy with the diverse communities (Matsuda, 1991). CRT affiliates with culturally relevant pedagogy (CRP) as both concepts foster "intentional behavior by a teacher to use gestures, language, history, literature, and other cultural aspects of a particular race, ethnic or gender group to engage students belonging to that in authentic student-centered learning" (Leonard, 2008, p. 8). In addition, CRT employs methods such as storytelling or counterstorytelling (including proverbs), chronicles, family histories, and narratives to illustrate the strengths of the varied experiences students bring to the classroom (Delgado, 1989; Delgado, 1995; Duncan, 2005; Solórzano & Yosso, 2000; Yosso, 2002). Indeed, Delgado (1995) asserts that many of the "early tellers of tales used stories to test and challenge reality, to construct a counter reality, to hearten and support each other and to probe, mock, displace, jar, or reconstruct the dominant tale or narrative" (p. xviii).

The above narratives underscore the rationale for the call for the inclusion of alternative epistemologies and pedagogies that utilize and recognize the experiential knowledge of diverse students as legitimate, appropriate, and critical to understanding alternative perspectives. Thus, educators should be cognizant of the fact that all students, regardless of ethnicity, carry their culturally influenced cognitive behavior and dispositions to school. However, at the same time we should be mindful of Caldwell (1995) admonition that "issues of experience, culture, and identity are not the subject of explicit legal reasoning" (p. 270), and that the lived experiences of underrepresented minority groups are generally marginalized, if not silenced from educational discourse. In effect, by allowing other narratives to be visible in the classroom as called for by CRT, the lived experiences of diverse students who continue to struggle for expression within the mainstream narratives would be acknowledged, instead of just toiling away in anonymity.

Critical literacy espouses that academic success can be achieved through culturally inclusive theoretical frameworks for research methods, assessment, as well as instruction. It "focuses on the critical family and community issues that students encounter daily" (Waxman & Padron,

1995, p. 52). Thus, critical literacy engages students in high -level cognitive activity and acknowledges issues of culture and language facility. Sleeter (2011) found several studies which acknowledged that when underrepresented minority students utilize learning resources that involve the study of people, events and experiences from their own race or ethnicity with which they can identify, they are typically more engaged and improve their academic performance.

Thus, utilizing CRT, critical literacy, and CRP helps students to identify, analyze, and transform debate and engage in discussions about the current mainstream narratives which have become "sanctified epistemological paradigms with which data and scholarship from all corners of the universe should come to terms if they are to attain "mainstream" recognition" (Yankah, 1999, p. 12).

CRITICAL THINKING SKILLS, SOCIAL JUSTICE AND CITIZENSHIP EDUCATION IN SOCIAL STUDIES EDUCATION

Critical Thinking in Social Studies

Though it is a household concept, it is such a complex process that the question of what critical thinking entails continues to defy definitional consensus. Critical thinking used to be considered the *silent partner* in the social studies curriculum (Grant & Asimeng-Boahene, 2006), but contemporary educators have strongly advocated to make critical thinking a pivotal segment of everyday lessons (Asimeng-Boahene & Marinak, 2010). When students are engaged in critical thinking, they look for evidence to back up new ideas and beliefs and are willing to express their thoughts on a topic. These readily identifiable behaviors, which denote that students are thinking critically, can be developed by reading, discussion, and writing about African proverbs (Asimeng-Boahene, 2009). For children to develop citizenship skills suitable to a democracy, they must be adept at thinking critically about complex societal problems and global problems. The social studies curriculum standards demand the inclusion of experiences that prioritize for the study of cultures and cultural diversity in social studies programs (National Council for Social Studies [NCSS], 2001). Research indicates that there is merit in knowing how languages, stories, folktales, and artistic creations influence the behavior of people living in a particular cultural heritage (Cullinan & Galda, 1994; Maxim, 2010). Thus, in conclusion, when exposed to the authentic words and wisdom of diverse cultures, children become informed of and start to think critically about global interdependence and connections among world cultures (Asimeng-Boahene & Marinak, 2010).

Social Justice in Social Studies

Social justice may include the idea of a just society that gives individuals and groups fair treatment and a just share of the benefits of society (Bell, 1997). The theories of social justice are situated in traditions of liberalism that spotlight the moral worth of all human beings as having the right to equal dignity (Asimeng-Boahene, 2010). This is reflected in the way in which human rights are manifested, irrespective of life situations (Gaus, 1983). For example, as Bell (1997) opines:

> Social justice includes a vision of society in which the distribution of resources is equitable and all members are physically and psychologically safe and secure.... Social justice involves social actors who have a sense of their own agency as well as a sense of social responsibility toward others and the society as a whole. (p. 1)

The crux of social justice in social studies centers on the belief in the equal worth of every person and the willingness to act in espousing that belief. One of the key features of ideal social studies teaching and learning is captured in its vision that "social studies teaching and learning are more powerful when they are challenging" (NCSS, 2001, p. 4). This vision further identifies teaching about varying and conflicting opinions on sociopolitical issues like social justice in order to foster and challenge the students' thinking. Thus, the proponents of social justice work toward the understanding of a world not as it is at the moment but, rather, as it should be, where all members of a society, irrespective of background, have basic human rights and equal opportunity to their community's resources (Brooks & Thompson, 2005).

Citizenship Education in Social Studies

As a tool for national development, social studies provide, knowledge, skill, competencies, attitudes, and values that enable the students to be good citizens (Maxim, 2010; Parker, 2012). There are many ways in which social studies can be used to develop good citizenship among students and these, among others, include the diversification of the curriculum to capture the varied students in the class, the incorporation of civic education, and the promotion of inquiry-based learning. The curriculum could be diversified through reflection of objectives, content, method, and resources of the curriculum to be redirected to mirror the perspectives of the diverse students it is supposed to serve. Social studies education includes core values of citizenship, such as group interaction skills, political skills, and social and intellectual skills. It further promotes the development of good citizenship by guiding students to acquire skills in making reasoned decisions, resolving conflicts peacefully, and appreciating diverse democratic institutions by fully participating in diverse civic activities such as voting, accepting alternative views, and encouraging free expression of ideas and opinions (Grant & Asimeng-Boahene,2006; Maxim, 2010; Parker, 2012). Furthermore, citizenship is an interactive rather than cerebral experience, and until students have experienced this process, they might not appreciate its significance. Consequently, one of the most important characteristics of citizenship is social justice concerns, such as concern for the welfare of others, moral and ethical behaviors, and acceptance of diversity (Grant & Asimeng-Boahene,2006; Maxim, 2010; Parker, 2012). Thus, the social studies teachers' understanding of educating diverse students for citizenship in a democracy is crucial to the achievement of the major goal of social studies by providing all students with the knowledge, tools, and skills to succeed in a globally-connected world.

Rationale for Incorporating African Proverbs Into Critical Thinking Skills, Social Justice and Citizenship Education

The use of proverbs for teaching dates back to ancient times with proverbs by Aristotle, Confucius and category of Chinese proverbs (Asimeng-Boahene, 2009). Furthermore, the use of proverbs in teaching different disciplines and empirical evidence on their learning benefits clearly support the expanding application of proverbs in the classrooms. Moreno and Di Vesta (1994) offer empirical support for the learning benefits of proverbs. They find that proverbs aid students in the comprehension and retention of new material as proverbs make main ideas more noticeable and relevant through the application of the selective attention.

It is therefore not surprising that these days an African proverb, "it takes a whole village to raise a child," has to a large extent been used to motivate communities throughout the U.S. to participate in the challenges of educating U.S. children (Grant & Asimeng-Boahene, 2006). This recent attention to African proverbs could provide a catalytic force essential to uncork the secret powers of African proverbs as cultural and pedagogical resource tools in a country like the United States, reputed for its support and promotion of innovative thinking. Other benefits for using proverbs as tools for social justice, critical thinking skills, and citizenship education include the following:

a. African proverbs create a galvanizing avenue for critical thinking for both individuals and community, for example, "If you want to go fast, go alone; if you want to go far, go with others." This Ghanaian proverb is used to help children develop a sense of community through creative thinking.

b. Proverbs strengthen children's analytical ability through the use of critical thinking skills, social justice concepts, and citizenship education, for example, a proverb such as "If you see a stick that will pierce your eye, break it off" is a case in point

c. Cognitively, the proverb "One head does not exchange ideas" (Akan, Ghana), which means two heads are better than one," can help to promote a concept of good citizenship.

d. Proverbs provide insight into how Africans revere the elderly. The proverb, "The word of the elder is more powerful than the *Suman* (an amulet with supernatural power), illustrates the point (Achebe, 1994; Appiah-Kubi, 1999; Grant & Asimeng-Boahene, 2006; Gyekye, 1996; Jones, 1995; Korem & Abissath, 2004). Consequently, African proverbs are significant pedagogical tools for education of children, for they promote cross-cultural tolerance and transcend universal philosophical intellectualism, which are increasingly important in current "global village." In very siuccinct ways, African proverbs provide powerful pictures of real life and as is commonly believed, a picture is worth more than a thousand words.

Interrelationship Between the Dispositions of Social Justice, Critical Thinking Skills, Citizenship Education, and African Proverbs

Tables 7.1-7.3 provide useful typologies that conceptualize, delineate, and apply the dispositions of social justice, citizenship education, critical thinking skills, and corresponding African proverbs. Table 7.1, which models the relationship between social justice and African proverbs, can usher in a new conceptualization of social justice for preparing diverse students for global knowledge with better informed global perspectives, which continue to appear too distant for them because of the mainstream curricular approach. The table further conceptualizes the African world view that values oral tradition of proverbs as elements of indigenous wisdoms for citizenship preparation and education. This

Table 7.1.   Tenets of Social Justice and African Proverbs With Social Justice Themes: Methodological Applicability

Tenets of Social Justice: Underlying Values	African Proverbs	Influence/Value/Lesson on Social Justice Education
Fair entitlement	"Treat the days well and they will treat you well." (Zimbabwe)	We should return kindness when it is shown to us.
Valuing difference in race	"If you are wearing shoes, you don't feel the thorns." (Sudan)	We should recognize the voice of the other. All people are created equal. Every person's culture. race/ethnicity, values, and beliefs are to be respected and valued.
Social norms	"The left arm washes the right arm and the right arm washes the left arm." (Ghana)	We should all be concerned about the welfare of others.
Intellectual flexibility	"The cattle are as good as the pasture in which they graze." (Ethiopia)	We should keep an open mind. Continuous learning is critical to the development of mind, body, and spirit.
Personal perspectives	"There is no better guidance than lessons learned from experience." (Kenya)	We should recognize the concept of human dignity and human life.
Appreciating diversity	"Knowledge is like a baobab tree; a single person's hand cannot embrace it." (Ghana)	Community of practice. Each of us possesses unique and diverse insights, perspectives, and experiences.
Promoting equity	"A tree that grows in the shade of another one will die small." (Senegal)	We should treat others as we want to be treated.
Advancing broadmindedness	"One head does not exchange ideas." (Mali)	We should be open to multiple interpretations. Embrace the wisdom and knowledge that each person brings.
Encouraging voice and expression	"If you cannot be a lighthouse, be a candle." (N. Africa)	Encourage creativity and encourage people to speak what is in their hearts.

Source: Asimeng-Boahene. (2010).

idea embraces the articulation of the World Commission on Culture and Development Report titled "Our Creative Diversity" that seeks to promote cultural diversity among international societies by advocating for the elimination of discrimination, prejudice, and domination with tolerance, equity, and productive coexistence in every sphere of our human endeavors (UNESCO, 1995).

Table 7.2. Tenets of Citizenship Education and African Proverbial Themes on Citizenship: Theoretical Delineation

Principles	*Virtue/Morality*	*Knowledge*	*Responsibility*	*Humanity/ Community*
Knowledge	Virtue has its reward. (Ghana)	"Caution is not cowardice; even ants march armed." (Uganda)	Footprints in the sands of time are not made by sitting down. (Liberia)	The way to overcome cold is to help each other. (S. Africa)
Thinking skills	If you want a better tomorrow, be good today. (Zambia)	"Too many bends on a foot path do not prevent one from reaching one's destination." (Cameroon)	A fly that dances carelessly in front of a spider's web risks the wrath of the spider's teeth. (Nigeria)	Teamwork without coordination brings confusion. (Zambia)
Democratic beliefs	Sharing brings a full stomach; selfishness brings hunger. (Africa)	"There can only be one ruler or leader, but not two." (Botswana)	If you warn someone of their behavior, you are not harming them. (Uganda)	It takes all kinds to make the world. (Kenya)
Active civic participation	When you love a person, you do not fold your arms. (Ethiopia)	"The person who aims at nothing will surely hit it." (Cameroon)	There is no other thing you get out of laziness than poverty. (Ghana)	Be a neighbor to a human being and not a fence. (Kenya)

Table 7.2 conceptualizes the interrelationship of traditional themes in Africa proverbs (virtue/community, knowledge, responsibility, and humanity/community). The basic tenets of citizenship education (knowledge, thinking skills, democratic beliefs, and active participation), as articulated in

Table 7.3, can be used to enhance a new epistemological conceptualization for preparing global citizens. Table 7.3 illustrates the relationship between critical thinking and African proverbs. This illustration can usher in a new epistemological conceptualization and methodological applicability of critical thinking for preparing diverse students for global knowledge with better informed global perspectives.

How can teachers utilize the intersections of African proverbial themes and the essentials of critical thinking skills, social justice, and citizenship education among diverse students in a culturally conscientious social studies classroom? Notwithstanding the fact that conventional educators operate within paradigms set by Western thought and scholarship, including methodology, language, and epistemologies, the above task could be addressed, among others, by equipping oneself with the suggested teaching strategies discussed below with references to the three tables discussed earlier.

Examples of Using African Proverbs as a Pedagogical Device and Sample of Instructional Activities

Social studies and language arts teachers can easily incorporate the use of African proverbs to promote critical thinking skills, social justice, and citizenship education into almost any content area lesson or grade level instruction to foster global understanding. Following are several ideas for integrating this culturally conscientious instruction.

First and foremost, teachers should use learning resources that engage all students in higher- order intellectual challenges. They should master diversity-related pedagogical skills, by incorporating a variety of materials that reflect the cultural diversity of their school, the community, the nation and the world. In other words, the teacher should model and promote "hands-on, minds-on" learning experiences that create a classroom climate that encourages cooperative learning, individual and group empowerment, student-shared experiences and knowledge, and respect for self and others to support positive social interactions (see Merryfield & Wilson, 2005). For this to happen, teachers, according to Kohn (1996), should establish an enabling classroom as:

> a place in which students feel cared about and are encouraged to care about each other. They experience a sense of being valued and respected; the chil-dren matter to one another and to the teacher. They have come to think in the plural: they feel connected to each other; they are part of an "us." (p. 101)

As an example, social studies teachers could develop thematic units around the various tenets of social justice/critical thinking/citizenship education

Table 7.3. Interrelationship Between Dispositions of Critical Thinking and African Proverbs: Epistemological Conceptualization

Dispositions/Attributes	*Critical Thinking Skills*	*African Proverbs*
Intellectual curiosity	Seeking answers to various kinds of questions and problems; investigating the causes and explanations of events; asking why, how, who, when, where.	A good wind is no use to a sailor who does not know his direction. (Zambia)
Objectivity	Using objective factors in the process of making decisions.	A person is a person through persons. (Xhosa, S. Africa)
Open-mindedness	Willingness to consider a wide variety of beliefs as possible being true, making judgment without bias or prejudice.	Hunt in every jungle, for there is wisdom and good hunting in all of them. (Africa)
Flexibility	Willingness to change one's beliefs or methods of inquiry, dogmatic attitude, and rigidity.	There is method in some people's madness. (Uganda)
Intellectual skepticism	Postponing acceptance of a hypothesis as true until adequate evidence is available.	Speech (talk) is one thing, wisdom is another, (Akan, Ghana)
Intellectual honesty	Accepting a statement as true when there is sufficient evidence.	A bird that is not flying cannot discover where there is harvest. (Burundi)
Being systematic	Following a line of reasoning consistently to a particular conclusion.	Judge each day, not by the harvest, but by the seeds you plant. (Guinea)
Persistence	Supporting points of view without giving up the task of finding evidence and arguments.	He who has not reached his destination, never gets tired. (Kenya)
Decisiveness	Reaching certain conclusions when the evidence warrants.	Knowledge alone is useless, unless it leads to achievement. (Kenya)
Respect for other viewpoints	Listening carefully to other points of view and responding relevantly to what was said.	Wisdom is not in the head of one person. (Akan, Ghana).

Source: Asimeng-Boahene (2009).

using the "big idea" approach. In this approach, the teacher begins with a focus on the major ideas or generalizations related to the content and then select activities designed to helps students develop those big ideas.

Teachers may start a lesson by using proverbs to review previously studied material. Complementing previously presented concepts to underlying concept-based proverbs will allow for quick interesting review.

1. Geography (social studies): This can be taught by identifying the people or ethnic groups of the countries from which the selected proverbs originated on a map of Africa. This project helps develop students' research skills that incorporate another area of study and are useful for teaching curricular standard themes of Culture and Global Connections (NCSS, 2001). These activities can show how all subject matter can be integrated to foster better understanding of using African proverbs as counterstories in promoting social justice in urban school settings.

2. Teachers can use Service Learning as central part of assignment (example: "It takes a whole village to raise a child.") or "The way to overcome cold is to help each other" (see Table 7.2). Since there should be a complementary relationship between the school and the community (Maxim, 2010; Parker, 2012), this learning is an experience in which students learn through active participation in thoughtfully organized service experiences that meet a community need. For it to be relevant, it must prepare students for active civic participation and social justice action. For example, in terms of Service and Advocacy, students can embark on a service project, like creating posters to bring awareness to the problem of homelessness as a social justice issue. This can raise consciousness on the importance of kindness, compassion, and understanding in the school and community. By inviting students to participate in service projects that embrace social justice and global understanding, the students will develop a consciousness about their community and the world.

3. To promote culturally linguistically responsive family, community engagement and an inclusive climate, teachers could use community learning resources to adapt instruction. Having the proverb: "The way to overcome cold is to help each other" in mind, teachers could extend the invitation to community members for a speaker who speaks African languages and is versed in African cultural heritage or contact the Consulate of an African country for a speaker to discuss oral literature like proverbs and how they are related to critical thinking/social justice/citizenship education.

4. In a technology-driven society, the teacher can make effective use of technology to enhance the lesson:

   a. Plan a web-based virtual tour of an African country, or conduct a web quest to look for cultural connections to common proverbs

   b. Use videos to promote critical thinking skills, social justice, citizenship education and demonstrate agent and target roles in eliminating oppression and discrimination; appreciate differences in race; advancing broad-mindedness; and demonstrate how a web of racism is built. For instance, a video on racism (e.g., *Understanding:* Racism) addresses the concept of interpreting social justice, conflict resolution, and interpersonal problem solving. The teacher can connect the video's discussion with African proverbs that have a social justice theme, for example, "If you are wearing shoes, you don't feel the thorns."

5. In integrating language Arts into social studies lesson, teachers can ask students to collect proverbs on critical thinking skills, citizenship education, and social justice from around the world to share or establish an anthology similar to a poetry anthology.

   a. Teachers could initiate debate about social justice/citizenship education or one aspect of the critical thinking dispositions (see Tables 7.1-7.3), e.g., respect for other viewpoints with its accompanying African proverb, "One head does not exchange ideas" (Mali) (Table 7.1). This debate can promote social and linguistic skills, which are significant ingredients in critical thinking.

   b. Teachers could establish a "proverb of the week" concept and have students come up with proverbs that relate to the social justice/citizenship or critical thinking dispositions.

This challenging activity is likely to engender a critical spirit, social justice, citizenship education, and a propensity for and capability in critical thinking among students.

Closing Activity: Putting all Together

As a culminating activity, students could role play using African proverbs, such as "knowledge is like a baobab tree; a single person's hand cannot embrace it" (Ghana) (see Table 7.1) to depict a valuable lesson on citizenship education, critical thinking skills, and social justice education.

These activities accentuate the benefits of using traditional oral communication as pedagogical tools to develop students' ability to think critically about social issues to promote citizenship, social justice, and communicate often-complex issues to an audience.

CONCLUSION

In conclusion, it is important to state that the discipline of African oral literature has great prospects as a pedagogical tool. In addition, drawing on critical race theory, culturally relevant pedagogy, and critical pedagogy as theoretical frameworks, I have argued that the use of indigenous proverbs can develop meaningful curriculum that embraces the narratives that draw from the cultural riches of other communities besides the dominant culture as literacy cannot be viewed separately from social power. I have suggested through instructional activities how the use of African proverbs as tools can enhance critical thinking skills, citizenship education, and social justice among diverse children in the social studies education classroom. With this in mind, I have explored some of the traditional knowledge-based teaching and learning strategies teachers can employ to develop the interpretative and communicative skills of students. Specifically, the strategies outlined seek to enhance students' ability to interpret/analyze critical social issues to determine their meaning; explain (or account for) the social issues addressed; examine (or reflect on) the social implications of an issue portrayed in a situation; and communicate (in writing) the knowledge and understandings derived from the analysis of the situation. Consequently, with technological advances bringing all world cultures closer together, not only can the use of proverbs as resource tools in the social studies education curriculum help children develop critical thinking skills, but also build bridges nurturing the development of a global community that exploits teaching and wisdom from diverse perspectives in a caring and safe learning environment. Such an approach carries the potential of a diverse, action-oriented educated citizenry committed to social justice in a globalized world.

REFERENCES

Abbam, C. M. (1994, October-November). Developing education. *West Africa, 4022,* 1870-1871

Achebe, C. (1994). *Things fall apart.* New York, NY: Doubleday.

Andrzejewski, B. W. (1985). Oral literature. In B. W. Andrzejewski, S. Pilaszewicz, & W. Tyloch (Eds.), *Literatures in African languages: theoretical issues and sample surveys.* (pp.129-157). Cambridge, England: Cambridge University Press.

Appiah, P., Appiah, K. A., & Agyeman-Duah. (2007). *Bu me be: Proverbs of the Akans.* Boulder, CO: Lynne Rienner.

Appiah-Kubi, K. (1999). *The Akan of Ghana, West Africa: A cultural handbook for reference*. Bloomfield, CT: Cowhide Press.

Asimeng-Boahene, L. (2009). Educational wisdom of African oral literature: African proverbs as vehicles for enhancing critical thinking skills. *International Journal of Pedagogies and Learning, 5*(3), 59-69.

Asimeng-Boahene, L. (2010). Counter storytelling with African proverbs. A vehicle for teaching social justice and global understanding in urban, U.S. schools. *Equity & Excellence in Education, 43*(4), 434-445.

Asimeng-Boahene, L., & Marinak, B. A. (2010). Well-chosen words: Thinking critically about African proverbs. *Social Studies and the Young Learner, 23*(1), P1-P4.

Bell, L. A. (1997). Theoretical foundations for social justice education. In M. Adams, L. Bell, & P. Griffin (Eds.), *Teaching for diversity and social justice* (pp. 3-15). New York, NY: Rouledge.

Boateng, F. (1983). African traditional education: A method of disseminating cultural values *Journal of Black Studies, 3*, 321-336.

Brooks, J. G., & Thompson, E. G. (2005). Social justice in the classroom. *Educational Leadership, 63*(1), 48-52.

Caldwell, P. (1995). A hair piece: Perspectives on the Intersection of race and gender. In R. Delgado (Ed.), *Critical race theory: The cutting edge* (pp. 267-277). Philadelphia, PA: Temple University Press.

Calmore, J. (1992). Critical race theory, Archie Shepp, and fire music: Securing an authentic intellectual life in a multicultural world. *Southern California Law Review, 65*, 2129-2231.

Cooper, C. (2004). *Bizarre superstitions: The world's wackiest proverbs, rituals, and beliefs*. London, England: PRC.

Cullinan, B. E., & Galda, L. (1994). *Literature and the child*. Fort Worth, TX: Harcourt Brace.

Delgado, R. (1989). Storytelling for opportunists and others. A plea for narrative. *Michigan Law Review 87*, 2411-2441.

Delgado, R. (1995). *Critical race theory: The cutting edge*. Philadelphia, PA: Temple University Press.

Duncan, G. A. (2005). Critical race ethnography in education: Narrative, inequality and the problem of epistemology. *Race, Ethnicity and Education, 8*(1), 93-114.

Finnegan, R. H. (1970). *Oral literature in Africa*. Oxford, England: Clarendon.

Freire, P., & Macedo, D. (1987). *Literacy: Reading the word and the world*. Westport, CT: Bergin & Garvey.

Gaus, G. F. (1983). *The modern liberal theory of man*. New York, NY: St. Martin's Press.

Grant, R., & Asimeng-Boahene, L. (2006). Culturally responsive pedagogy in citizenship education: Using African proverbs as tools for teaching in urban schools. *Multicultural Perspectives, 8*(4), 17-24.

Gyekye, K. (1996). *African cultural values: An introduction*. Philadelphia, PA: Sankofa.

Jones, A. (1995). *Larousse dictionary of world folklore*. New York, NY: Laroussse Kingfisher Chambers.

Kohn, A. (1996). *Beyond discipline: From compliance to community* (10th anniv. Ed.). Alexandria, VA: ASCD.

Korem, A. K., & Abissath, M. K. (2004). *Traditional wisdom in Africa: 1915 proverbs from 41 African countries.* Accra, Ghana: Publishing Trends.

Leonard, J. (2008). *Culturally specific pedagogy in the mathematics classrooms: Strategies for teachers and students.* New York, NY: Routledge.

Matsuda, M. (1991). Voices of America; Accent, antidiscrimination law, and a jurisprudence for the last reconstruction. *Yale Law Journal, 100,* 1329-1407.

Maxim, G. W. (2010). *Dynamic social studies for constructive classrooms: Inspiring tomorrow's social scientists* (9th ed.). Boston, MA: Allyn & Bacon.

Merryfield, M. M., & Wilson, A. (2005). *Social studies and the world: Teaching global perspectives.* Silver Spring, MD: National Council for the Social Studies.

Mieder, W. (2004). *Proverbs: A handbook.* Westport, CT: Greenwood Press.

Moll, L. C., Amanti, C., Neff, D., & Gonzalez, N. (1992). Funds of knowledge for teaching: Using a qualitative approach to connect homes and classrooms. *Theory into Practice, 31,* 132-141.

Moreno, V., & Di Vesta, F. J. (1994, April). Analogies (Adages) as aids for comprehending structural relations in text, *Contemporary Educational Psychology 19,* 179-198.

National Council for the Social Studies. (2001). *Expectations of excellence: Curriculum standards for social studies.* Silver Spring, MD: Author.

Parker, W. C. (2012). *Social studies in elementary education* (14th ed.). Boston, MA: Pearson. Retrieved from http://pages.uoregon.edu/mourund/dave/quotations.htm

Participatory management and local culture: Proverbs and paradigms. (2000, March). *IK Notes, 18,* 1-4.

Reagan, T. (2005). *Non-Western educational traditions: Indigenous approaches to educational thought and practices* (3rd ed.). Mahweh, NJ: Erlbaum.

Siqwana-Ndulo, W. (1989, Fall). Proverbs: The aesthetics of communication in Africa. *African Studies Center Newsletter,* pp. 20-22.

Sleeter, C. E. (2011). *The academic and social value of ethnic studies; A research review.* Washington, DC: The National Education Association.

Solórzano, D. G., & Yosso, T. J. (2000). Critical race methodology: Counter-storytelling as an analytical framework for education research. *Qualitative Inquiry, 8*(1), 23-44.

UNESCO. (1995). Our creative diversity: report of the World Commission on Culture and Development. Retrieved from http://tigger.uic.edu/-victor/Reviews/creativediversity.pdf

Waxman, H., & Padron, Y. (1995). Improving the quality of classroom instruction for students at risk of failure in urban schools. *Peabody Journal of Education, 70,* 44-65.

Woodson, C. G. (1933). *The mis-education of the Negro.* Asmara, Eritrea: Africa World Press.

Yankah, K. (1999). African folk and the challenges of a global lore. *African Today, 2,* 9-27.

Yosso, T. (2002). Toward a critical race curriculum. *Equity and Excellence in Education, 35*(2), 93-107.

CHAPTER 8

RIDDLES AS COMMUNICATIVE AND PEDAGOGICAL TOOL TO DEVELOP A MULTICULTURAL CURRICULUM IN SOCIAL STUDIES CLASSROOM

Kwadwo A. Okrah and Lewis Asimeng-Boahene

INTRODUCTION

The use of riddles, among other African oral traditions, can stimulate knowledge, skills, attitudes and beliefs that could be learned through interactive process, even among illiterate communities. To expand the dimensions and approaches that could advance global, multicultural and social studies curriculum, there have been calls to include in the curriculum the perspectives of underrepresented classes with the hope of improving the academic performance of students who are culturally, ethnically, racially and linguistically diverse. This demand is further supported and emphasized by inclusion of "global perspectives" in the National Council

African Traditional and Oral Literature as Pedagogical Tools in Contest Area Classrooms: K-12, pages 129–144
Copyright © 2014 by Information Age Publishing
All rights of reproduction in any form reserved.

129

for the Social Studies (NCSS) standards, a principle that has created a renewed interest in globalization of education and the introduction of cross-cultural awareness in schools (NCSS, 2001).

However, such pleas and efforts have been limited to short descriptive piece of literary writing, which have not been integrated and merged into the curriculum. Thus, non-Western oral literature, especially African oral art has been pushed to the fringes of mainstream curricula considerations in any curriculum development in America. With the minor literary status accorded African oral literature and oral art in the curriculum, it is not surprising that Western scholarship lacks any real exposure to non-Western educational traditions and philosophies. The result of such a scenario of ignorance is that many educated and noneducated Western scholars live with the attitude of multicultural and global deficiency that produces stereotyping and prejudice.

The intent of this chapter is to provide a new philosophical viewpoint that will advance a discussion to explore the use of riddles as a communicative and pedagogical tool to develop a multicultural curriculum in social studies classroom. The following areas will be covered in our discussion:

1. The history and motivation for the development of riddles—how African riddles are conceptualized and their ability to promote cognitive skills, psychomotor skills and affective skills.
2. The relationship between African riddles as philosophical thoughts and Western philosophical concept of critical thinking.
3. The development of a curriculum that is culturally responsive and integrates multicultural and global literacy; using riddles as a pedagogical vehicle for critical thinking and formation of traditional philosophies.
4. Developing classroom-based activities and practice with riddles to promote critical thinking and philosophy formation among students.
5. Discussion of the place on African riddles as pedagogical tool in American Social Studies and multicultural classroom.

The capacity of the teacher to facilitate active learning of all children using appropriate diverse materials and all available human resources in the classroom is one of the strengths of inclusive schooling (Asimeng-Boahene, 2009; Asimeng-Boahene, 2011). This assertion is supported by the emergence multicultural and global education curriculum in the United States, which has created a renewed interest in education in other cultures (Ladson-Billings, 1995; Nieto, 1999; Oakes & Lipton, 1999; Reagan, 2005). With the growing number of immigrants in the United States, and the resolve by most African Americans to return to their African roots, the use of African oral traditions including riddles can stimulate the knowledge, beliefs and attitudes that could be learned through interactive process. Thus, attempts are already underway to reduce the principles of Kwanzaa, the African American end of year festival, into African symbols and proverbs. Consequently, Delpit (1995), Gay (2000) Howard (2003), Ladson-Billings (1995), have called for the inclusion of the perspectives of underrepresented classes into the curriculum with the hope of improving the academic performance of ethnically, racially, culturally, and linguistically diverse students. Indeed, the efforts should extend beyond the traditional window-dressing method of few additions of short descriptive pieces of literary writings and contributions of few individuals and celebrations of heroes from minority groups. There are many oral literary traditions that have been relegated to the periphery of Western academia, but whose educational and intellectual ideals are substantial. Riddles remain one of the casualties of these neglected, unexplored areas, which need to be studied to reveal its inherent value of informal education.

Okrah (1995) reinforces this contention when he pronounces that the contributions of indigenous education have been great and indispensable in all areas of socialization. Therefore, as the West is reexamining the educational system, which was designed to train people to become for example, factory workers, we will come full circle and draw on indigenous wisdom to help meet today's needs for creative problem solving and critical thinking. Okrah further states that as educational systems the world over are being revised, we are again realizing the importance of rhythm and movement, of musical, kinesthetic, spatial, interpersonal, intrapersonal intelligence (all of which are indigenous form of education) as well as the long recognized verbal and mathematical intelligence. These modalities are to be addressed if all children are to be given their best chance for success.

Conceptualization of Riddles

In traditional societies, both elders and children cherish riddles. Riddles are statements and questions, asked in a play form, which are meant to test the ingenuity of the players. The answer can be an explanation or a solution to a problem raided. Riddles and puzzles may be used interchangeably in many African cultures. They are verbal art forms that have been handed down by forefathers and mothers. In Finnegan's (1970) discourse, riddles are witty questions often imbued with wisdom. They require two parties, one to pose the question and the other to respond. Generally, riddles are readily distinguishable by their question-and-answer statement form and by their succinctness. Very often, a riddle is a simple form of a phrase or statement referring to some familiar item in more or less shrouded language.

There are many riddles in Akan and African literature and, they are as popular as proverbs, poems and folktales. Like critical thinking, riddles, considered oral literature, have been viewed differently by different scholars. One school of thought believes that riddles belong to the social circle of human race as a mere folkloric game. However, Aristotle and others have amplified the close relationship between metaphorical articulation and riddles (Chatton, 2010; Finnegan, 1970). To them, riddles constitute a game that challenges the intellectual adroitness of the riddler's peers. Therefore, the cognitive value of riddles as metaphorical expressions related to sociocultural paradigm should be sufficiently received to the ears and eyes of anthropologists, philologists, psychologists, or students of folklore. Thus, this form of oral literature constitutes both game and intellectual exploration.

Riddles could therefore be used to supplement critical literacy as a guide to frame the rationale for teachers to develop meaningful curriculum for critical thinking that draws from the cultural riches of the African American family and community. This topic on riddles employs critical and cultural responsive teaching as a theoretical framework. As discussed by Waxman and Padron (1995), critical literacy argues that academic success can be achieved through inclusive instruction, as critical teaching is seen as the type of instruction that, like riddles, focuses on the critical family and community issues that students encounter daily. Thus, African cultural heritage is nurtured through the pedagogic creed of African oral literature in the form of culturally sensitive teaching (Asimeng-Boahene, 2011).

In Lee's (2000) illustration, culturally responsive teaching signifies a form of social discourse in the African American community, which has the potential to serve as an effective scaffolding device for teaching complex skills in the interpretation of literature. Evidently, the same role can be said of riddles for its universal and persuasive significance in African communities as a means of communication to stimulate and encourage intellectual growth through exchange and discussion of viewpoints. Okrah (2003) identified riddles as mind tools for critical thinking. In his statement, "Riddles are ... used to train the mind of both children and adults to think independently and critically about all issues through observation and experience of the individual" (p. 73)

African Riddles as Philosophical Thoughts

We are privy to the development of riddles of ancient times including the classical riddle of the *Sphinx* solved by Oedipus (Chatton, 2000).

Among the Akan of Ghana, riddles were originally called *Agya rekoro ogyaa me adee bi* implying, wisdom is always the preserve of the elders. Therefore, anything considered puzzling or intellectually perplexing is attributed to the elders. Literary, *Agya rekoro* means "when father was departing, (going away/leaving)," as is the reminder of the intelligence and the philosophy one's father bequeathed to them before he died or on being left to start an independent life (Okrah, 2003). *Akans* are not boastful about their intelligence. For this reason, even if one propounds own theory or creates something of educational value with in-depth wisdom, the credit is given to the elders. This is also true with other sayings, especially proverbs.

Subsequently, after Europeans invaded and colonized Africa riddles assumed the term *abromme* meaning "the White man's proverb." Even though they resembled proverbs, they were as complicated as Europeans themselves when they first came in contact with Africans. Gradually, African oral literature is assuming position of importance, especially with the emergence of multicultural, social studies and global education in the United States of America. Interest in African cultures have impressed upon non-Africans to accept the presence of sophisticated values and educational implications of indigenous literary practices. No one accepts the Anglo centric positions of earlier European writers like Burton in the 1800s cited in Finnegan (1970) who wrote about Africa as "the savage custom of going naked, we are told, has denuded the minds, and destroyed all decorum in the language. Poetry there is none.... There is no metre, no rhyme, nothing that interests or soothes the feelings, or arrests the passion" (p. 26). However, some scholars are sometimes unconsciously swayed by such biased and uninformed assumptions about the descriptions of literary traditions among non-literate peoples. A discussion of riddles within the confines of critical thinking would help refute the myth held [by some] about Africa as a continent either devoid of literature until its engagement with so-called civilized nations, which precipitated publications in European languages or having just rudimentary or unrefined literary construct not requiring systematic study (Finnegan, 1970; Harries, 1971). The procedure for riddles is simple but not without rules. They are considered to be a type of art form, and like proverbs, they are expressed briefly and concisely. They involve analogy, whether in meaning, sound, rhythm or tone. Riddles also sometimes have close connections with other aspects of literary expression—with such forms as enigmas and dilemma tales with stories and epigrams. In spite of such connections, however, riddles emerge as a distinct type of literary expression in most African countries (Finnegan, 1970; Reagan, 2005). Generally, the purpose of posing a riddle is to outwit the respondent. As Cole-Beuchat (1957) argued, riddles combine recreational and educational needs to an unusual degree, providing and exercise in intellectual skill and quickness of wit and a test of memory.

Comparatively, riddles (or traditional quizzes) could be equated to present-day psychological tests that assess knowledge and creativity in associating, differentiating, establishing cause-and-effect and so on (Ishumi, 1980). Again, African riddles are important logical tools in the traditional education system (Gwaravanda & Masaka, 2008). They do not only function as socialization and recreation process, they also sharpen one's reasoning skills and quickness of wit and that riddles can foster quick mental flexibility on the part of the child as he or she grapples with different possibilities and probabilities in the search for correct answers to given ambiguities. In African oral literature therefore, the riddle is often posed with linguistic or contextual ambiguity in order to confuse the respondent and create difficulty in solving the problem.

Characteristics and Functions of Riddles

As discussed by Asimeng-Boahene (2011), riddles in African societies function like a sort of initiation into poetic expression and, it is a truly active learning process by which the intelligence of the individual is solicited. In the game of riddles, the efforts of the audience to find the correct answers are instructive. Incorrect answers are often as interesting as correct answers since they reveal the inductive mechanisms by which the listeners attempt to decode the images. Thus, the process of solving riddles involves logical inferences and justification for answers based on reasoned analysis of the posed riddle.

The following captures the manner by which African riddles are conceptualized and span and responded. Among the Akan of Ghana, The participants sit together in a circle and the initiator spins or calls and, the audience responds as follows:

call:	Bore me. (Dig into me).
response:	Merebore wo. (I am digging into you).
call:	Agya rekoro omaa/ogyaa me adee bi or Agya adee bi wo ho. (When father was going away/departing he left something with me.) or (There is something belonging to father.)

Even though the name "abromme" stands for "aborofo mme" (the White man's proverbs), it also comes from the call "bore me" which together form the word "abromme". It should be noted here that the Fante (the Akan group living along the coast in the central region of Ghana) mostly use the "bore me" as a call for riddles, while the Asante, Bono and Akuapem, the Twi speaking people, use the phrase "agya rekoro" to start a riddle. At present, when riddles are spun in schools, they begin in English as:

Call: riddle, riddle!

Response: riddle!!

The following are examples of Akan riddles:

Riddle: When father was departing he left two siblings with me. When the sun shines one is very happy, while the other one is in very serious trouble; But when it is raining, the first one is in trouble, while the other one is very happy. What is it?

Answer: Salt and cream—When the sun shines, the cream begins to melt, while the salt gets harder. If rain falls on the two of them, the salt melts while the cream solidifies.

Okrah (2003) found two kinds of Akan riddles, which were:

1. The rigid-formula (or one-answer) riddles. They have a single or short answer.
2. The discourse type of riddles (custom-laden and open riddles. They demand explanation and analysis in the answer to the riddle (p. 73).

One-Answer Riddles

This type of riddle has only one possible answer that the riddle initiator expects from the audience depending upon the environment in which they live. For example:

Riddle: When father was going away he left a very beautiful damsel with me. When she is sitting in the sun she feels happy. She is more comfortable when she is sitting by the fire, but she begins to cry the moment she sees water. What is it?

Answer: Salt.

Riddle: (Berber, Morocco): I riddle to you, a storage jar without an opening.

Answer: God will not tell you otherwise than that, it is an EGG.

Riddle: (Yoruba, Nigeria): We cut off the top and bottom, yet it produces wealth.

Answer: Drum (Ilu).

Riddle: (Akan, Ghana): A pair of shoes that are never worn out (mpaboa a enhi da).

Answer: A pair of feet (onipa nan).

Riddle: (Akan, Ghana): When father was departing, he left a gentleman; so long as he is alive, he is playful and harmless. But when he is dead, the least mistake you make trying to touch him, he will bite you seriously.

Answer: Bottle (the time of his death is when it is broken; it is only when it can cut someone).

Custom-Laden Riddles

The answer to this type of riddle depends upon the particular cultural or customary environment to which the people belong. The answer to the following riddle is dependent upon the Akan matrilineal system.

Riddle: A man was travelling with his mother, father and wife across a river.

The raft on which they were crossing the river capsized and all were on the verge of drowning. The man was the only one who could swim. At that instance, he could save the life of ONLY ONE of the three other people. Who would he save?

Answer: The mother—she is the only one who for sure can be trusted as being your blood relation. (An Ewe, one the ethnic groups in Ghana, however, would save his father as an Englishman might save his wife.)

Open-Ended Riddles

This type of riddle may also be referred to as the 'debate-type riddle'. Their solutions have to be convincing explanations that the audience will accept. For example:

Riddle: A certain man was abysmally poor. He had three wives. The first wife advised him to travel to seek fortune elsewhere; the second wife gave him some cloth to cover his nakedness and the third wife gave him some money for the journey. He embarked on a journey that took him to a town, far away, where the inhabitants were celebrating the funeral of their dead king. In this kingdom it is the custom that the person who gives the highest donation becomes the next king. With the amount given the man by the third wife, he was able to give the highest funeral donation and thus became the next king of this kingdom with all the honor, pageantry and the wealth that accompany such an enviable position. Within a twinkle of an eye the penniless, destitute man became luxuriously and fabulously rich. However, another custom of this kingdom is that a king is allowed to keep only one wife. The new king was at liberty to bring any of his three wives to rule with him. Which of the three wives has the edge over the other two to remain with the new king as his wife?

Answer: Any answer that is given will depend upon how it will be explained. However, the consensus is that the first woman who prompted the man to embark on the journey should be given the chance to enjoy her seniority. As the senior and the first wife, she has already shown years of resourcefulness and was responsible for planning the logistics for the journey that led him to his current position and fortune. This answer gives credence to the old adage, "The devil you know is better that the angel you don't know."

Like characters in most folktales, riddles have their own characters with which a riddler propounds his riddles. The following are the characters and accompanying examples of the riddles that go with them.

1. Parts of the body—examples of riddles that are based on observation of parts of the body abound. These personified body parts insulate the meaning, which is to be unwrapped by the audience in solving the riddle.

   Riddle: Two brothers live in the same room but each one always leans out of his own window in a way that neither sees the other. What is it?

   Answer: The room is the human head. The brothers are the two eyes and the windows are the eye sockets?

   Riddle: There is a very beautiful and light complexioned lady who is always surrounded by white plates. Without her one cannot determine the deliciousness of one's food. Who is she?

Answer: The beautiful, light complexioned lady is the tongue. The white plates are the teeth.

2. Animals, birds and insects/bugs—by observing the activities, color, the habitat, or the process of killing particular animals, riddles are propounded. For example:

    Riddle: A hunter killed an animal and carried it home. The animal was killed with a matchet but was opened for its meat with air. What is the animal?

    Answer: The aquatic snail (abebee).

    Riddle: Father ordered me to kill an animal, use only the intestines to prepare soup and throw away the actual meat. What is this animal?

Answer: An insect in eggplant/garden egg (obiripantampram).

3. **Riddles about plants:** Through observation of their characteristics we have riddles about plants like bamboo, oil palm, coconut, etc. Examples follow:

    Riddle: A stranger came to visit me. I gave him a chair to sit on but to my surprise he went away with the chair. Who is this stranger?

    Answer: The full palm nut sachet (bemuu).

    Riddle: My father owns a strange man. In his youth the strange man wraps his cloth neatly around himself, but when he grows old he takes off the cloth. Who is this man?

    Answer: Bamboo tree.

    Riddle: Father has some woman; when she buys a new cloth she doesn't wear it.   Instead, she uses it as an umbrella. She only wraps it around herself when the cloth has become old. Who is this woman?

Answer: The plantain plant ("borodoba")—the leaves are the cloth).

4. Riddles about other things, e.g., smoke, eggs, sandals, coffins, brooms, candles, hour-glass drums, guns, bottles, hearths, cooking pots, paths, shadows, cream, salt, bathrooms, sacks, and so forth. The following are examples of such riddles:

    Riddle: Father left me with a special friend. Whenever he is hungry he cannot stand up but once he is full, he stands up and cannot sit down. Who is this friend?

Answer: A sack.

Riddle: When father was going away he left two servants to serve me. The problem with these servants is that whenever one of them is indisposed the other one cannot work. Who are these servants?

Answer: A pair of sandals.

Riddle: Father left me in my care, a very old man. He is so old that when he sits in the house his beard can be seen outside a house. Who is this old man?

Answer: Smoke.

Riddle: When father was going away he left a very beautiful and elegant house to me. Strangely enough, the architect of the house does not like the house he himself built. The person who buys the house does not live in it himself; he only donates it for the use of a dear one. However, this dear one does not realize that he is living in such a beautiful house. What is this beautiful house?

Answer: Coffin.

Educational and Pedagogical Implications

Even though riddles serve as a source of entertainment, they also have inherent educational value. Besides portraying the richness and depth of the language, riddles demonstrate how the people can manipulate and weave vocabulary into a complex, thought-provoking and entertaining form. They also help children and elders alike to become eloquent, a quality greatly cherished in Africa. It takes skill to manipulate words and ideas into a riddle with an intelligible question demanding a specific answer. It also helps in the development of critical thinking, since one has to think deeply making associations and comparisons before one can solve a riddle. Riddles are also used to teach children about certain cultural and family values. Through riddles people learn to be observant of their environment and notice how their experience of the environment relates to their character, origin, function, and so forth. Thus, African communities uphold critical thinking using riddles in the traditional forms of education. The examples of riddles given in this chapter exposes the exercise of intellect, teaching of logic, and compelling individuals to engage in contemplation of a variety of paradoxes an enigmas to know about social norms, history, and sociocultural environment.

As observed from the foregoing analysis, types and examples of riddles, we can conclude that riddles, like critical thinking skills, are reflective and authentic with their capacity to ask questions that address the heart of the matter. They pose a problem and like the classical and modern Socratic method of teaching, try to answer a question raised or a problem posed by reasoning them out. Thus, players of riddles learn to solve riddles by thinking them through using the rudiments of reasoning. As Nosich (2009) has stated, riddling and critical thinking share common boundaries in the area of intellectual audacity, confidence in reasoning, intellectual firmness and intellectual autonomy.

- Intellectual audacity: Both riddles and critical thinking entail readiness to confront challenges about established principles and philosophical viewpoints. Thus they will both undeniably face up to deep-rooted ways of judgment or thoughts one may entertain.
- Confidence in reasoning: Both riddles and critical thinking provide willingness to try to figure things out, to rely on thinking through things, to the best of one's ability, rather than on all the other influences that shape thinking without knowing it.
- Intellectual firmness: Both riddles and critical thinking require a willingness to stick with and intellectual undertaking for as long as it takes to reach a realistic conclusion. This helps to push one's intellectual perseverance in the form of revising one's thinking.
- Intellectual autonomy: Both riddles and critical thinking entail the willingness to think for oneself using the best reasoning one is capable of, including elements, standards and discipline with awareness of the bigger picture (Nosich, 2009).

Hence, riddles can be considered as a tool that addresses epistemological import in any educational discourse by its advancement of the use of intellect to address issues and complexities. African riddles call to mind the different ways of seeing and learning. They also bring to light a different way of conceptualizing critical thinking skills making use of human parts and attributes, flora and fauna, cultural artifacts and customs. Understanding of these diverse ways of thinking and perception would provide linkages between cultures that can help students acquire global knowledge. Students would, in furtherance, learn to appreciate global perspective consciousness as it exposes them to other uncharted paradigms, which continue to appear too remote for them because of mainstream curricular approach (Maxim, 2010). In the view of Reagan (2005), with the tremendous challenges facing racially and ethnically diverse children in the United States, this model could create multiple perspectives for teachers to become aware of the need for culturally responsive teaching practices within schools for their diverse students. To further support Reagan's (2005) observation, he cites Gloria Snively's argument that:

If schools are to do justice to native students, they must not represent a culture that ignores and denigrates the indigenous culture. Oral traditions must be respected and viewed by the teacher as a distinctive intellectual tradition, not simply as myths and legends. If traditional beliefs, values, and ideas that have been taught to the children by their parents and grandparents are not important in the school curriculum, the message is obvious. (p. 128)

With the renewed interest in the education of other cultures engendered by contemporary globalism, the same can be said of the idea of utilizing African riddles as multicultural and critical thinking tools to improve the academic performance of students who are culturally, ethnically, racially, and linguistically diverse (Asimeng-Boahene, 2011). Thus, we should be cognizant of the fact that there is much in the educational paradigms of non-Western societies that is worthwhile and fertile to support global literacy. The value of riddles as an aspect of indigenous knowledge is not only pragmatic; it is also profoundly metaphysical, epistemological and axiological in nature. It is based on this conviction that we agree with Semali and Kincheloe (1999) for asserting that:

We find it pedagogically tragic that various knowledges of how action affects reality in particular locales have been dismissed from academic curricula. Such ways of knowing and acting could contribute so much to the educational experiences of all students; but because of the rules of evidence and the dominant epistemologies of Western knowledge production, such understandings are deemed irrelevant by the academic atekeepers.... Our intention is to challenge the academy and its "normal science" with the question indigenous knowledge raise about the nature of our existence, our consciousness, our knowledge production, and the "globalized future." (p. 15)

Activity

With appropriate activities in the classroom, riddles have the capacity to widen children's conceptual lenses. By acting as a catalyst for the development of critical thinking for both intercultural awareness and critical literacy, they have the capacity to promote cross-cultural communication across cultural and national frontiers (Asimeng-Boahene, 2011).

The Following Are Examples Of Activities That May Be Used in a Social Studies Classroom

1.   Create own riddle whose answer will fall into one of the categories discussed—human part, animals, insects, birds, plants.

2. Create a riddle that involves nonliving things, for example, bread, matches, a hole, and so forth.

3. Let students form groups of three. A set of group acts as riddle spinners and respondents. Another set will act as riddle critics who will categorize riddles as funny, insightful, challenging, or complex.

4. In groups of three students should think about their own riddles. The groups should compete among themselves with their riddles like a quiz competition or

5. "A riddles game of jeopardy" with a facilitator and teams with two or three respondents to perform to see who can out-riddle the other team.

6. In a small group, ask students to try to find at least four riddles for which they can determine the following:

   a. Riddle
   b. Answer
   c. Underlying value
   d. Influence on critical thinking

7. "Riddle box" game: Students write a riddle each and put in a box for the class. On the riddle day, students pick a riddle in turn and solve the riddle. This can be shared with other classes. This can also be converted into a bulletin board or even included in the school announcement.

8. Using a map of Africa, ask students to locate the countries of origin of riddles.

9. Let students conduct interviews with African citizens or immigrants face-to-face, online or by phone. They should find out about the culture and traditions, especially oral literature. Ask about favorite riddle and why it is his or her favorite.

10. Students can collect riddles and establish anthology of riddles from around the world to share.

11. Research proverbs from your own country of origin that use natural phenomena, plants or animals symbolically to make a point (Okrah & Taylor, 2004).

12. Write a how and why story with a moral about an animal or bird that lives in your area (Okrah & Taylor, 2004).

Some Examples of Riddles Related to Critical Thinking

1. What is it that always ends everything?
   The letter "g"

2. What runs around the entire yard without moving?
   The fence
3. What is it that is always before you, yet you can never see it?
   Your future
4. My children can build a house without water. Who are they?
   Termites

Conclusion

This chapter sought to explore the pedagogical values of African rhythms in multicultural classroom settings. In terms of methodological applicability, theoretical delineation, and epistemological conceptualization, this inquiry has spotlighted how riddles could be used as communication and pedagogical tool to promote a multicultural curriculum in a social studies classroom. We believe that educators that embrace such inclusive alternative paradigms can create an environment in which students gain skills, knowledge, and appreciation for their own linguistic background as well as those of others. As educators, we are continuously searching for new ways to help students seek for rich information and knowledge. African riddles can certainly be one of the avenues to that end.

REFERENCES

Asimeng-Boahene, L. (2009). Educational wisdom of African oral literature: African proverbs as vehicles for enhancing critical thinking skills in social studies education. *Journal of Pedagogies and Learning*, 5(3), 59-69.

Asimeng-Boahene, L. (2011). Riddles as Critical Thinking Tools. In V. Yenika-Agbaw & M. Napoli (Eds.), *African and African American children's and adolescent literature in the classroom: A critical guide* (pp. 33-52). New York, NY: Peter Lang.

Chatton, B. (2010). *Using poetry across the curriculum*. Oxford, England: ABC-CLIO.

Cole-Beuchant, P. D. (1957). Riddles in Bantu. *African Studies 16*(3), 133-149.

Delpit, L. (1995). *Other people's children: Cultural conflict in the classroom*. New York, NY: The New Press.

Finnegan, R. (1970). *Oral African literature*. Oxford, England: Clarendon Press.

Gay, G. (2000). *Culturally responsive teaching: Theory, research & practice*. New York, NY: Teachers College Press.

Gwaravanda, E. T., & Masaka, D. (2008). Shona reasoning skills in Zimbabwe: The importance of riddles. *The Journal of Pan African Studies*, 2(5), 193-208.

Harries, L. (1971). The riddle in Africa. *Journal of American folklore, 84*, 377-393.

Howard, T. C. (2003). Culturally relevant pedagogy: Ingredients for critical teacher reflection. *Theory Into Practice. 42*(3), 195-202.

Ishumi, A. (1980). *Kiziba: The cultural heritage of an old African kingdom*. Syracuse, NY: Syracuse University.

Ladson-Billings, G. (1995). But that's just good teaching! *Theory Into Practice, 34*, 159-165

Lee, C. D. (2000). Signifying in the zone of proximal development. In C. D. Lee & P. Smagorinsky (Eds.), *Vygotsky perspectives on literacy research: Constructing meaning through collaborative inquiry* (pp. 191-224). Cambridge, England: Cambridge University Press.

Maxim, G. W. (2010). *Dynamic social studies for constructive classrooms: Inspiring tomorrow's social scientists* (9th ed.). Boston, MA: Allyn & Bacon

National Council for the Social Studies. (2001). *Expectations of excellence: Curriculum standards for social studies*. Silver Springs, MD: Authur.

Nieto, S. (1999). *The light in their eyes: Creating multicultural learning communities*. New York, NY: Teachers College Press.

Nosich, G. M. (2009). *Learning to think things through: A guide to critical thinking across the curriculum* (3rd ed.). Columbus, OH: Pearson/Prentice Hall.

Oakes, J., & Lipton, M. (1999). *Teaching to change the world*. New York, NY: McGraw-Hill.

Okrah, K. A. (with Taylor, S.). (1995). *Ghana: Arts and culture for home and classroom*. Villanova, PA: Rainbow Child International.

Okrah, K. A. (2003). *The wisdom knot: Toward an African philosophy of education*. New York & London: Routledge.

Okrah, K. A., & Taylor, S. (2004). *African indigenous knowledge and science*. Haverford, PA: Infinity.

Reagan, T. (2005). *Non-Western educational traditions: Indigenous approaches to educational thought and practice* (3rd ed.). Mahwah, NJ: Lawrence Erlbaum.

Semali, L. & Kincheloe, J. (Eds.). (1999). *What is indigenous knowledge? Voices from the academy*. New York, NY: Falmer.

Waxman, H., & Padron, Y. (1995). Improving the quality of classroom instruction for students at risk of failure in urban schools. *Peabody Journal of Education, 70*(2), 44-65.

CHAPTER 9

THE METAPHOR OF GHANAIAN CLOTH

Decoding the Symbols in Ghanaian Wax Prints

Kwadwo A. Okrah

Introduction

In addition to the many Ghanaian artifacts and relics, the Ghanaian textile is one of the most obvious features of the material culture. Pottery, metal casting, woodcarving, leatherwork, and architecture, all have symbols in the form of phonographic, ideographic and pictographic meanings attached to the piece of art. Thus, the Akan of Ghana make extensive use of a system of ideographic and pictographic symbols (Arthur, 2001). However, it takes distinctive knowledge to unravel the connotations buried in the pictures and ideas expressed in the symbols. Consequently, the Akan of Ghana have used cloth not only for personal adornment, but also metaphorically as a powerful expressive medium of communication. Individually, each symbol is associated with a specific proverb, saying or a

African Traditional and Oral Literature as Pedagogical Tools in Contest Area Classrooms: K-12, pages 145–181
Copyright © 2014 by Information Age Publishing
All rights of reproduction in any form reserved.

concept rooted in the Akan experience. Collectively, these symbols form a system of writing, which preserves and transmits the accumulated cultural values of the Akan people. This chapter focuses on recapturing the value-laden symbols that are on the verge of disappearance. Again, attempt would be made to restore not only the import and worth that go with Akan cloths, but also the educative implications.

In order to make pedagogy a central area in improving education, teacher preparation, equity and diversity, there is the need to investigate the intersection of culture and teaching that rely on a culturally relevant theory of education (Ladson-Billings, 1995). Building on Ladson-Billings (1995) conception of culturally relevant pedagogy, Nieto and Bode (2012); Gollnick and Chinn (2013), have discussed the relevance of positioning multicultural education within such theoretical framework.

Culturally relevant pedagogy is based on the theory that the learning process relies on social interaction and is related to students' cultural experiences (Ladson-Billings, 1995). Truly, cultural variables are powerful tools for learning and it has been agreed that learning is both socially constructed and socially mediated to the extent that it occurs when students participate in culturally meaningful activities. When these factors are overlooked, the school fails diverse, nonmainstream children because culturally diverse students may have a set of values, beliefs and norms that is often incongruous with middle class cultural norms and behaviors of schools. Gollnick and Chinn (2013) therefore suggest an educational strategy in which students' cultures are used to develop effective classroom instruction and school environments. African and African American students who desire some grounding in their ancestral philosophies are denied the opportunity because of the hiatus that have existed between the generations. Among the many elements of African philosophy, practices and reflections on symbols provide a way to define and recognize culturally relevant pedagogy. Sometimes, the symbols and patterns serve as a writing system.

Writing system is a set of visible or tactile signs used to represent units of language in a systematic way (Blackwell Encyclopedia, 2007). This simple explanation encompasses a large spectrum of writing systems with vastly different stylistic and structural characteristics spanning across the many regions of the globe. Many nonwriting cultures often pass long poems and prose, sometimes referred to as oral literature, from generation to generation without any change. But for those living in a culture where textiles play no significant role, it is difficult to appreciate the profound position [they hold in traditional societies] (Dawson, 1990).

In traditional societies, whenever a cloth is presented as a gift the receiver shows appreciation based on the name of the cloth, which is determined by the patterns in the cloth. Ghanaians, like the historic indigenous people of Mexico, Guatemala, Panama, and ancient Americans of Peru share a special reverence for cloth. They collectively and unconsciously recognize that textiles form a most democratic and economic format for communicating essential messages about themselves (Dawson, 1990). It is only the most jaded visitor to these places who would not be impressed by the brilliance and abundance of traditional costume.

At Ghanaian traditional gatherings and festivals both in and outside Ghana, non-Ghanaians, especially Europeans and Americans note with a mixture of awe and curiosity the importance Ghanaians bestow on their traditional cloth and dress. It becomes obvious to the uninitiated visitor that the impressive craft, color, and rich materials communicate status, wealth and prestige. Sometimes the embroidery and the pattern of sewing are used to communicate the more subtle information about a particular group, for example, marital status, age, social rank, religious role, and so forth. Combining the requisite social information with ancient refined aesthetic formats does not only give the traditional cloth and costume its power and appeal; it also makes available and possible for the group to collectively understand the nonliteral symbolic messages (Dawson, 1990).

In exploring and determining the meanings, the wisdom and educational implications of the pictographic and ideographic symbols in Ghanaian wax prints, it was found that among Ghanaians, cloth patterns and symbols form part of the ancestral wisdom. This knowledge is an inescapable foundation of the Akan cultural being, which is relevant to their identity and cultural health. To the Akan of Ghana, wisdom is the aggregate of all experiences and pertains to what is true, what is right or what is lasting. As stated by Opoku (2002), wisdom also means learning, reasonableness or good judgment, the ability to discern inner qualities and relationships.

The Akan symbolic literacy, which is mostly, found in cloths, therefore project the moral aspect of their existence in the sense that a wise person can distinguish between what is right and what is wrong just by interpreting a symbol in a cloth. Thus, clothing in Ghana, as elsewhere, has long served more than one purpose. In addition to satisfying human needs for covering and adornment, textiles and clothing provide media for artistic expression for weavers, dyers, tailors, and clothing designers (Arthur, 2001). Hence, cloth has become an important art object that constitutes a code in which Ghanaians have deposited some aspects of the sum of their knowledge, fundamental beliefs, aspects of their history, attitudes and behaviors towards the sacred, and how their society has been organized.

The symbols, designs, and patterns encoded in Ghanaian cloths are linked to proverbs, stories, songs, maxims, beliefs and everyday expressions. These symbols in essence constitute a writing system with which the Akan [of Ghana] communicate (Arthur, 2001). Accordingly, the language of the patterns and symbols, when beautifully expressed in words, serve as dynamic tools by which proverbs and pithy sayings are used to solve problems, communicate and express cultural ideas and concepts.

This chapter explores the means of literacy, symbolism as instrument of literacy, different types of cloth, proverbs as a symbol, cloth as a metaphor and the educational and pedagogical implications of cloth patterns and symbols. In synthesizing the findings of cloth symbols and meanings within the context of culturally relevant pedagogy, I have made categorical and analytical connections between the patterns and names of Ghanaian cloths and their relevance to the themes under which they are grouped. The description of these precepts in a social studies context would advance the concept of designing an inclusive curriculum in K-12 social studies classroom.

Means of Literacy

Encouraging a wider description of literacy has the potential of leading students who come from nonwritten cultures to develop and improve their socioemotional status. The dictionary definition of literacy as the ability to read and write is myopic and unclear in as much as it does not expand to include the ability to locate, evaluate and communicate, using a wider range of resources including text, visual, audio, and video sources (Okrah, 2007). Literacy could be merged in multicultural and global education by encouraging a sense of understanding other people. Thus, the need to understand literacy in a wider perspective would be a prerequisite.

A study of the Akan cloth reveals that any form of symbolism that conveys meaning or contributes to communication is a vehicle to literacy. In other words, literacy and communication are intertwined and we can only claim literacy as global citizens when we have a way of understanding the other person and their means of communication. Literacy in the 21st century should also be defined beyond reading and writing, to include the ability to understand one another and, understanding of different concepts in different disciplines. Literacy should also include the ability to locate, evaluate and communicate, using a wider range of resources including text, visual, audio, and video sources (Okrah, 2007).

Symbolism as Instrument of Literacy

Symbols hold a powerful attraction for people. Even today, in an age in which materialistic perspectives rule human thought, many ancient symbols such as the ankh, the yin/yang, American Indian designs, pyramids, and many other symbols are quite popular in jewelry and in the home

(Warren, 2012). Symbols are the vehicles through which language is carried and communication made possible. Writings, verbal and road signs, sounds, cues, fine art and sculpture all serve as types of symbols that convey meaning. For example, art is not produced solely for its aesthetic ends; rather it is deeply embedded in the belief patterns of the society. All art forms are therefore symbolic and representative rather than abstract and representational.

Symbology, the study of symbols, sounds like a very complicated subject, but interestingly enough, we already have some knowledge about it because, as mentioned above, we are surrounded by, use and wear symbols every day. Warren (2012) states that, the word symbol means something which contains something else. A symbol transmits something, a symbol reflects something, and it has been said that the best type of symbol is the symbol, which transmits most purely that which it is reflecting and keeps almost nothing for itself. In analyzing symbology as a science, Warren warns us not to get stuck in one's own cultural perspective. In other words, if the only perspective one is able to perceive is one's own, which was shaped by the society, the culture, the religion or politics in which one was raised, then everything is always going to look foreign. In that case the one is not going to be able to see symbols or understand symbols; he/she is just going to see foreign looking things. To understand others and other symbols then, we need to try to understand sincerely. Sincere understanding requires us to go a little higher, and take a little bit higher perspective, a little more subtle understanding, and a little more in-depth understanding.

Warren (2012) goes further to in his discourse by explaining that in order to get a better glimpse of the lost science known as symbology, let's take as an example a symbol which is quite popular these days: the Ankh. It looks like a circle or an oval sitting on top of a capital "T." The Ankh is a perennial favorite in jewelry. It is interesting that the Ankh, which hasn't had a living religion associated with it for a couple of thousand years, is so popular today. The ankh is from Ancient Egypt. In the temples of the Ancient Egyptians, it is found in the hands of the Gods. It signifies Eternal Life. It is called the Key of Life, and is the key to the Mysteries of Nature. It is used to open doors between the visible and the invisible worlds. As it regards the individual human being, this refers to the difference between physical existence and spiritual existence.

The ancients believed that everything has a soul. Plants, animals, even stars have souls, very great souls. The soul of a chicken is obviously not the same as the soul of a human (although the behavior of some humans these days does make you wonder sometimes!). In modern times, the Department of Transportation (DOT) for example, uses a set of 50 pictograms to convey information useful to travelers without using words (DOT Pictograms,

2013). Such images are useful in airports, train stations, hotels, and other public places for foreign tourists, as well as being easier to identify than strings of text.

As discussed by Okrah and Taylor (2004), West African societies express their convictions of their moral values in their ceremonies, such as those connected with birth, on their drums, sandals, stools, umbrellas, through their horns or through linguist staffs. These symbolic objects record certain cherished values. For example a hand holding an egg, usually found on top of a linguist staff or an umbrella, says "power is like holding an egg in the hand. If you hold it too tightly it breaks and if you hold it too loosely it drops." Power must therefore be handled with great care.

Different Types of Cloth

Other art forms amongst Ghanaians include the symbols in kente and adinkra cloths with different designs. For example, "Abusua ye dom" (The family is a force), "Gye Nyame" (Except God).

Adinkra is the screen and block-printed cloth with designs that are derived from various sources—proverbs, historical events, human attitudes, animal behavior, plant life and shapes of objects, both celestial and man-made

Kente is a hand-woven cloth that is not only valued for its aesthetic quality, but also for its symbolic and expressive quality.

Wax print is a factory-made wax resistant dyed fabric printed by a textile industry. (The three Ghanaian textile industries are located in Akosombo, Tema and Juapong).

Color is also used as a symbol to represent different thought and actions. For example gold or yellow represents royalty; white represents purity; green represents newness and fertility; black and red represent deep feelings of melancholy; blue represents love and tenderness, and so forth.

Proverbs as Symbols

In traditional African society, proverbs are effective mode of communication. They are used to state metaphorically certain general truths about life. As Okrah (2003) and Asimeng-Boahene (2009) have discussed, proverbs are pithy sayings that are used to explain a thought or to give it credence and potency. Proverbs confirm and clarify the meanings of lengthy statements in summary form. When they are critically examined, one may observe that proverbs are to language as gems are to stones. Proverbs may also be described as the insulator of the language, accenting a particular theme with a series of expressions, which clearly uncover the speaker's intention. Among the Akan, when a speech is interspersed with appropriate proverbs, the conversation is considered much more interesting. An eloquent person, who is especially well versed in proverbs and idioms, is considered an orator.

Proverbs are used to advise and educate both the youth and elders about values in a society. The proverbs are constructed or created based on expected behavior in the society. They describe analogies made from observation and experience within the community, for example, "Aserewa su agyenkuku su a ne to pae" (If the little humming bird, [aserewa] tries to shout or chirp like the big *agyenkuku*, it ends up bursting its anus.); "Okoto nwo anoma" (The crab does not beget a bird.); "Awadee nye nsafufuo na yeaka ahwe" (Marriage is not like palm wine, which is tasted before a choice can be made.)

In education circles, proverbs and pithy sayings are composed into mottos for institutions. For example, "He who rests rusts," "Knowledge is power," "One head does not form a council," "Obi dan bi" (We all depend on one another or no man is an island), and so forth. When properly understood, they serve as vehicles for dispositional training for schools and students. When properly used, literacy in symbols that draw lessons from proverbs can shape character and solve conflicts in schools and work places.

Cloth as a Metaphor

To study the language of the symbols in the Akan (Ghanaian) cloth is to learn about Nature, to learn about the laws which rule the Universe. The symbols, patterns, and sometimes the color are meant to instruct and to assist the spiritual evolution of the human being, or to record some historical lesson for educational purposes. In addition to these, there are unique symbols and emblems, which represent schools of thought or religions. This is similar to the hieroglyphs (ancient Egyptian writings), cuneiform (ancient Sumerian writings) and ideograms of all ancient civilizations, which were also symbols.

It is the belief of the Akan that nature is full of symbols. For example, a flower, the geometric patterns in the veins of a leaf, the markings on animals or insects, the constellations in the nighttime sky, even dreams; all these are symbols with hidden meanings. So we live in a world of symbols. Thus, the Akan of Ghana also believe that sacred symbols help us by reminding us of our invisible part. Symbols also remind us about the immortality of the soul and serve as universal maps of consciousness. These symbols, in many cases, inspire us when they are rendered beautifully.

Following is a list of Ghanaian cloth samples with names and lessons that reveal and reflect back possible experiences we encounter personally and professionally in our lives. These symbols function as internal and external mirrors for the mental, emotional, spiritual, and physical levels of consciousness. Whether political, economic, religious, or cultural, all the symbols educate people to reach explicit and implicit understanding of the body politic and expediency of the society. Thus, they help people in counseling, coaching, teaching, managing conflicts and understanding the self and society at large. The following are pictures of different cloth symbols from Ghana.

Cloth Symbols With Political Implications

Politically there are cloth patterns that serve as a tool for guiding systematic and analytic appraisal to uncover partially hidden meanings about philosophy and theory of governance. They may also show or comment on personalities in government, power and power relations. They tell a history or give credit to a government or discuss an aspect of traditional or modern system of government. The following cloth patterns have political implications.

1. NKRUMAH PENCIL (or PEN). From 1958 to about 1964, Kwame Nkrumah, the first President of Ghana had a penchant to use his pen to sign deportation and detention orders as a method of controlling political opponents. Some political opponents had resorted to violence. His political opponents made several unsuccessful attempts on his life. His pen was, therefore, considered mightier than the sword. This cloth was named Nkrumah pencil (or Nkrumah pen) to obliquely reflect the political reality of those times. When Nkrumah's government was overthrown by the military in February 1966, the name of the cloth suddenly became pencil (or pen). In recent years, as part of the rehabilitation of the positive image of Nkrumah, the cloth has taken on its former name of Nkrumah pencil (or Nkrumah pen).

2. *ODEHYEE KYINIIE*—ROYAL UMBRELLA. Symbol of AUTHORITY, LEGITIMACY, PROTECTION and SECURITY. From the expression: Nea kyiniie si ne so ne ohene. Literal translation: He who has umbrella over his head is the king.

3. Senkye bridge or The Adomi bridge—to honor the only suspension bridge in Ghana at Adomi in the Eastern region of Ghana under the Nkrumah presidency.

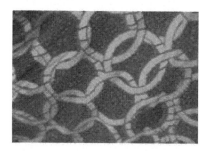

4. *Abankaba*—handcuffs. From the expression: Efie ye a anka abankaba nna me nsa. An indication that all is not well else I would not be in handcuffs. This implies law and justice in modern system of government with policemen as servants of the executive branch of government.

5. *Bonsu*. Named after and in honor of the Asantehene Mensah Bonsu who chased the White man to the Atlantic Ocean. Afterwards he was honored with the nickname Bonsu (Whale), the greatest sea fish. It demonstrates and encourages brave leadership.

6. Yaw Donkor—(An Akan name meaning: Yaw—Thursday boy; Donkor— Servant. From the expression: se akoa som som-pa a otumi di akonnwa. If a servant serves well he can rise to become a king. (The cloth is named after a servant whose ingenuity impressed the king of Asante to raise him to a position of responsibility in his kingdom.). It reassures social justice and inspires empowerment of all without recourse to social class.

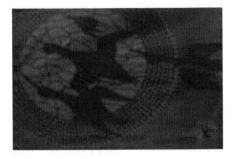

7. *Ahemfie*—**(The palace).** A cloth that was made during the death of the Asante king Osei Agyemang Prempeh in 1970. It was worn to enter the palace to mourn the king. It is also an expression of the power and sanctity of the dwelling place of the leader.

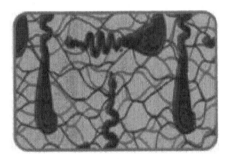

8.   Akofena—*Ohene   afena*— **(Sword of war).** The sword is a symbol of office. A symbol of traditional authority and the chief's military might. It is a symbol of courage and valor. To incorporate some aspects of tradition into the modern system, Ghanaian presidents are sworn into office with a traditional sword in hand; a sword bearer always leads the president in a procession to parliament.

9. *Dehyee nsu:* **Royalty does not lament.** (A person from the royal family is does not lack anything so he will not mourn or weep). A child at the doorstep of power does not grief; after all, he/she is not deprived of anything.

10. *Akuffo.* This cloth design was named after the first state linguist of Ghana, Okyeame Boafo Akuffo, appointed by the first president of Ghana (Kwame Nkrumah) in his attempt to incorporate traditional system of governance into the newly independent nation of Ghana. The state linguist is the presidential praise poet and the cultural consultant at the state protocol office.

Cloth Symbols With Educational/School Implications

Educatively, cloth patterns and symbols provide reflective judgment to people who use them. Some of the symbols serve as a way of improving users' reasoning, which must be of great interest to educators and policymakers. They encourage both children and adults to be able to make informed decisions in their personal lives, in the workplace, and in their communities. Elements of both formal and informal education are reflected in the symbols and patterns of cloths.

Some of the symbols encourage people to practice their reasoning skills in many settings whilst others discuss controversial, ill-structured issues. Eventually, cloth symbols simultaneously become a resource that shows the factual basis and lines of reasoning for several perspectives. When used appropriately, cloth symbols may create many opportunities for people to analyze others' points of view for their evidentiary adequacy and to develop and defend their own points of view about controversial issues. The following cloth patterns provide information and inferences to educate and school people:

1. *ABC*— ALPHABETS. (Literacy and numeracy) From the proverb: *Suukuu nko na nyansa nko.* Literal translation: Attending school does not mean that one would be wise. "Knowledge is different from wisdom/intelligence." Expression: *Nea onnim no sua a ohunu* Literal translation: Knowledge can be acquired by anyone who is willing to learn (life-long education).

2. *Ludu aba* (DICE of the game of ludu). Expression that "all work and no play makes Jack a dull boy." It is also a reminder of the importance of learning mathematics and logic through play.

3. ACHIMOTA. This cloth commemorates the founding of the Achimota School and College in 1927 by the then Governor of the Gold Coast, Gordon Guggisberg. The first Principal, Rev A. G. Fraser was assisted by Dr. Emmanuel Kwegyir Aggrey, a Ghanaian. The Aggrey-Fraser-Guggisberg Memorial Lectures series, given by the University of Ghana, honors the contribution of these three men to the development of formal education in Ghana. The logo of Achimota, the black and white keys of the piano (as shown on the top part of the picture on the left), symbolizes harmony and unity in diversity.

4. Konkuro/Konini ahahan—The leaves of the kola-nut tree. "Konini ne bese ahaban, yetase no obanyansafoo." Literal translation: Only the intelligent and wise person can distinguish similar leaves from different trees. School and education must provide a person with the knowledge and skills to differentiate between issues and solve problems.

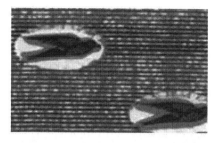

5. *SIKA WO ATABAN*—MONEY HAS WINGS. From the maxim: "Sika; etu se anomaa." Literal translation: Money has wings; it can fly like a bird. Money not properly handled will be lost. Bad investment decisions will cause one to lose one's money.

6. *"Fa akonnwa"*—Take a seat. From the expression: *"Wobeka me ho asem a fa akonnwa/ wote me ho asem a fa akonnwa"* (If you want to talk about me, take a seat—because you will need more time. In order words, good deeds fear no gossip.)

7. *"ANI BERE A, ENSO GYA"*—GRIEVING EYES DO NOT SPARK FIRE. Symbol of PATIENCE, SELF-CONTROL, SELF-DISCIPLINE, SELF CONTAINMENT. From the proverb: *"Anibere a, enso gya." Or, "Enye obiara a ne bo fu a omuna."* Literal translation: No matter how flaming red one's eyes may be, fire is not sparked in one's eyes. Or, every frowned face does not necessarily depict anger.

Cloth Symbols With Economic Implications

Cloth symbols also speak to the occupation of people and deal with income and other monetary cost that one bears for something to get in return. The symbols also educate and sometimes, inform the people's financial and social lifestyles (economics). Through the explicit and implicit meanings of symbols the people are led to understand that if they do not properly manage their economy, scarcity will directly affect their ability to grow crops, create and maintain jobs. The following cloth patterns provide information and suggestions about work, career and income:

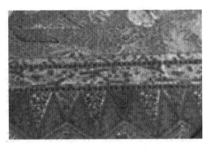

1. *KOFORIDUA FRAWASE/ NHWIREN — KOFORIDUA FLOWERS.* Symbol of **URBANIZATION, ECONOMIC PROSPERITY,** and **CONSPICUOUS CONSUMPTION.** From the expression: *"Koforidua nhwiren, dee mede wo reye!"* Literal translation: Koforidua flowers, what use do I have of you? The ideograph stems from the conspicuous consumption by some rich people during the rapid urbanization of Koforidua following the success of the cocoa industry, and later the diamond mining industry in the Eastern Region of Ghana at the turn of the 19th century.

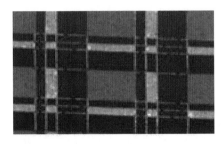

2. BLOCKS. From the expression: *"Wonni sika a wonntwa blocks."* Or, *"Yebisa wo fie a woasi, nnye wo sika dodo a wowo."* Literal translation: You do no build a block house if you do not have money. Or, we ask to be shown one's house, not how much wealth one has acquired. **OR** *HUHU-HUHU*—(RUMORS) from the expression: *Huhu-Huhunye me hu.* Literal translation: Rumors do not scare me.

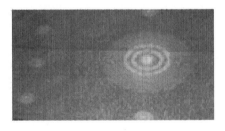

3. *Gramofone mpaawa*—**(Record player discs).** This cloth pattern was made to mark the appearance of Western style of recording music in Ghana when Gramophone was also introduced.

4. Sitia bekum driver—The driver may die behind the steering wheel. (A committed professional is never afraid of his death while in the line of duty).

5. Dadee mpadua- (Iron bedstead). (A sign of good living—A person's wealth is determined by his sleeping place.

6. Asobayere doto (The yam tendrils). Honor to farmers: A good farmer whose farm produces the king of crops—yams)

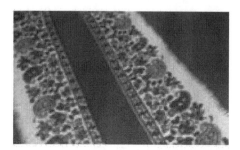

7. Asetena pa—(Good living). From the expression: Asetena-pa ma awerefire. Success or prosperity leads to forgetfulness

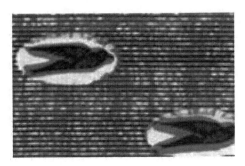

8. SIKA WO ATABAN—MONEY HAS WINGS. From the maxim: *Sika; etu se anomaa.* Literal translation: Money has wings; it can fly like a bird. Money not properly handled will be lost. Bad investment decisions will cause one to lose one's money.

Cloth Symbols and Patterns That Honor Personalities (Special Names)

Honor, honesty, integrity, and sincerity are considered high moral principles and people are encouraged to live up to such values. Strict conformity to such morality confers high honor upon one in society. Also, people who go far beyond what was expected in contributing to the community are honored with a symbol the will immortalize their names in society. Special cloth symbols and patterns are therefore named after such personalities as a sign of honor. Following are some cloths named after some people:

1. Amma Serwaa. Amma Serwaa wuo ye ya—Amma Serwaa's death is painful or sorrowful. (Particular cloths have been named for the funerals of certain individuals. Popular ones include Major Kwame Asante and Amma Serwaa). Amma Serwaa was a powerful Ashanti queen that parents wanted to name their daughter after. It became a saying From the expression: *Akwagyan Nana, woma me ntoma a ma me Amma Serwaa, na se mannwo ba a mede aye badin.* A call to Akwagyan Nana (a praise name for a husband) that when deemed necessary to give me a gift of cloth, I prefer "Amma Serwaa" from which I will have some consolation even if I don't beget a child of my own.

2. *Akuffo*. This cloth design was named after the first state linguist of Ghana, Okyeame Boafo Akuffo, appointed by the first president of Ghana (Kwame Nkrumah) in his attempt to incorporate traditional system of governance into the newly independent nation of Ghana. The state linguist is the presidential praise poet and the cultural consultant at the state protocol office.

3. FELICIA. Like Amma Serwaa, Felicia is just a woman's name and the source of this name for a cloth design was not available.

4. *Angelina*. From the hit music "Angelina" by the Ghanaian musician A.B. Crentsil.

5. *Bonsu*. Named after and in honor of the Asantehene Mensah Bonsu who chased the white man to the Atlantic Ocean and given the nickname Bonsu (Whale). It demonstrates and encourages brave leadership.

6. *Bonsu nketewa.* (miniature version of Bonsu). A variation of Bonsu (above).

7. *Yaw Donkor*—(An Akan name meaning: Yaw—Thursday boy; Donkor—Servant. From the expression: *se akoa som som-pa a otumi di akonnwa.* If a servant serves well he can rise to become a king. (The cloth is named after a servant whose ingenuity impressed the king of Asante to raise him to a position of responsibility in his kingdom.). It reassures social justice and inspires empowerment of all without recourse to social class.

Cloth Symbols With Relationship, Marriage, and Love Implications

"Awadee nye nsafufuo na yeaka ahwe" meaning "marriage is not palm wine to be tasted by any passerby." Or (marriage is not like palm wine, which is tasted before a choice can be made). This saying suggests the sanctity of marriage and so people are advised to enter into a marriage relationship with sincerity and seriousness. Cloth symbols related to marriage and relationship reminds people to salvage troubled marriage or relationship by learning and maintaining the virtues of patience, love, understanding, sincerity, forgiveness, and mutual respect. They also advise that it takes efforts and dedication to keep the fun and romance alive. Again, people learn from the proverbs and sayings depicted in some of the symbols to make even the happiest marriage better. In fact most of them are expressions of love and gratitude to partners. Cloth with the following patterns provides facts and pieces of advice to couples.

1. *OKUN PA*—GOOD HUSBAND.
From the expression: *Okunpa ho ye na*. Literal translation: A good husband is hard to come by. This is an expression claiming that all men must strive to become responsible in any relationship, especially in marriage.

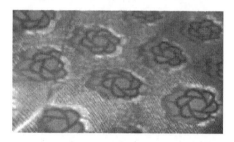

2. *Odo "chain"* (Lover's necklace).
An expression of unbreakable love (looks like it will break but it continues). This is an expression that encourages spouses and lovers to keep the love link intact.

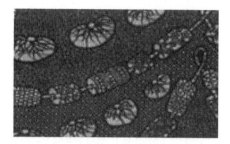

3. *Obaa-pa*—The Ideal Woman.
Literal translation: A good wife is hard to come by. This is an expression claiming that all women must strive to become responsible in any relationship, especially in marriage.

4. *Me kraa ko aburokyire*—My soul is already abroad. (A symbol of self-assurance)

5. *Akoma ntoasoo* (**Linked heart**). Expression of understanding and agreement) **OR** *M'akoma mu toffee* (**Kiss love**): (**The love of my heart (expressed as the "candy of my heart"**) (This is a modern cloth pattern/design that expresses love).

6. *ADUKURO MU NSUO— GROVE WATER.* From the expression: Adukuro mu nsuo akọnnọ-akọnnọ, merenya bi ama me dofo anom! Literal translation: May I find some sweet grove water to offer to my lover! (An expression of unconditional love.)

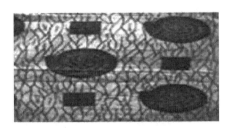

7. *WOAFA ME NWA—YOU HAVE TAKEN ME AS CHEAP AND EASY AS A SNAIL.* (You take me for granted). From the expression: if you drink for free from the water pot, you will have to pay to drink from the wine pot. This is a patient woman's warning to her ingrate husband.

Cloth Patterns With Conflict Resolution Implications

Conflict is a fact of life and, if not managed properly they may lead to threatening a valued relationship. The Akan of Ghana believe that conflict is a problem to be solved in a sensible way to benefit both parties. To them the best outcome of conflict is to identify the preferred style of both parties so they can manage and influence the conflict to a conclusion that would result in a win-win situation for both parties.

Through pictographs and ideographs in the cloth symbols and patterns, they advise, encourage and solve conflicts. Most of the names pertaining to these symbols are couched in pithy sayings that have been passed on to posterity by elders and, therefore accepted with respect and reverence. When such statements are quoted or referred to during arbitration, conflicting parties accept them as a custom and statement of law. Following are some cloth names that solve conflicts:

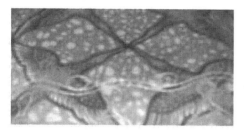

1. *Ano ne ano hyia a ntotoo mma.* (Together the mouth can solve every conflict). From the expression: *Asem ye den sen ara a yede yen anonaeka; yemfa sekan na etwa.* Dialogue is the best mediator to solve any conflicts; No knife can cut through a case.

2. *NIPA TIRE NYE BOFERE*— (THE HUMAN HEAD IS NOT LIKE THE PAPAYA FRUIT). From the proverb: *Nipa tire nye borofere na yeapae mu ahwe dee ewo mu.* Literal translation: The human head/mind is not like the papaya fruit to be split open to see what is on the inside.

3. *ANI BERE A, ENSO GYA*— GRIEVING EYES DO NOT SPARK FIRE Symbol of PATIENCE, SELF-CONTROL, SELF-DISCIPLINE, and SELF-CONTAINMENT. From the proverb: *Anibere a, enso gya. Or, Enye obiara a ne bo fu a omuna.* Literal translation: No matter how flaming red one's eyes may be, fire is not sparked in one's eyes. Or, every frowned face does not necessarily depict anger.

4. *Nkwadu-sa* (**Banana bunches**). From the expression: *Wosum borodee a sum kwadu; na wonnim dee obehwe wo kom bere mu.* Advice to accord similar tender care to both plantain and the banana—you may never know which of the two will survive severe weather or famine. (Treat all you children equally; you may not know when you may need brain or brawn.

5. *AKYEKYEDEE AKYI*—**TORTOISE SHELL**. From the proverb: *Huriee si akyekyedee akyi a, osi ho kwa. Or, akyekyedee a ope ne yere amanee na ose wo m'akyiri mmesa ma me.* Literal translation: The tsetse fly sits on the back of the tortoise in vain; it cannot suck any blood through the hard shell. Or, when the tortoise wants to get his wife into trouble he asks her to plait the hair on his hairless back. Engaging in futile enterprise serves one no good.

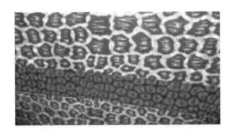

6. *Efie aboseaa*—**Courtyard pebbles.** From the expression: *Se ofie aboseaa twa wo a eye ya sen abonten so dee.* A cut from your own courtyard pebbles is more painful than a cut from outside pebbles. (In other words, exploitation/mistreatment/ manipulation from a relative is more hurtful than any abuse from a stranger.

Cloth Symbols as Proverbs

Generally cloth symbols are verbally expressed in order to appreciate the meaning and unfold the code concealed in the pattern. In fact, the different symbol themes discussed—political, educational/school, economic, relationship marriage, conflict, and so forth, are mostly expressed in proverbs. This demonstrates the importance placed on proverbs among the Akan. Proverbs simplify a long discussion and are revered as a source of legal injunction at any traditional court of arbitration (Okrah, 2003). A person who can weave a discourse with proverbs is not only considered intelligent, he/she is also revered for his/her linguistic astuteness and insight. The respect for the use of proverbs in African culture is further reinforced by Achebe's (1959) assertion that proverbs are the palm oil with which words are eaten. Proverbial symbols in cloth are represented in pictograms and ideograms.

The distinctive difference between a pictogram and an ideogram lies in the words themselves. A pictogram uses a picture of an object and an ideogram uses a symbol made to represent an idea (Papadopoulos, 2010). Thus both pictograms and ideograms are part of a tradition of pictorial art. The difference is that pictograms represent particular images in a consistent way, which can be described as a form of picture writing. Essentially, **pictogram** represents symbols that everyone use in a similar form to convey a similar meaning. Thus, a conventional relationship exists between the symbol and its interpretation.

Ideogram on the other hand is a picture developing into a more fixed symbolic form, to be used for ideas behind the picture and the picture itself. For example, the picture of a sun (pictogram) can be used for "heat" and "daytime," as well as for "sun." As the symbol extends from "sun" to "heat." it is moving from something visible to something conceptual (and no longer a picture). This type of symbol is then considered to be part of a system of idea writing, or **ideograms.** The distinction between pictograms and ideograms is essentially a difference in the relationship between the symbol and the entity it represents. The more "picture-like" forms are **pictograms** and the more abstract derived forms are **ideograms.**

The following ideographic and pictographic cloth symbols are explained by different proverbs that advise the people in everyday life. Some of them cast insinuations euphemistically to speak, warn or threaten one's enemy whilst some function as a catalyst to discourage socially unacceptable conducts. The following ideographic and pictographic symbols would suffice for the discussion:

A. IDEOGRAPHIC SYMBOLS

1. *Nsuaehunu* **(empty threats).** A sign of resilience and advice to disregard petty jealousies from one's adversaries.

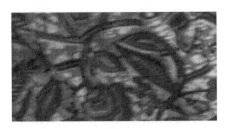

2. *AHWENEPA NKASA—* **PRECIOUS BEADS MAKE NO NOISE.** From the proverb: *Ahwenepa nkasa.* Literal translation: Precious beads make no noise. That is, empty barrels make the most noise. A good person needs not blow his/her own horns.

3. *AFE BI YE ASIANE—* **INAUSPICIOUS YEAR.** Symbol of misfortune, bad lick, and unfavorable/discouraging times. From the expression: *Afe bi ye asiane.* Literal translation: Some years are inauspicious or unlucky.

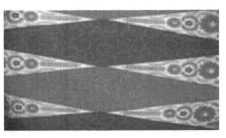

4. *Otan nnim akorokoro*—**No amount of indulgence will mitigate hatred.** (Don't waste your time and energy seeking love from your avowed enemy.)

5. *Eboo- fa; dadee-fa*—Half stone; half iron A symbol of moderation—avoiding absolutes.

6. *Kotodwe* (**Knee cups**). A symbol of strength.

B. PICTOGRAPHIC SYMBOLS

1. *WO NSA AKYI*—**THE BACK OF ONE'S HAND (your knuckles)**. From the proverb: *Wonsa akyi beye wo de a, ennte se wo nsayamu.* Literal translation: The back of one's hand does not taste as good as the palm does.

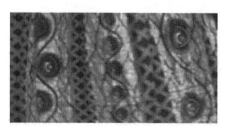

2. *Aniwa nnim awerehoo*—**The eye does not know grief/the eye does not feel grief.** From the expression: Aniwa nnim awerehoo; anka mesi ho a na mereda? The eye does not feel grief otherwise it would not catch sleep.

3. *Obaatan-* **Nursing Mother.** From the expression: Obaatan Na Onim Dee Ne Mma Bedie. (Only mothers know what is best for their children.)

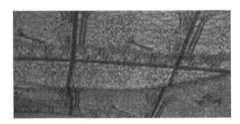

4. *Duakoro*—**The single tree.** From the expression "duakoro gye mframa a ebu" a single tree cannot withstand a storm; it would fall. (A notice from an industrious son to his parents to advise the other children who do not show concern for the upkeep of the parents.)

5. *Ahwede-po*—**The sugarcane.** From the expression: *Ahwedee nye de nkosi ne nkon (Abrabo ye nkosoo ne nkoguo)*, A single sugarcane is not sweet throughout to the tip (Life experiences comprise successes and failures)

6. *Owuo atwedee*—**the ladder of death OR Sakadom—scattered crowd.** From the expression: *Owuo atwedee, obaako mforo.* No one escapes the ladder of death/ the ladder of death is not reserved for only one person; we will all climb it—an expression of human mortality

7. *Nkyemfere* (**Broken pot**). From the expression: *Dee okoo aware ase kane na ne nkukugo dooso*. Many broken pots in a woman's kitchen are an indication of marital experience.

8. Kotoko—symbol of the porcupine. From the expression: *Asante kotoko: kum apem a apem beba*. Asante, the porcupine, if you kill a thousand, a thousand more will resurface (expression of formidable force).

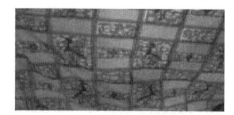

9. *Akonfem tikoro* (**the stray guinea fowl**). From the expression: *Akonfem-tikoro te se aboa ako; ofiri dodo mu nti wohu ono nko a mento no boo*. Guinea fowls are like parrots; they move in groups. So don't take advantage of her loneliness for her group may be nearby.

10. *Kete-pa*—(**sleeping mat**). From the expression: *Kete-pa ne sumuie—pa ma adwen pa*. A better sleeping mat with a better pillow produces sound sleep and sound thoughts. (It is also a symbol of good marriage)

11. *Fa akonnwa*—Take a seat. From the expression: *Wobeka me ho asem a fa akonnwa/ wote me ho asem a fa akonnwa* (If you want to talk about me, take a seat—because you will need more time. In order words, good deeds fear no gossip.)

12. *Akokonini*—The Cockerel. From the expression *akokonini-abankwaa: dee ebeye me ara na aye me yi.* The cock in loneliness says, "Destiny is inescapable."(After all the benefits the cock provides for mankind, especially as the sole announcer of daybreak to the entire community, his reward is to be killed on festive occasions.)

13. *Aburoo ne nkatee*—roasted maize and peanuts. (a symbol of complementarities, close-ness, attachment, and insepa-rability)

14. *Woato pete tuo*—Wasted your bullet on a vulture (a symbol of futile and unproduc-tive undertaking. (Note that the vulture is a bird that feeds on the dead animals and filthy food and nobody eats it.)

15. *Kata wodee so na bue me dee so*—**cover your misdeeds and open mine** (a symbol of jealousy—one who tries to put others down and cover one's own mistakes).

16. *Akwadaa bo nwa na ommo akyekyedee* **(A child cracks the shell of a snail NOT the shell of a tortoise).** A child's behavior should reflect his age and position in the family, community and neighborhood. This is a symbol of advice to recalcitrant, disobedient, and disrespectful children.

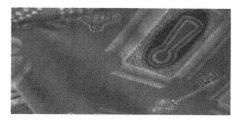

17. *Nsafoa* **(Keys).** From the expression: *Dee okita safoa na edan ye no dea.* (The holder of the key is the owner of the room.) OR *Etire nni safoa.* (There is no key into the head). It is impossible to see what one is thinking.)

Miscellaneous Symbols

Other cloth symbols come in the form of images of nature. They can be insects, animals, plants, crops, water bodies and other objects in nature. These may have specific proverbs created around them or a specific ideographic perceptions attributed to the image. Following are a few of the images that are found in Ghanaian cloth.

1. *Aya*—**Ferns**—Expression of endurance and resourcefulness. The fern can withstand all types of weather.

2. *Nsubura* **(creeks/patches of river).** (A symbol of fertility.)

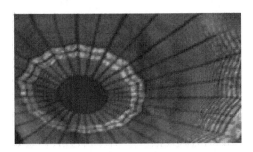

3. *Ananse ntentan* **(Spider's web).** Expression of wisdom and creativity.

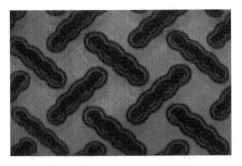

4. *Nkatehono*—**(peanut/ground-nut shells).** In honor to a good farmer.

5. *Kotoko*—symbol of the porcupine. From the expression: *Asante kotoko: kum apem a apem beba.* Asante, the porcupine, if you kill a thousand, a thousand more will resurface (expression of formidable force).

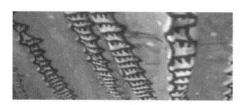

6. *Nsafoa* (Keys). From the expression: *Dee okita safoa na edan ye no dea.* (The holder of the key is the owner of the room.) OR *Etire nni safoa* (There is no key into the head). It is impossible to see what one is thinking.

7. *Ahwede-po*—The sugarcane. From the expression: *Ahwedee nye de nkosi ne nkon (Abrabo ye nkosoo ne nkoguo.)* A single sugarcane is not sweet throughout to the tip (Life experiences comprise successes and failures.)

Contemporary White Funeral Cloths

Of late, Ghanaians use white cloth for funerals of parents who die at a ripe age. Also, funerals are followed by church service on the Sunday after the funeral. Family members order special white cloth for the funerals. The designs vary but they collaborate with the textile designers to write a befitting inscription in the cloth. The following are examples of some of the messages written as a reminder of grief of family members:

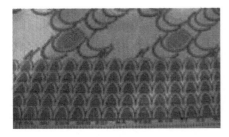

1. *Ena mu ena ben bio na yebenya te se wo* (How can we ever replace you with another mother of your caliber?)

2. *Obaatan pa a osom bo afiri yen mu* (A worthy mother has left us.)

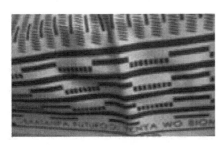

3. *Obaatanpa futufoo, yenya wo bio* (A good mother and adviser, we will never have you again.)

4. *Owuo ama adepa bi afiri yen nsa* (Death has taken away from us a valuable thing.)

Funeral Cloths

Generally, funeral cloths are in the colors of red, black, and brown. These colors symbolize grief and sadness. For this reason, all the cloth patterns catalogued above can be used as funeral cloth if they come in any of the funeral colors. But it would be more appropriate if the name of the cloth speaks to issues of death and sympathy. For example: *Dua koro gye mframa a ebu (the single tree); Obaatan (na onim dee ne ba bedie) (the nursing mother); Afe bi ye asiane (unfavorable/gloomy year); Ani bere a enso gya (grief in the eyes does not spark fire);* The following few examples will suffice for further clarification:

1. *Owuoatwedee*—**the ladder of death OR Sakadom—scattered crowd.** From the expression: *Owuo atwedee, obaako mforo.* No one escapes the ladder of death/ the ladder of death is not reserved for only one person; we will all climb it— an expression of human mortality

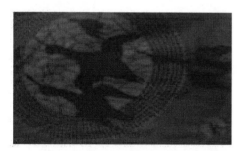

2. *Ahemfie*—**(the palace).** A cloth that was made during the death of the Asante king Osei Agyemang Prempeh in 1970. It was to be worn to be admitted to the palace or around to mourn the king. It is also an expression of the power and sanctity of the dwelling place of the leader.

3. *Fa akonnwa*—**take a seat.** From the expression: *Wobeka me ho asem a fa akonnwa/ wote me ho asem a fa akonnwa* (If you want to talk about me, take a seat—because you will need more time. In order words, good deeds fear no gossip.)

Educational Implications

Noticeably, modern education does little to teach the distinction between symbols and things. In Lutus (2001) assertion, most "educated" people cannot tell the difference between a fact and an idea, the most common confusion of symbol and thing. Most believe if they collect enough facts, this will compensate for their inability to grasp the ideas behind those facts. And, because of this "poverty of ideas," most cannot work out the simplest conceptual questions, such as "why is the sky dark at night?"

As a result of this educational deficit, our individually inspired sense of well being; our direct participation in those actions that assure our continued survival; our sense that we must create our own reasons for living, have been replaced by a kind of conceptual totalitarianism, which has as its cornerstone a deliberate blurring of symbol and thing (Lutus, 2001). But without understanding the underlying meaning of a thing used as a symbol, we will not be able to decipher and maintain the import of nonverbal language and its significance.

From the foregoing, it is clear that symbols and patterns (art forms) contribute to intellectual development since the related pictures can be understood and ideas formulated only by reason. Understanding the nature of art forms and their implications facilitate the process of any educational endeavor and its etiological implications. Also, cultural literacy helps people to function well in society and likewise, intercultural literacy contributes to global conflict resolution. Again, cultural literacy records cherished values, teach rules and precedents, and ensure dispositional and moral training. Furthermore, not only does the study of cloth metaphor introduce multiculturalism in literacy education; it also widens the scope for multicultural education and global literacy in a global village.

Also, teachers need to investigate all contents that directly teach multicultural and global content by analyzing all curriculum materials for appropriate content and concepts (Brown & Kysilka, 2002). Teachers must know that they have wonderful resource available in their local communities and beyond. Working with individuals and groups to develop these resources can be time consuming, but the rewards are well worth the effort. As stated by Brown and Kysilka (2002), teachers and schools can no longer afford to be isolated from their local and greater communities. The world of today reaches into the classroom even if the teacher has tried to close the door. Effective teachers realize the importance of allies in educating their students. They understand that they alone cannot provide all the resources and information necessary to lead their students toward active participation in the local and global societies.

Finally, a study of this kind completes the claim to literacy as global citizens through a way of understanding others and their means of communication. In this information age, collaboration is vital (Brown & Kysilka, 2002).

Conclusion

Literacy in its wider perspective cannot be defined in a vacuum. Literacy means reading, writing, speaking and explaining signs, symbols, and gestures within and beyond one's own culture. Intercultural communicative competence is the ability to adapt one's behavior toward another in ways that are appropriate to the other person's culture (Beebe, Beebe, & Redmond, 2008), which will improve if we develop a knowledge that will enhance understanding of others who differ from us. To accomplish this, we need to seek information about the other culture; that is, learning about the other culture's worldview, art forms, and signs or symbols.

The development of intercultural communicative competency has the potential to afford our world that is strife with conflicts and wars a better sense of understanding one another. It should also be understood that same words may mean different things in different cultures just as similar signs and symbols have different meanings in different cultures. Since literacy is the first step to education, it is important to widen the scope of literacy to encompass its wider perspective so that children will come out of school with another dimension of multicultural and global literacy that will help them to function in a world that has become a global village.

Activities

Cloth as a metaphor is likened to art combined with critical thinking. Therefore, appropriate activities in the classroom would expand children's imaginative skills, as well as help them to appreciate nature and art forms. Appropriately delivered and guided, their conceptual visions would stimulate them to develop discerning philosophies in multicultural and global education. Such beliefs and attitudes would generate for both intercultural awareness and critical literacy as they combine literary resources to promote both the aesthetic and ethical functions of the African fabric.

The following are examples of activities that may be used in a social studies classroom.

1. Identify some symbols known to you and describe their meanings
   You may describe different religious symbols known to you. Explain

the pattern or picture and connect it to the meaning given to the symbol for example, the cross, the yin yang, the crescent and the star, and so forth.

2. Identify some gestures and explain the generally accepted meanings. Create or imagine your own meaning and explain your choice.

3. Make your own art piece using a sheet of paper or plain cloth. Cut or carve your own design into an eraser, a calabash or any soft, fluffy material.

4. Poke small sticks into the back of the stamp to serve as a handle With mixed color or paint use your cut design to make series of rows between straight lines, which separate one design from another. Create a proverb to go with the symbol, pattern, design, or combination of symbols. Explain the meaning of the picture or the idea behind the picture or the pattern.

REFERENCES

Achebe, C. (1959). *Things fall apart*. New York, NY: Fawcett Crest.

Arthur, G. F. K. (2001). *Cloth as metaphor: Reading the adinkra cloth symbols of The Akan of Ghana*. Accra: Cefiks Publications.

Beebe, S. A., Beebe, S. J., & Redmond, M. V. (2008). *Interpersonal communication: Relating to others*. Boston, MA: Allyn & Bacon.

Blackwell Encyclopedia of Sociology. Ritzer, George. (Ed.). (2007). Blackwell reference online. Retrieved from http://www.blackwellreference.com.libproxy.lib.unc.edu/subscriber/tocnode?id=g9781405124331_chunk_g978140512433113_ss1-16

Brown, S. C., & Kysilka, M. L. (2002). *Applying multicultural and global concepts in the classroom and beyond*. Boston, MA: Allyn & Bacon.

Dawson, D. (1990). *Traditional textiles from Mexico, Guatemala and Panama*. Chicago, IL: Mexican Fine Arts Center Museum.

DOT Pictograms. (2013). Department of transportation symbols. Retrieved from www.en.wikipedia.org/wiki/DOT_pictogam

Gollnick, D. M., & Chinn, P. C. (2013). *Multicultural education in a pluralistic society*. Boston, MA: Pearson.

Ladson-Billings, G. (1995). Toward a theory of culturally relevant pedagogy. *American Education Research Journal, 32*(3), 465-491.

Lutus, P. (2001). How we confuse symbols and things. Retrieved from www.arachnoid.com/lutusp/symbols.html

Nieto, S., & Bode, P. (2012). *Affirming Diversity: The sociopolitical context of multicultural education* (6th ed.). Boston, MA: Pearson.

Okrah, K. A. (2003). *The wisdom knot: Toward an African philosophy of education*. New York & London: Routledge.

Okrah, K. A. (2007). Rethinking literacy: Preparing children for multicultural and global literacy. *Journal of African Educational Research, 7*(2), 100-104.

Okrah, K. A., & Taylor, S. (2004). *African indigenous knowledge and science* Haverford, PA: Infinity.

Opoku, K. A. (2002, October). *The wisdom of the ancestors: Advancing proverbial Knowledge.* Unpublished paper presented at the 14th annual Cheikh Anta Diop International Conference, Philadelphia, PA.

Papadopoulos, A. (2010). Difference between pictograms and ideograms. Retrieved From   http://www.ehow.com/info_8434995_difference-between-pictograms-ideograms.html#page=0

Warren, A. (2012). The power of symbols. Retrieved from www.newacropolisuk.org/articles.php?artid=10

CHAPTER 10

ADDRESSING CULTURE AND CONTEXT FOR URBAN STUDENTS IN THE CONTENT CLASSROOM

Recognizing Oral Tradition and Drama as Cultural Tools

Rachel A. Grant

"Tell me and I will forget.

Show me and I will remember.

Involve me and I will understand."

—Native American Proverb

*African Traditional and Oral Literature as Pedagogical Tools in
Contest Area Classrooms: K-12,* pages 183–200
Copyright © 2014 by Information Age Publishing
183

Introduction

When Africans were captured, transported, and held as slaves in distance lands Europeans displayed unimaginable cruelty in their efforts to wipe-out all aspects of the languages and cultures that defined an African identity. "Masters made every attempt to control their captives' thoughts and imaginations, indeed their hearts and minds. Maintaining a system of bondage in the Age of Enlightenment depended upon the master's being able to speak for the slave, to deny his or her humanity, and to draw a line between slave consciousness and human will" (Williams, 2005, p. 7). It is clear, that in spite of the real and symbolic violence imposed upon them, enslaved Africans managed to pass on to future generations the ways of doing, knowing, and being that connected their spirit and identity to Africa. Although Europeans sought to destroy the beliefs and practices, attitudes and perspectives, memories. and even the stories of Africa, a uniquely African cultural identity emerged in every land where Africans were held in bondage. As a critical educator and scholar who has focused on the teaching and learning needs of racially and linguistically diverse learners, I have come to realize the importance of drawing upon the cultural wealth of community as a resource for fully engaging learners, supporting literacy development and elevating academic achievement (Grant, 2011, 2012).

In addressing the psycho-social, emotional and learning needs of diverse learners, I stress the centrality of culture for connecting with students as they try to make sense of school in the context of their own lives. This is particularly important for African American students in urban schools who fair less well than their European American counterparts. Achieving high educational goals for all students, especially those who historically have been shortchanged in schools and larger society by racism, classism, sexism, and linguistic bias, must begin, first, with a belief in the "infinite capacity" of students. Delpit (2012) describes this as a belief in the inherent intellectual capability, humanity, physical ability, and spiritual character of students.

In an account of African American education in a rural southern community, Walker (1996) provides an example of how schools served as a cultural extension in many rural African American communities that were racially segregated and under resourced. Walker (1996) detailed ways that school and community operated around shared traditions, displayed common ways of acceptable communicative patterns, and shared beliefs about children's abilities to reach their highest potential. In this chapter my goal is to address the role of culture, employing the arts, specifically drama as cultural tools within the context of urban schools and in content area classrooms. I begin by discussing the implications for using culture to support learning in school, connecting this to African and African American oral tradition and literature. Next, I provide support for using the arts, particularly drama as a resource for incorporating culture, motivating interest and engaging students in literacy and learning content. I conclude the chapter by purposing a process for helping prepare teachers to infuse culture by using strategies such as reader's theater as a way to support literacy and learning in the content area classroom.

Theoretical Underpinnings: Culture, Cultural Responsiveness, and Contextual Relevance

In its broadest sense culture consists of the beliefs, behaviors, objects, and other characteristics common to the members of a particular group or society. Culture is reflected in certain societal practices that among other things include language, customs, values, norms, mores, rules, tools, technologies, products, organizations, and institutions. Culture is also associated with ways of doing, being, knowing, and reacting. Hollins (2008) notes that, "culture is difficult to define because it is the essence of who we are, and how we exist in the world" (p. 18). Race and ethnicity are manifestations of culture; however, culture transcends these attributes because it is multidimensional and fluid. Culture evolves over time, across locales and over generations within a given society. The boundaries of culture are not necessarily fixed because qualities associated with culture intermingle. Intermingling or hybridity are easily seen as we consider the impact of European exploration and colonization on indigenous cultures of the Americas or in the ways that a shared history and territorial boundaries create a national identity and national culture. As Ibrahim (2003) points out, we can see the interrelationship of race, culture, language, and identity through the enormous influence of Hip-Hop cultural and linguistic styles. The youth the world over now reach across national, racial, and ethnic borders to appropriate this African American music genre and Black Stylized English as a "symbolic space for identification, bonding, investment, and desire" (p. 170).

Hollins (2008) addresses the centrality of culture and social ideology within the context of school by identifying teachers' perspectives of culture as falling into three types that connect pedagogical practices to their definition of culture, their ideological stance (i.e., characterizing one's orientation as Afrocentric or Western, liberal, or conservative) and their conceptualization of learning (e.g., traditional or culturally mediated, student-centered or teacher-centered). In turn, teachers' positionalities relative to ideology and conceptualization of learning influence teaching practices. Hollins demonstrates this in a framework that connects teachers' perspectives on culture, learning, and ideology (for a complete description see Hollins, 2008, pp. 6-7). Table 10.1 presents an overview of teacher types and some of the instructional approaches identified by Hollins.

Table 10.1.   Summary of Culture Definition and Instructional Practices for Teachers

	Type I	*Type II*	*Type III*
Definition of culture	Artifact and behavior	Social and political relationships	Affect, behavior, intellect
Instructional approaches	Generic teaching strategies Individualization Remediation = repetition	Learning styles Background experiences Individualization	Culturally medicated instruction Cultural accommodation Personalization

Source: Hollins (2008, pp. 6-7).

According to Hollins (2008),

> schools are shaped by cultural practices and values and reflect the norms of the society for which they have been developed [and] the existence of the culture of schooling can be inferred from the uniformity of values and practices across school districts. (pp. 33-34)

Lee's (2007) work with African American urban students provides an exploration of the life context and cultural resources these students bring to the classroom. Lee posits that these resources are accessible "only to a teacher who can provide affirmation for students' intelligence, support them in risk-taking, and create culturally connected bridges from what they know to the academic forms of knowledge application expected in school" (p. xix). Using the centrality of culture as a framing concept, this chapter also connects with two overlapping perspectives, *culturally responsive teaching and contextually relevant practices* that inform work on culture and schooling. The ideological connections of these perspectives undergird this chapter and provide the basis upon which to build pedagogical practices. According to Ladson-Billings (1994), culturally responsive teaching is a pedagogy that recognizes the importance of including students' cultural references in all aspects of learning.

Instruction is culturally mediated when it incorporates and integrates diverse ways of knowing, understanding, and representing information.

Instruction that is culturally responsive places teaching and learning in an environment that encourages diverse viewpoints and allows for inclusion of knowledge that is relevant to the students. Learning happens in culturally appropriate social situations; that is, relationships among students and those between teachers and students are congruent with students' cultures (Gay, 2000; Grant & Asimeng-Boahene, 2006; Nieto, 2002). Gay (2000) asserts that culturally responsive pedagogy is validating, comprehensive, multidimensional, empowering, transformative, and emancipatory. Teachers who utilize approaches that embrace students' cultures and lived experiences as well as local contextual realities offer opportunities for students to establish meaningful connections because instruction is better suited to meeting their pedagogical needs.

Contextual relevance, the second pedagogical perspective addressed here, subsumes all elements of culturally responsive teaching and also places emphasis on the geopolitical and sociohistorical circumstances in which teaching and learning take place. Contextual relevance takes into account that, teaching and learning take place within a context and that due to migratory shifts and changing demographics, teachers increasingly work with students whose "historical, cultural, social, economic, religious, and political environments reflect practices and realities that may differ sharply from their own" (Grant, 2011, p. 206).

The relevance of context allows teachers to consider, for example, that although African American students share a broader culture, the examples we draw from and resources we utilize may require adjustments in accordance with locale, rural versus urban, or region, north versus south. Taking context into consideration may also help teachers avoid essentializing cultural membership by acknowledging that cultural groups have both intergenerational stability and diversity (Lee, 2007). The situated context of learning encourages teachers to employ curriculum and teaching practices that are inclusive and particularistic as we take into account not only what we teach, but who we teach, and where we teach. Because this chapter offers, for your consideration, practices that engage culture, instructional strategies, and the arts (i.e., drama) it is important to note that embedding multicultural practices through artistic expression in the content classroom offers opportunities to expand learning within nonverbal and sensory communication by using gestures, emotions, feelings, sound, symbols, movement, shapes, color, patterns, and even designs to present information and demonstrate learning. I believe that when classrooms are imbued with these qualities learning becomes anchored within the lives of children and potential for achieving is boundless.

Connecting African and African American Orality and Literary Forms

Oral tradition, oral culture, and oral lore are cultural materials and traditions that have been transmitted by word-of-mouth from one generation to another. Essentially oral tradition is a way for keeping a culture alive. Oral tradition for African Americans was especially potent for transmitting culture because during slavery they were denied a formal education and had virtually no access to print literacies. Even after emancipation, African descendant people struggled to gain access to European forms of literacy, especially reading and writing. It is through oral tradition one can see the vivid imprint of Africa on African American culture Scheub (1985). Like the ancient African griots, African American elders passed on cultural artifacts such as stories, songs, poems, folktales, and family histories to expose the memories of a life before, during and after enslavement. Orality and verbal lore reveals everyday tradition within a culture. Verbal art forms show that Africans and African Americans share an unbroken continuity with literary forms by bearing witness to a staggering sum of experiences that reflect common, everyday ways of knowing, being, doing, expressing, and reacting.

Genres generally associated with the ordinary ways a culture operates often are referred to as its folk life, folk lore, or folk ways. These genres include: verbal, materials, custom, belief, motion, music. and song. The strength of oral tradition in everyday life is seen in African literature, especially in the classic work of Chinua Achebe's (1958) well known and best-selling novel *Things Fall Apart*. Achebe uses song, proverbs, riddle, and lyric poetry to link history with fiction to show every day African life. In an article addressing the use of African oral tradition in literature, Scheub (1985), points out the vitality of the relationship between the oral and written word in African literature. "Oral culture is a cultural component that distills the essences of human experiences, shaping them into rememberable, readily retrievable images of broad applicability with an extraordinary potential for eliciting emotional response" (p. 1).

Cultural traditions as evidenced through the epics, epigrams, poems, songs, and folk tales of Africa, until recently were all spoken and recited. As availability of print forms expanded efforts were undertaken to capture African oral tradition in modern literacy forms making it accessible to everyone. African novels, especially Achebe's, became the proponents of African oral culture and revitalized interest in Africa. Scheub (1985) characterizes the use of oral genres within the African narrative as a metaphorical process, that is, "product of pattern and image; and, being prescriptive rather than descriptive, they resolve themselves into models for human and cultural behavior, falling into a cyclical, not linear, mode" (p. 2).

All children enter school already possessing a narrative style or have been exposed to storytelling traditions that reflect their cultural/ethnic roots, and storytelling traditions vary around the world. The very qualities that distinguish African American oral narrative style from European narratives are often less familiar to many teachers. This may also be the case for other non-European oral narratives. As a result teachers may judge as deficit the oral and storytelling traditions of African American and other cultural groups. This is important because narrative text shapes school instruction in the early grades and narratives frame the basis for most of the emergent reading and writing instruction. It is important to consider that a student's way of hearing or telling a story may vary from how stories are shared and how they operate in school. To see how oral storytelling can vary, Table 10.2 summarizes qualities associated with the oral narrative style of African American, Japanese, Native and Aboriginal peoples (North America), and Latino cultures. It is clear that these oral traditions offer unique literary and cognitive complexities that could enhance opportunities for intellectual growth. Teachers would do well to consider how to incorporate the range of storytelling traditions that reflect the cultures and experiences of their students.

Table 10.2.   Narrative (Storytelling) Qualities by Cultural Group

Cultural Group	Narrative Qualities
African American	Dramatic, lengthy, embellish facts to heighten interest; explicit or implicit improvisation on a theme; use of teasing, metaphor, alliteration, rhyme, refrains and other poetic devices; linked to various musical traditions, dance, and visual art forms; use of African American English
Latino	De-emphasize event sequencing; emphasize description with much detail about the appearance of objects; stories often centered around family or extended fictive kin; may overlap their narrative with the narrative of others during the story sharing process
Native and Aboriginal peoples (North America)	Historical stories based on cultural heroes; stories shared to educate or control; may link multiple episodes thematically or by repetition sequences
Japanese	Influenced by cultural proscriptions of verbosity; short succinct collections based on similar experiences unified into one discourse
China (Suzhou chantefable)	Singing, instrumental music, and a complex mixture of narrative registers and dialogue

Sources: McCabe(1996); Bender (1998).

An important characteristic of oral tradition is the linguistic form (i.e., language, dialect, rhetorical style) and cultural nuances used in sharing a story or experience. The language that many black children come to school knowing often has been demonized and labeled as low-class or inferior to the variety of English spoken in school. Estimates are that millions of African Americans speak, at one time or another, a variety of English variously known as African American English, African American Vernacular English, Ebonics, Black English. As teachers consider how to engage cultural tools of a community, they must also take note of what it means to allow students to use the language form through which they are best able to demonstrate what they know and who they are.

Historically, the use of African American English, orally and in writing, has been problematic in school settings (Richardson, 2003). In order for teachers to fully realize the resource of culture in the classroom they must come to terms with their own raced and classed attitudes about teaching "other peoples 'children' " and then look for ways to utilize students' first languages and cultural traditions in support of learning. Indeed how can teachers incorporate language as part of the cultural toolkit that provides a bridge from where students *are* to the places we wish to *take* them? Demographic evidence suggests that U.S. students are becoming increasingly more diverse, yet our teaching force remains overwhelmingly female, white and middle-class (Ball & Tyson, 2011; Delpit, 2012). So, an important question is, how can we engage instructional practices that utilize the cultural tools of community in support of learning and academic achievement for all students? Indeed, how can we accomplish this at a time when culturally and linguistically diverse students are more likely to have teachers who are from different racial, class, and linguistic backgrounds? It is my belief that how we respond to these questions will be critical to closing what I see as an opportunity gap as we seek to stem the tide of underachievement for African American students, English language learners and urban schools.

Connecting the Arts With Opportunities for Learning Content

Arts programs have long been used to help people communicate, share beliefs, learn skills and communicate information. Teachers who understand the ways that the arts can help students connect to culture and community will be able to use the arts to make learning exciting, meaningful, and support literacy development and learning in the content classroom. When teachers incorporate different ways of knowing, being, and doing by encouraging students to draw upon their own cultural, community, and familial literacy practices and artistic expression they are employing culturally responsive teaching practices (Pirbhai-Illich, Turner, & Austin, 2009).

Latta and Chan (2011) suggest that through the arts diverse learners are engaging a type of thinking, that is, artistic thinking, that supports relational processes including making, composing, performing, adapting, building, and meaning making. Further, Latta and Chan stress that the arts support learners by strengthening: attentiveness, personal investment, emotional commitment, dialogue and interaction, alertness and participation, and enhance one's sense of freedom and self-knowledge. Recent brain research proves that emotions are linked with learning. When learners connect to the concept emotionally, they will have a better understanding of it. When teachers use the arts we are linking students' prior experiences with new stimuli (Haley, 2009).

In a recent themed issue of *Harvard Educational Review* (HER) on the arts and education, Clapp and Edwards (2013) noted that the

> current educational landscape is fixated on standardized tests, measurable outcomes in rigid content areas, and increased "achievement" at all costs that may be at the expense of having school serve as a place where we make meaning of ourselves, our environments, and our sociocultural interactions. (p. 5)

This special issue of HER focuses on the need to reposition the arts within and outside traditional notions of where and how "we make art" as a way to "humanize our schools, strengthen our communities, and create a healthier society" (p. 3). One point made clear through the various articles in the issue is how education in and through the arts can meet the "sophisticated demands of today's students within the complex social and political landscapes that they inhibit" (p. 7).

Arts advocates and educators have recently started to explore the use of drama as an integrated way of learning across the curriculum. Using this particular art form as a conduit for learning extends content by engaging learners in representations of understanding that combine teaching art forms and disciplines. Simply put, using the arts to support learning academic content means that teachers are helping learners creatively interpret and re-design what they know in ways that are an essential part of 21st century learning (Grant & Austin, 2013). Using the arts is not haphazard but a skill of making decisions about the use of conventions, norms and practices of cultures, institutions and societies' values to convey a message to a particular audience for particular purpose (Ivanic, 1998). When teachers find ways to incorporate the arts to teach content, students engage in planning, writing, revising, editing, and negotiating meaning. These are decisions that are carried out in collaboration with peers and in student conferencing with the teacher (Grant & Austin, 2013). Teachers would do well to remember that drama is not only performance; this is just the final product of a whole learning process. This is especially the case in social studies teaching, specifically history, because the subject matter is ripe with topics that are open to dramatic interpretation. Drama involves the students' imaginations because the content addresses real life events, real people, and real circumstances. This encourages students to think actively, logically and emotionally about the human situations, problems and challenges they encounter in unfolding events. Drama is powerful because it offers a unique balance of thought and feeling.

Combining the arts with content subject matter allows for projects that build multiliteracies because teachers can utilize multilingual and multicultural resources and engage multimodalities that provide access to learning for even otherwise reluctant students. Moreover, they become the most memorable lessons valued long after the class is over (Grant & Austin, 2013). Here are additional ways dramatic arts, integrated with content subject matter can benefit students.

- Facilitates a learner-centered approach allowing learners to become actively involved in the text and be active participants in the teaching and learning.
- Promotes collaborative engagement with peers, increasing motivation and decreasing anxiety because learning is motivating and fun.
- Builds academic language and content knowledge because vocabulary is used with a clear purpose and contextualized in a specific context and its content becomes more relevant for learners.
- Involves the development of the four linguistic skills integrated (listening, speaking, reading and writing) and builds fluency.
- Fosters interaction and the negotiation of meaning among learners.
- Develops social and interpersonal skills, stimulates imagination, cooperation, creativity, and critical thinking.

Teachers wishing to include the arts have an extraordinary range of options in designing lessons. This could mean that instead of having students write a summary at the end of a unit about the industrial period, they might view one of the many films about this era and then role play what life was like for workers. Afterwards, they could create a collage of images to demonstrate their understanding of people and issues of the period. The teacher could assign students to use interactive writing in developing a script to role play the juxtaposition of laborers and factory owners. Teachers working with older students many of whom who hold part-time jobs could ask them to share perspectives about their own work environment.

Connecting the Arts With Opportunities for Learning Social Studies

Social studies an interdisciplinary concentration in the social sciences and humanities draw upon various fields, including sociology but also political science, history, economics, religious studies, geography, psychology, anthropology, and civics. Considering the diverse composition of students, that is, African American, English learners, and as well, large numbers of students living in poverty who attend urban schools, meeting their needs can be particularly challenging for all teachers given the text-dependent nature of content areas (Cruz & Thorton, 2009).

Social studies teaching, especially within the vast areas of history content, provide the substantive, factual framework of information that learners can use in bringing the distance or recent past to life through drama and role play. As such, drama develops nondeterministic open-ended and creative thinking which makes links and connections and enables children to deepen their understanding of historical events and how individuals respond within a historical period. It is this depth of engagement that produces critical thinking as students engage in observation, interpretation, analysis, inference, evaluation, explanation, and metacognition; these skills are essential for comprehension and meeting the demands of academic content learning.

Under the guidance of a skillful and culturally competent teacher, there might also be opportunities for using mixed medium such as film and public debate. Using the film "The Great Debaters" (Black, Forte, Roth, & Winfrey, 2007) as stimulus, teachers could teach historical content and focus on techniques for debating. Later, they can design activities encouraging students to utilize debating devices like those used by characters in the film. This would help students to not only learn about the tenets of debating, they could move on to conduct research on important debates in U.S. history (Malcolm X: the Ballot or the Bullet, 1964; Malcolm Oxford Debate, 1964; Kennedy vs. Nixon Presidential Debate, 1960; Lincoln vs. Douglas Presidential Debate, 1858; Obama vs. Romney Presidential Debates, 2012) and later, students could participate in classroom debates on current topics under study.

There also are cross-curricula possibilities, especially in the areas of social studies and science. For example, issues surrounding the theory of scientific evolution and intelligent design, global warming, or waste management and environmental racism. The possibilities are limitless as culture and context could serve as guides for teachers in determining how and why certain topics can be used to "draw" students into learning in school by connecting them to their own communities and circumstances.

Because music has such a powerful influence on popular and youth culture, students could research the music of a particular period and see how musical genres have been used at various times throughout history as social and political commentary, much like some of the Hip Hop and rap songs they enjoy. An assessment option could be to write a song or poem of their own to depict the burning issues of our times. The directions could be adjusted for developmental appropriateness across a range of ability, linguistic levels, interests, and cultures. Activities associated with the arts can be used for helping students respond during reading and other literacy activities to make learning exciting.

According to McDonald and Fisher (2006), "the making and doing of the arts can also uniquely stimulate the senses and provide active pathways to perceptions about the world around us" (p. 5). Typically the arts comprise four areas: music, visual arts, theater and drama, and dance and movement (see McDonald & Fisher for a comprehensive list of activities students can do in the four arts). Because large numbers of students who attend urban schools also are English language learners, teachers should be aware that a growing body of research indicates the arts can support literacy for them as well. According to McDonald and Fisher and other scholars (see DiPietro, 1987; Egan, 1992) English learners benefit because using the arts is:

- Enhancing and motivating other learning because students can access other systems (e.g., attentional, cognitive, emotional, etc.).
- Including all students especially those who are marginalized, underserved, or at risk.
- Increasing literacy skills in traditional areas (e.g., reading, writing, etc.) and other literacies, including opportunities to use language in concrete ways.
- Supporting doing and creating.
- Teaching and learning cross-curricular content.
- Affecting creativity and increasing satisfaction.
- Stimulating image-based nonlinguistic thinking in interpreting & expressing understandings of vocabulary and concepts.

Teachers who work with English learners could encourage them to include the stories and music of their own cultures, especially those written in their first languages. For English learners, oral language development paired with the arts can increase student involvement and language development. "These skills are critical to students' overall literacy development, as well as important in their understanding of the ways humans communicate" (McDonald & Fisher, 2006, p. 82).

The final section of the chapter discusses reader's theater, a popular strategy for combining literature, drama, cultures and literacy development. In closing, I introduce a procedure I have used in guiding preservice teachers through a process for developing cultural responsive and contextual relevant literacy lessons for teaching academic content.

Readers Theater, Drama, and Teaching Content

Research indicates that using drama in the classroom as a means of teaching helps students learn academically, socially, and developmentally (see Clark, Morrison, & Wilcox, 2009; Keehan, Harmon, & Shoho, 2008). While all of the arts can be influential learning tools, drama is especially powerful. *Readers Theater*, a well-seasoned literacy strategy makes it possible for teachers to combine drama and content teaching, and with appropriate modification Readers Theater (RT) can be used to incorporate culturally responsive and contextually relevant pedagogies into day-to-day content teaching.

RT has been recognized as a reading strategy that influences factors associated with positive reading performance (Clark, Morrison, & Wilcox, 2009; Keehan, Harmon, & Shoho, 2008; Martinez, Roser, & Strecker, 1999; Tyler & Chard, 2000). In 2000, Tierney and Readence (1999) described RT as a repeated reading procedure that integrates the language arts, reading, writing, speaking, and listening, as well as increases motivation to read. According to Keehan, Harmon, and Shoho (2008), RT involves oral reading practice as readers prepare for a performance and is a well-documented intervention shown to increase fluency. Important factors for learning academic content are being able to read and demonstrate understanding of the range of topics covered. Investigations of the effects RT has on reading have included studies involving how this repeated reading strategy influences fluency and other factors including motivation and confidence (Clark et al., 2009); comprehension and vocabulary (Keehan et al., 2008); and reading engagement (Martinez et al., 1999). Above all else, RT is considered to positively influence fluency, that is, factors such as accuracy, smoothness, pace, expression (e.g., stress and pitch), volume, and phrasing (Clark et al., 2009). Although easily modified, the steps in RT usually include:

1. *Selecting materials*—the teacher generally selects the materials, text with a strong plot, strong characters, and high interest;
2. *Getting started*—open ended classroom discussion about how to change a particular text to a play, when first introducing students to RT the teacher should select the story;
3. *A sample to see and read*—introduce students to an example of a short story for which a script exists, students read and discuss the adjustments made from the story to the script;
4. *Plan for adaptation*—using the sample script (step #3) as a model, students select a story from which they will create a script;
5. *Adapt the story*—students or teacher create the actual script;
6. *Preparing for the theatrical production*—rehearsal time is provided, during this time students read and re-read the script multiple times as they develop fluency and confidence in reading with peers, this is also a good time to discuss the elements of dialogue and its relationship to plot development; and
7. *Performing the play and follow-up*—students perform the script and the class discusses aspects of the script (i.e., characters, possible revisions or refinement of the script).

Utilizing Culture and Context Within the Framework of Readers Theater

Shelton and McDermott (2010) stress that using literature and drama is important for helping teachers, especially preservice teachers, engage in critical thought about diversity, equity, democracy, and power relationships. This is important for several reasons noted earlier in this chapter: (1) the vast majority of current and future teachers represent backgrounds (i.e., language, social class, race/ethnicity) that differ from the students they teach; (2) demographic trends that confirm the United States' school-aged population is becoming more racially, linguistically, and socially diverse; and (3) current academic indicators suggest that culturally and linguistically diverse students who attend urban schools fair less well than their middle-class White peers. If we are to stem the tide of low expectations, disengagement, and less than desirable school performance for diverse students in urban schools, we must help teachers develop dispositions that support learning for all students; and we must prepare teachers who know how to deploy a broad range of culturally and contextually appropriate strategies for meeting the needs of all learners.

A critical focus for modifying any strategy is to expose teachers to critical pedagogies (e.g., critical race theory, critical multiculturalism, cultural responsive and contextually relevant teaching) and then help them discover ways to use this knowledge in transforming praxis (Lensmire, 2012). Teachers, especially those who work in the urban context, need to understand that they will have unique opportunities for using culture, literacy and content as tools to help students (Freire & Macedo, 1987). An important goal is to help the students we teach to see that what they learn in school really could have meaning within the context of their own lives.

Shelton and McDermott (2010) planned workshops to guide urban pre-service teachers (PST) through a process to help them understand the complexity of meaning making. This can be important for teachers who work in diverse urban communities for helping them better understand the life experiences of those unlike themselves. The goal of the project was to engage pre-service teachers in critical thought about diversity, equity, democracy, and power. Using African American children's literature and drama the teachers participated in a procedure that revealed how personal engagement or experience, their cognitive and subconscious processes, and their social and cultural roles, attitudes and perceptions lead to personal meaning construction. Informed by Freirian principles of literacy that include understanding that literacy is a tool for 'reading the word and reading the world' Shelton and McDermott also incorporated Boal's *Theatre of the Oppressed* techniques. Boal (1995) defines *Theater of the Oppressed* as a system of physical exercises, aesthetic games, image techniques and special improvisations which have the objective to protect, develop, and reshape this human vocation, by turning this practice of theater into a meaningful resource for the comprehension of social and personal problems, as well as the search for their solutions.

In my own work with urban preservice teachers, I developed the *culturally and contextually responsive readers' theater* (CCR-RT) approach. The goal is to shed light on how preservice teachers problematized and resolved issues, as they discovered how to develop culturally responsive and contextually relevant literacy and content lessons. The process for teachers consists of four components: *Phase I script development* provides opportunity to discuss culture and context (This initial stage serves as a way for teachers to consider how language and dialect, race and class, locale and circumstance will influence the scripts.); *Phase II literacy extension* during which they identify ways to extend literacy in other areas (reading, writings, or other multiliteracies); *Phase III team debriefing* is used for teachers to "deconstruct" the team building and decision-making process and how they addressed issues of culture and context; and *Phase IV self-analysis/reflection* is the time when the teachers "turn the mirror on themselves" to reexamine their role in the CCR-RT process, how their own attitudes and beliefs about culture and context influenced how they advocated for or against various elements of the script or literacy activities.

With the continued use of the CCR-RT process, I am encouraged that preservice teachers see the project as "motivating and fun," "a way to work through their own language bias and urban stereotypes," "a way to understand how to teach reading," "a chance to do something that's not boring, but fresh," and as "an opportunity to work through their feelings about teaching in the 'hood.'" These future teachers consistently stress the importance of the project for helping them apply theory about language, learning, and culture in developing literacy activities that are relevant in the urban context.

Conclusion

The potential for using culture and the arts to address the various literacy and content area needs of racially and linguistically diverse learners in urban schools is exciting, and thus far, remains underutilized. Active and engaged students learn more. It is my hope that this chapter served as a resource to help you understand culturally responsive and contextually relevant teaching and provided ideas for teaching in an era of accountability and test-consciousness. It is my strong belief that if we continue failing in our efforts to utilize the cultural tools, familial and community resources of students, if we remain indifferent to understanding who and where we teach, if we consider thorny issues that question US commitment to urban schools, then we will become resigned to the opportunity chasm for urban children.

REFERENCES

Achebe, C. (1958). *Things fall apart*. New York, NY: Anchor Books.

Ball, A. F., & Tyson, C. A. (Eds.). (2011). *Studying diversity in teacher education*. Lanham, MD: Rowen & Littlefield.

Barack Obama vs. Mitt Romney Presidential Debates. (2012, October 17). 2012 Presidential Debates. [Video files]. Retrieved from www.youtube/watch?v=QEpCrcMF5Ps

Bender, M. (1988). Suzhou Tanci storytelling in China: Contexts of performance. *Oral Tradition*, *13*(20), 330-376.

Black, T., Forte, K., Roth, J., & Winfrey, O. (Producers). (20007). The great debaters [DVD]. Retrieved from http://thegreatdebatersmovie.com/

Boal, A. (1979). *Theatre of the oppressed*. New York, NY: Theatre Communications Group.

Clapp, E. P., & Edwards, L. A. (Eds.). (2013). Expanding our vision for the arts in education. *Harvard Educational Review*, *83*(1), 5-13.

Clark, R., Morrison, T. D., & Wilcox, B. (2009). Readers' theater: A process for developing fourth-graders reading fluency, *Reading Psychology, 30*, 359-385.

Cruz, B. C., & Thornton, S. J. (2009). *Teaching social studies to English language learners*. New York, NY: Routledge.

Delpit, L. (2012). *Multiplication is for white people: Raising expectations for other people's children*. NY: New Press.

DiPietro R. J. (1987). *Strategic interaction: Learning languages through scenarios*. Cambridge, England: Cambridge University Press.

Egan, K. (1992). *Imagination in teaching andlLearning ages 8-15*. London, England: Routledge.

Gay, G. (2000). *Culturally responsive teaching: Theory, research, and practice*. New York, NY: Teachers College Press.

Freire, P., & Macedo, D. (1987). *Literacy: Reading the word and the world*. Westport, CT: Bergin & Garvey

Grant, R. A. (2011). African American female literacies and the role of double Dutch in the lives and literature of black girls. In V. Yenika-Agbaw & M. Napoli (Eds.) *African and African American children's and adolescent literature in the classroom: A critical guide* (pp. 90-105). Bern, Switzerland: Peter Lang.

Grant. R. A. (2012). Double Dutch as community cultural wealth in the writing of African American middle school girls. *Languages and Linguistics, 29-30,* 15-38.

Grant, R. A., & Asimeng-Boahene, L. (2006). Culturally responsive pedagogy in citizenship education: using African proverbs as tools for teaching in urban schools. *Multicultural Perspectives, 8,* 17-24.

Grant, R. A., & Austin, T. Y. (2013). Literacy and English language learners. In M. H. Haley & T. Y. Austin, T. Y. (Ed.), *Content-based second language teaching and learning* (pp. 194-236). Boston, MA: Pearson.

Haley, M. H. (2009). *Brain-compatible differentiated instruction for English language learners*. New York, NY: Allyn &Bacon.

Hollins, E. R. (2008) *Culture in school learning: Revealing the deep meaning* (2nd ed.). New York, NY: Routledge.

Ibrahim, A. M. (2003). "Whassup, homeboy?" Joining the African diaspora: Black English as asymbolic site of identification and language learning. In S. Makoni, G. Smitherman, A. F. Ball, & A. Spears (Eds.), *Black linguistics: Language, society, and politics in Africa and the Americas* (pp. 169-185). London, England: Routledge.

Ivanic, R. (1998) Writing and identity: *The discoursal construction of identity in academic writing*. Amsterdam: John Benjamins.

Keehan, S., Harmon, J., & Shoho, J. (2008). A study of readers theater in eight grade: Issues of fluency, comprehension, and vocabulary. *Reading & Writing Quarterly, 24*, 335-362.

Kennedy-Nixon Debate. (1960, September 26). Re: Kennedy-Nixon debate. Retrieved from www.jfklibrary.org/Asset-Viewer/

Ladson-Billings, G. (1994). *The dreamkeepers: Successful teachers of African American children*. San Francisco, CA: Jossey-Bass.

Latta, M. M., & Chan, E. (2011). *Teaching the arts to engage English language learners*. New York, NY: Routledge.

Lee, C. D. (2007). *Culture, literacy, and learning: Taking bloom in the midst of the whirlwind.* New York, NY: Teachers College Press.

Lensmire, A. (2012). *White teachers: Stories of fear, violence, and desire.* Lanham, MD: Rowen & Littlefield.

Lincoln-Douglas Debates. (1858, June 16). Retrieved from www.digital history. uh.edu/teachers//lesson_plans/pdfs/unit5_13.pdf

Martinez, M., Roser, N. L., & Strecker, S. (1999). "I never thought I could be a star": A readers' theatre ticket to fluency. *The Reading Teacher, 52,* 326-334.

McCabe, A. (1996). *Chameleon readers: Teaching children to appreciate all kinds of good stories.* New York, NY: McGraw-Hill.

McDonald, N. L., & Fisher, D. (2006). *Teaching literacy through the arts.* New York, NY: Guildford Press.

Nieto, S. (2002). *Language, culture, and teaching: Critical perspectives for a new century.* Mahwah, NJ: Erlbaum.

Pirbhai-Illich, F., Turner, K. C. N., & Austin, T. (2009). Digital technologies in addressing the persistent academic inequities for Aboriginal adolescents' education: A Middle School   Intervention. *Multicultural Education and Technology Journal, 3*(2), 144-162.

Richardson, E. (2003). *African American literacies.* London, England: Routledge

Scheub, H. (1985). A review of African oral traditions and literature. *African Studies Review, 28*(2/3), 1-72.

Shelton, N. R., & McDermott, M. (2010). Using literature and drama to understand social justice. *Teacher Development, 14,* 123-135.

Tierney, R. J., & Readence, J. E. (2000). *Reading strategies and practices: A compendium* (5th ed.) Boston, MA: Allyn & Bacon.

Tyler, B. J., & Chard, D. J. (2000). Using readers theatre to foster fluency in struggling readers: A different twist on the repeated reading strategy. *Reading & Writing Quarterly, 16,* 163-168.

Walker, V. S. (1996). *Their highest potential: An African American school community in the segregated south.* Chapel Hill, NC: The University of North Carolina Press.

Williams, H. A. (2005). *Self-taught: African American education in slavery and freedom.* Chapel Hill, NC: the University of North Carolina Press.

X., Malcolm. (1964, April 3). Re: The ballot or the bullet. Retrieved from www. excahnge.org/multicultrual/speeches/malcolm_x_ballot.html

X., Malcom. (1964, December 3). Re: Oxford union debate. Retrieved from malcomfiles.blogspot.com//oxford-union-debate-december-3-1964.html

CHAPTER 11

LIBATION

Human Ingenuity as a Pedagogical Tool of Dialogic Performance and Competence

Osei Mensah

"(Some) children come to school everyday and have their culture validated and (other) children have theirs invalidated, even berated, daily."

—Linda Darling-Hammond

Introduction

Preparing students to function effectively in this diverse and interconnected world will require students to develop a sense of intercultural awareness and a desire to be proactive as responsible global citizens. The other option will be to encourage and enable students to develop awareness and understanding of others' perspectives, values and attitudes. I therefore, argue that libation could be utilized to develop human ingenuity skills among American students in the United States.

African Traditional and Oral Literature as Pedagogical Tools in Contest Area Classrooms: K-12, pages 201–216
Copyright © 2014 by Information Age Publishing

In an ever-changing diverse and multicultural world, the access to significant concepts from other cultures can promote understanding of cultures, for one's own, and those of others broaden perspectives, and help students appreciate how they are connected with the larger world (Grant & Asimeng-Boahene, 2006). It can be argued that within the aims and objectives of the humanities' curriculum in schools, there are concepts that students must be addressed and integrated into unit and essential questions. These are the big ideas and issues that are necessary for students to retain for years into the future. Libation is one of such powerful concepts that can help students to develop an understanding of key humanities' concepts such as time, place and space, change and global awareness in terms of its social and religious importance.

The purpose of this chapter is first, to examine libation as concept of conversations that communicate gratitude, complaints, rebuke, bargains, and serve as reminders about mutual obligations between God, deities, living dead (or ancestors) on one hand and community members on the other. Second, the discussion focuses on the matter used for libation, the ceremony of libation, instances of libation, and the purpose of libation, its cognitive, religious and social significance. The conceptual framework underpinning this discussion is then presented and finally, samples of classroom activities of how to use libation as teaching tool will be discussed.

Conceptualizing Human Ingenuity and Global Awareness

According to Merriam-Webster Collegiate Dictionary (1998), ingenious means skilled in inventing or thinking out new ideas; curious or clever in design. Ingenuity means cleverness, resourcefulness, being able to think up new and clever solutions to things. The International Baccalaureate Organization describes human ingenuity as much more than the presentation of a product or concept as an example of human achievement. For them, human ingenuity can lead to a reasoned judgment of scientific, ethical, aesthetic, and technological transformations and an appreciation of their consequences. This may result in the celebration of this achievement or the recognition of negative consequences—in many cases, it will lead to both (MYP, 2008). Human ingenuity, therefore, is the sum total of the ingenuity of all people. Human ingenuity has been an agent of creative and innovative involvement of the whole clans and tribe in presenting a holistic view of human activity, both in the past and in the present.

Human Ingenuity in Education

As one of the areas of interaction, human ingenuity in the IB Program encourages students to see the relationships between diverse subjects, as it can be used to inquire into a broad range of human activities. These include systems, communication, thought, art, and culture, rituals and customs (MYP, 2008). In the classroom context and for the purpose of our discourse, human ingenuity provides students with opportunities to explore the very nature of the subject disciplines themselves. It can prepare them for the demands made by courses such as the theory of knowledge in all academic pursuits. Ingenuity students develop creative thinking while working on projects. Original works are created as a means of expression and students develop cultural understanding and global awareness. Students also contribute to project teams to learn the importance of teamwork, communication, and collaboration when assigned tasks and how to work successfully as a team.

Conceptual Framework

To contextualize the issues to be discussed in this discourse, critical race theory, post colonial theory and culturally relevant pedagogy will be discussed as a way of highlighting the theoretical underpinnings that inform this discourse. Postcolonialism is a postmodern theory which focuses on reactions to, and analysis of the cultural legacies of colonialism. According to Loomba (1998), postcolonialism comprises a set of theories found amongst philosophy, film, political science, human geography, sociology, feminism, religious and theological studies, and literature. The ultimate goal of postcolonialism is overcoming the enduring the vestiges of colonialism on cultures. It is concerned with recouping past worlds and learning how the world can move beyond this period together, towards a place of mutual respect. Postcolonialist thinkers recognize that many of the assumptions which underlie the "logic" of colonialism are still active forces today (Schwarz & Sangeeta, 2000). The introduction of Christianity saw concerted attacks on indigenous cultural practices including the pouring of the libation which were regarded as heathen and idol worshipping by the invading colonialists, masquerading as missionaries (Assimeng, 1989; Baffoe, 2005). The debate about Christians' negative attitude towards libation still persists. African theologians such as Pobee (1977) are determined to have their traditional cultures given the respect they have always deserved by drawing out the areas of continuity between past and present religions. Sarpong (2010) has suggested a middle ground by proposing that Christians could invoke saints instead of deities during libations.

Critical Race Theory

Ladson-Billings and Tate (1995) introduced critical race theory (CRT) to education and explained how using CRT as a conceptual framework could be applied to our understanding of educational inequity. CRT focuses on the ongoing adverse impact of racism and how institutional racism privileges Whites in education while disadvantaging racial minorities. Other writers like (DeCuir & Dixson, 2004) assert that, the notion of the permanence of racism suggests that racist hierarchical structures govern all political, economic, and social domains. Such structures allocate the privileging of Whites and the subsequent "othering" of people of color in all arenas, including education.

As indicated above, Christian missionaries denigrated libations, as was their attitude with many other traditional practices. The tension between Christian beliefs and libation ideology has persisted since. In light of this, the discussion of the cognitive, religious and social significance of libation in other cultures will go a long way to combat stereotypical thinking and enhance cross-cultural awareness and communication. CRT places particular importance on the voices and experiences of people of color; their insights into the operation of racism and their understanding of being racially minoritized (Delgado, 1989). Such accounts sometimes take the form of storytelling or counternarrative, a tenet of CRT, and may be semiautobiographical or allegorical in nature. As a tool, story-telling can act as a powerful means of enabling racially minoritized groups to "speak back" about racism and facilitate a means for psychological and spiritual empowerment in response to the depleting effects of racism (Tate, 1997). CRT scholars are not making up stories: they are constructing narratives out of the historical, sociocultural, and political realities of their lives and those of people of color (Ladson-Billings, 2006). Similarly, Akan (Ghana) libations are full of stories, oral histories, proverbs, similes, and metaphors and these poetic devices can be utilized in libation as a persuasive and transformative tool to make political commentary on issues in the Akan (Ghana) societies without fear of consequences.

Culturally Relevant Pedagogy

Culturally relevant pedagogy is based on the theory that the learning process relies on social interaction and is related to students' cultural experiences. Lev Vygotsky (1978) argued that learning is socially mediated and occurs when students participate in culturally meaningful activities with the assistance of someone who is more competent than they are. Vygotsky's sociocultural theory acknowledges the importance of culture in the teaching and learning. A culturally relevant pedagogy builds on the premise that how people are expected to go about learning may differ across cultures (Villegas & Lucas, 2002). In order to maximize learning opportunities, "teachers must gain knowledge of the cultures represented in their classrooms, then translate this knowledge into instructional practice" (p. 22). However, student achievement is not the only purpose of a culturally relevant pedagogy. Teachers must also assist students to change the society not simply to exist or survive in it. As more and more students from diverse backgrounds populate 21st century classrooms, and efforts mount to identify effective methods to teach these students, the need for pedagogical approaches that are culturally responsive intensifies. Today's classrooms require teachers to educate students varying in culture, language, abilities, and many other characteristics (Gollnick & Chinn, 2002).

Price-Williams and Ramirez (1971) and Hillard (1992) have indicated that we tend to view environment as a whole rather than parts. This presupposes an affirmation of ideological hegemony, racism, sexism, and other forms of social domination and intolerance in our curricula. But curriculum making should incorporate the sociocultural contexts of subject matter. This leads to the realization that multiple perspectives on truth exist. As the world is becoming a global village we need to embrace other cultures with rich and alternative paradigms. This why I think libation is a good resource for human ingenuity. It is for these reasons that the issues raised by critical race and postcolonial theories as well as culturally relevant pedagogy strengthen our rationale for using libation as a pedagogical tool for enhancing human ingenuity.

Akan (Ghana) Libation as a Case Study

Of the major types of rituals in Akan society, libation is one of the most important. The term "libation" is derived from the Latin word *"Libare"* which means "to take a portion," "to taste" Sarpong (2010). Libation is essentially a drink offering; pouring out of a small quantity of a wine, milk or other liquid as a ceremonial act. The Akan word for libation in general is *Nsaguo*, word made up of two words, *nsa* (a drink), *gu* (to pour). There are two other words *Mpae* or *Mpaebo* or *Mpaeyie* mean praying. Any kind of liquid is used for libation. These include water, palm wine, European imported drink, both soft and strong, schnapps, whisky, rum, beer and gin. Libation involves the pouring of the liquid and the invocation of the Supreme Being or the *"abosom"* (gods) or the *"nsamanfo"* (ancestors/living dead) which accompany the act of pouring.

The procedure begins with the libator if he is a man removes any headgear he may have on, lowers his cloth a little from his shoulders to mid-body and also removes his sandals. S/he then takes his right hand a calabash or a cup or a glass containing the liquid. The libator invokes the spirit of the Supreme Being (***Onyankopon***), mother earth (***Asaase Yaa***) and pours some of the liquid on the ground. The libator continues with the invocation of the national or household gods, the spirits of the ancestors a special request asking them to come and drink, those spirits believed to be hovering around the place, pouring a little of the liquid at the end of each invocation and addressing to each. At the end of the invocations and prayers, he empties the calabash completely on the ground. He puts on his sandals, dresses up and retires to the group saying "I have discharged the task" and the group answers' "Well done." During the ceremony, the group throws in at different intervals, words expressing approval or giving assent to what is being prayed for and at times even gives the libator suggestions and reminders of what to add. The contents of the prayer depend on the purpose or occasion on which the libation is poured.

Adjaye (2004) classifies the occasions of libation into three categories: obligatory, preferred, and optional. The obligatory or mandatory are those times that tradition demands that the ancestors be invoked or propitiated. Instances in this category are the ritual calendrical days such as **Odwira, Adae**, all ***"da bone"*** (bad days) days, annual festivals, child naming, marriage, installation and destoolment of chiefs and queen mothers and war times (Sarpong, 2010; Owusu, 2010; Pobee, 1977).

The second category includes meetings of elders, the welcoming and bidding farewell of important visitors, the construction of schools, in times of crisis such as famine, droughts, wildfires, natural disasters and inexplicable family calamities, before a journey and on returning home from a journey, after a long absence, the arrival of an important guest, the beginning of the building or any enterprise (Owusu, 2000). Third, because libations are forms of prayer they may be performed at any gathering, even private, involving two or more people as a way of asking for blessings and other favors for he intended recipients (Mbiti, 1969; Sarpong, 2010).

Although the libationary prayer varies depending on the occasion, the prayer seems to follow a certain pattern. First is the invocation of the person or persons to whom the libation is being offered. These are the Supreme Being, the national deities or local deities, the ancestors, the good dead chiefs and the dead person. Second is the reason or the occasion for the assembly and for the pouring of the libation. Third is the supplication or petition which has occasioned the pouring of the libation. The next aspect is the general prayer for common blessings and favors for all members of the family or community both present and absent. Finally, the libator asks those addressed at the very beginning of the libation to receive the drink and the remains of the drink in the calabash or glass is poured onto the ground (Assimeng, 1989; Sarpong, 2010).

Akan Libation: Dialogic of Performance and Competence

As part of the need to increase multicultural collaboration, intercultural communicative competence is now generally seen as an overarching goal in foreign language education. It involves essentially a capacity for encountering cultural diversity in intercultural communication between people coming from different sociocultural settings. It also emphasizes the importance of being able to critically reflect on one's cultural identity and values and to develop an awareness of the complex relationships between language, society and cultural meanings (Byram, 2003). I believe libation through human ingenuity can be utilized in the classroom to emphasize the importance of cultural identity and diversity.

An analysis of Akan libation indicates that it is a coded verbal performance which is formalized, coordinated poetic enactment (Adjaye, 2004). It is quite different from ordinary, everyday speech. The libator plays with words and invokes a number of great spirit of the sky (*Onyankopon*), mother earth (*Asaase Yaa*), national or household gods, and the spirit of ancestors and those spirits believed to be hovering around the place. The prayer involves address to each a special request asking them to come and drink through the application of rich and witty interplay of verbal resources, competence in the complex Akan system of metaphysical thought, and familiarity with the contextual situations. The officiant through his/her ingenuity makes a conscious effort to carry his/her audience along with his utterances to get them emotionally charged. S/he does this by eliciting or stimulating the spontaneous responses from participants. The group throws in, at different intervals, words expressing approval or giving assent to what was being prayed for and at times even gives the libator suggestions and reminders of what more to add. With the assistant leading the way, any member of the audience can interject interlocutory responses such as *sio* or *wiee* (both meaning "yes" and *amp*a (true). What comes out of the coded verbal performance of libation is human ingenuity of the Akan using critical thinking and analytical skills. These are skills that can be utilized and encouraged in our classroom instructional delivery (Asimeng-Boahene, 2010). Libation performance is, therefore, not only agent centered but also, it reveals the active participation of the audience as a knowledgeable group even if their participation is minimal (Adjaye, 2004; Owusu, 2000; Sarpong, 2010).

Libation is considered as a component of distinctive frames or units, that is, subtexts, each of which can be rendered extractable for effective discourse analysis (Owusu, 2000). The context of libation indicates where two sets of experiential engagements intersect: one from a cultural perspective about the nature of human relations with the invisible forces of the spiritual world, the other derived from ability and the oratorical skills of the performer to stimulate the spontaneous reaction of the audience (Adjaye, 2004). The traditional Ghanaian does not compartmentalize the world into a natural and a supernatural world. Life after death is, for him, in a world closely continuous with the present one; and our departed ancestors are conceived still to be participating members of their families. The pouring of libation is, accordingly, intended as an invitation to them to come and take part in important undertakings of the living and to grant them their propitious auspices.

Competence: Who Pours Libation?

An important component of libations is competence. Using Chicano case studies, Briggs (1988) demonstrated that "competence" is judged differently in different genres, such as historical discourses, proverbs, religious performances, legends, and prayers. Similarly, the Akan libation requires competence in Akan worldview, especially knowledge of national, local or household deities, knowledge of family, lineage, and clan history and genealogy. Familiarity with the former enables him to invoke the appropriate gods and goddesses whereas the knowledge of the latter endows him with the ability to call on the relevant ancestors and address them by their appropriate appellations. The prayer part of libation calls upon an individual's rhetorical skill and creativity in the use of the *Twi* language. Prayers in any libation consist of metaphors, proverbs and many other figurative expressions. Libation needs no specialists. However, since the libation ritual is basically religious, individuals who are articulate in the *Twi* language and culture perform elaborate libation because they possess the necessary understanding of the Akan belief system. This explains why during ceremonial occasions the chiefs, the linguists, priests, priestesses and the elders, the key Akan traditional bearers would be excellent in the performance of libation than would others (who are less conversant with Akan tradition) in an informal situation (Owusu, 2000). Generally, men and women can pour libation but it is generally performed by grown-ups. On public occasions, it is usually done by men or linguists or official spokesmen rather than women. Normally, libation is poured by the head of the family or clan, senior male members of the royal family or the duly appointed master of ceremonies or a traditional priest. These people are expected to be people who command social, political, economic, and religious respect in the community.

The libator should be able to move the performance. He must be able to control the flow of the performance. His oration must be such as to inspire, legitimize, recreate, reaffirm, question, or provoke cross-contextual associations in the minds of the audience. In addition to content knowledge, libators require linguistic competence. The libator is likely to impress the audience if he commands the ability to render his invocation at a high energy level in a continuous flow, except at the end of appropriate frames, where he pauses for dramatic effect. Again the libator uses his ingenuity to mesmerize their listeners and make them captive by identifying key questions and problem issues of the family, community and tribe.

Rationale for Infusing Libation Into Concepts of Human Ingenuity for Minority Students

North American classrooms have become culturally and ethnically diverse, but the teaching population has originated from European American, and suburban experiences. Most current and future teachers have not had sustained relationships with people from different ethnic, cultural and lower socioeconomic backgrounds (www.centerforpubliceducation. org). As a result much of their knowledge about diversity has been shaped by media stereotypes. School curriculum, methods and materials usually represent European-America or White culture and ignore the backgrounds and experiences of students and families from lower socioeconomic levels and different ethnic and cultural backgrounds. Many teacher programs do not adequately prepare teachers for culturally relevant pedagogy. When cultural differences are ignored in the classroom, students' fears and alienation increase. Consequently, this disconnect has become a national problem whose influence has been linked to poor literacy development and high dropout rates among students from urban and rural poverty areas (Schmidt, 2003). That being said, the biggest obstacle to successful culturally responsive instruction for most educators is disposing of their own cultural biases and learning about the backgrounds of the students that they will be teaching.

According to Ladson-Billings (1995), an important criterion for culturally relevant teaching is nurturing and supporting competence in both home and school cultures. Teachers should use the students' home cultural experiences as a foundation upon which to develop knowledge and skills. Content learned in this way is more significant to the students and facilitates the transfer of what is learned in school to real-life situations (Padron, Waxman, & Rivera, 2002). The processes necessary for preparing to teach in a culturally responsive classroom can be broken down into three general categories: exploring one's own culture, learning about other cultures, and learning about students' cultures. This explains why some progressive scholars are championing the cause of indigenous pedagogies such as storytelling, proverbs, riddles, myths, and legends (Kubow, 2007; wa Thiong'o, 1986).

There is the need for a classroom environment where students will receive equal opportunities, and to achieve their full potential regardless of race, gender, economic status, and ability; also a need for an educational setting where, prejudice reduction will prevail and content will be infused with examples, and histories from wide range of cultural groups. Moll and some other scholars (see Moll, Ananti, Neff, & Gonzalez, 1992; Moll & Greensburg, 1990) using cultural responsive teaching have established that by capitalizing on household and other community resources the quality of classroom instruction can be enhanced. The significant aspect of the two paradigms is the fact that teaching is used to promote racial, ethnic, linguistic and economic equality for all students (Grant & Asimeng-Boahene, 2006). Moreover, learning is a socially mediated process (Goldstein, 1999; Vygotsky, 1978).

To implement the above models, human ingenuity skills need to be utilized in the classroom situation. With human ingenuity, students can inquire into subject content and reflect on the ingenuity of humans from various perspectives. We advocate the use of concept libation in promoting ingenuity skills of diverse students in North American classroom because of its oral arts and because it is one of the most important of the major types of rituals in African societies. This cultural practice of pouring libation is deeply rooted in the African psyche and it is a strong is belief system that most African families, even among sophisticated urban Christians, continue to pour libation during the rites of passage.

Example of Libation: Libation and Oral Traditional Histories

The following examples taken from oral traditional histori as enunciated by Owusu (2000), will illustrate the meaning of certain aspects of libation in the Akan oral narrative. For example, history is extremely important in the libation performance. Genealogies and events are sometimes recited in the prayer in order to make the audience ready for the history about to be narrated after the libation

Twi Text

1. *Nana Dwaa Hemaa*
2. *Begye nsa nom o*
3. *Wo ne wotwa kwan yi, ne wode mma ne mmanana yi nyinaa beware Hene Ameyaw Kwakye.*
4. *Se enne dadua yi a, yegyina ha seisei.*
5. *Asem nnee aba ne se, enne, Abrofo besi fam he, bia mpaninnsem he, bemma no nyera.*
6. *Esese nee bia wokyerekyere wo mpanninsem.*
7. *Woduru Amanfoso a, na wakae yaanom,*
8. *Mebo Nananom ho din no, wayo me awerehosem, wayo me anibresern.*
9. *Me ne me mma ne me mmananamon, a wonnim nyinaa ate.*
10. *Ne seisei wayo beya*
11. *Se nee nka tumii yewo, ne nneema (nnooma) nca: eye a, ma oko baee, nneema he asee he nyinaa, yekeka enti wama waha ye.*
12. *Nti mebo din saa he, esese mema ho nsa nom.*
13. *Woabegye nsa anom, Amanfoo: Wie! Mmo ne kasa.*

English Translation

1. Nana Dwaa Hemaa (Name of the Aduana Queen mother).
2. Come and drink wine.
3. It was you who travelled with the children and the grandchildren to marry King Kwakye Ameyaw.
4. Today we are present here.
5. What has happened is that, when the white men came, they did not want anyone's history to be left out.
6. It is the duty of everyone to tell his/her history.
7. When I reached a ruin of the ancestors, I remembered my people.
8. When I mentioned the elders' name, this has made me sad, this has made me distressed.
9. My children and my grandchildren, those who do not know have heard it.
10. They are now worried.
11. That the power we had and the things we had destroyed during the war are all mentioned, and this makes them worried.
12. Therefore when I mention your name, I must give you wine to drink.
13. Come and get wine and drink. Audience: Amen! Well done for talking.

Apart from the above libation's emphasis on oral traditional histories it reveals its poetic devices demonstrating the use of simile, metaphors, and stanzas and rhyming.

The Significance of Libation

Analysis of libation shows the human ability to adapt to and work with an environment, and the desire for Akans to explain their environment. Libation through human ingenuity finds expression in the following:

- The Akans have reacted and dealt with health and social issues in the past (Assimeng, 1989; Sarpong, 1974).
- The Akans address moral issues regarding health and social values and ways in which they deal with them (Assimeng, 1989; Pobee, 1977).
- They express the belief in God the Supreme Being (Assimeng, 1989).
- The belief of the people in the deities/gods and the ancestors and shows their dependence on these supernatural powers (Assimeng, 1989; Hammond-Tooke, 1989; Mbiti, 1969; Ngubane, 1977).
- The relationship between the Supreme Being on one hand and the ancestors and divinities on the other (Pobee, 1977; Sarpong, 2010; Ngubane, 1977).
- Libation tells us that the specific messages conveyed to the ancestors, the deities and other supernatural (Malefijt, 1968; Ngubane, 1977).
- Libation brings about unity and brotherliness (Mbiti, 1969; Sarpong, 1974).
- Libation performances serve as a binding factor, linking those alive with those in the ancestral world (Adjaye, 2004; Sarpong 2010).
- They indirectly teach the virtues of friendship and hospitality (Adjaye, 2004; Sarpong, 1974; Owusu, 2000; Sarpong, 2010).
- Most importantly, libation gives a sense of security and confidence in the officiants (Hammond-Tooke, 1989; Ngubane, 1977).
- In contemporary times libation is poured to project the Ghanaian personality since many state functions begin with the pouring of libation (Sarpong, 2010).
- Libation is an aspect of community and service since it touches on identity and indirectly organizes individual and groups (Mbiti, 1969; Ngubane, 1977).

- Proverbs, similes and other traditional metaphors are embedded in libations which help to give meaning to performance (Adjaye, 2004; Sarpong, 2010).

Sample Instructional Libation Activities

a.   Educators could develop concept maps in their integrated units around universal themes of libation.

b.   Teachers with their students could create a gallery of pictures/ photos, posters and audio that will continue to be added to as resources become available. In this situation, teachers could act as guides, mediators, consultants, instructors, and advocates for the students, helping to effectively connect their culturally- and community-based knowledge to the classroom learning experiences.

c.   Teachers and students could embark on the collection of examples (libation poured) by chiefs, linguists, traditional healers, head of families, and so forth. Here, teachers could act as guides, mediators, consultants, instructors, and advocates for the students, helping to effectively connect their culturally, and community-based knowledge to the classroom learning experiences. Teachers should use the students' home cultural experiences as a foundation upon which to develop knowledge and skills.

d.   Students could interview their parents or members of their community who have knowledge about libation and compile a report to share out with class.

e.   Families could be encouraged to support the teaching and learning of oral literature as a communication tool by discussing the importance of libation and their experiences and knowledge of the concept.

f.   Guests (chiefs/traditional leaders, adults/head of families and traditional healers in the diaspora could be invited to give presentations/talks to class. To maximize learning opportunities, teachers should gain knowledge of the cultures represented in their classrooms and adapt lessons so that they reflect ways of communicating and learning that are familiar to the students.

g.   Students could be assigned differentiated Group and Individual projects to research aspects on libation. Learning is a socially mediated process (Goldstein, 1999; Vygotsky, 1978). Through this children develop cognitively by interacting with both adults and more knowledgeable peers. These interactions allow students to hypothesize, experiment with new ideas, and receive feedback (Darling-Hammond, 1997).

h.   Students could write a letter to a friend about libation poured during a naming, burial, or marriage ceremony s/he witnessed in his/
her community.

Conclusion

The chapter examined the act of libation which contains a rich mixture
of religious, social, and cultural ingredients which can be utilized as tools
for enhancing ingenuity among diverse students in social studies education. Again, we argued that the use of libation can provide an equity, content integration, and knowledge construction. The article drew on postcolonial and critical race theories as well as culturally responsive pedagogy
to justify the principles for teachers to develop a meaningful curriculum.
This helps to promote prejudice reduction, content integration, equity
pedagogy, and influence of sociocultural histories of other communities
besides the dominant culture. We are of the view that the existing structures of curriculum and instruction promote feelings of ethnocentrism,
hegemony, and devalue other world cultures. It is our belief that libation
as a powerful cultural pedagogical tool can help foster intercultural understanding in North American classroom.

REFERENCES

Adjaye, J. A. (2004). *Boundaries of self and other in Ghanaian popular culture.* Westport: Praeger.
Assimeng, M. (1989). *Religion and social change in West Africa: An introduction to the
sociology of religion.* Accra, Ghana: Ghana Universities Press.
Asimeng-Boahene, L. (2010). Educational wisdom of African oral Literature: Afri-
can proverbs as vehicles for enhancing critical thinking skills in social stud-
ies. *International Journal of Pedagogies and Learning, 5*(3), 59-69.
Baffoe, M. (2005). *Demonizing African culture in the name of Christianity, Crusade
watch.* Montreal, Quebec: Black Studies Center.
Bell, D. (1992). *Faces at the bottom of the well: The permanence of racism.* New York, NY:
Basic Books.
Byram, M. (Ed.). (2003). Intercultural competence. Strasbourg, France: Council of
Europe Publishing.
Briggs, C. (1988). *Competence in performance: The creativity of tradition in Mexicano
verbal art.* Philadelphia, PA: University of Pennsylvania Press. Retrieved from
www.centerforpubliceducation.org
Darling-Hammond, L. (1997). *The right to learn: A blueprint for creating schools that
work.* San Francisco, CA: Jossey-Bass.

DeCuir, J. T., & Dixson, A. D. (2004). "So when it comes out, they aren't surprised that it is there": Using critical race theory as a tool of analysis of race and racism in education. *Educational Researcher, 33*(5), 26-31.

Delgado, R. (1989). Storytelling for oppositionists and others: A plea for narrative, *Michigan Law Review, 87,* 2411-2441.

Goldstein, L. (1999). The relational zone: The role of caring relationships in the co-construction of mind. *American Educational Research Journal, 36*(3), 647-673.

Gollnick, D. M., & Chinn, P. C. (2002). *Multicultural education in a pluralistic society* (6th ed.). Upper Saddle River, NJ: Pearson Education.

Grant, R. A., & Asimeng-Boahene, L. (2006). Culturally responsive pedagogy in citizenship education: Using African Proverbs as tools for teaching in Urban Schools. *Multicultural Perspectives, 8*(4), 17-24.

Hammond-Tooke, D. (1989). Rituals and medicines. *Indigenous healing in South Africa.* Johannesburg: Ad Danker.

Hilliard, A. (1992). Africentrism and multiculturalism. *The Journal of Negro Education, 61*(3), 370-377.

Kubow, P. K. (2007). Teachers' constructions of democracy: intersections of Western and indigenous knowledge in South Africa and Kenya. *Comparative Education Review, 51*(3), 307-328.

Ladson-Billings, G. (1995). But that's just good teaching! The case for culturally relevant pedagogy. *Theory into Practice, 34*(3), 159-165.

Ladson-Billings, G. (2006). From the achievement gap to the education debt: Understanding achievement in U.S. Schools. *Educational Researcher, 35*(7), 3-12.

Ladson-Billings, G., & Tate, W. F. (1995). Towards a critical race theory of education. *Teachers College Record, 97,* 47-68.

Loomba M. (1998). *Colonialism/post-colonialism.* New York, NY: Routledge.

Malefijt, A. (1968). *Religion and culture.* New York, NY: Macmillan.

Mbiti, J. S. (1969). *African religions and philosophy.* London, England: Heinemann.

Ingenious. (1998). In *Merriam-Webster's Collegiate Dictionary.* (1998). Retrieved from http://www.merriam-webster.com/dictionary/ingenious

Moll, L. C., Amanti, C., Neff, D., & Gonzalez, N. (1992). Funds of knowledge for teaching: Using a qualitative approach to connect homes and classrooms. *Theory into Practice, 32*(2), 132-141.

Moll, L. C., & Greensburg, J. (1990). Creating zones of possibilities: Combining social context for instruction. In L.C. Moll (Ed.), *Vygotsky, and education* (pp. 318-348). Cambridge, England: Cambridge University Press.

MYP: From Principles into Practice. (2008). *Humanities subject guide teacher support material: International Bacalaurete Organization.* Chippenham, England: Antony Rowe.

Ngubane, H. (1977). *Body and mind in Zulu medicine: Ethnography of health and disease in Nyuswa Zulu thought and practice.* London, England: Academic Press.

Owusu, B. (2000). Libation in highlife songs. *Research Review New Series, 16*(1), 39-57.

Padron, Y. N., Waxman, H. C., & Rivera, H. H. (2002). Educating Hispanic students: Effective instructional practices (Practitioner Brief #5). Retrieved from http://www.cal.org/crede/Pubs/PracBrief5.htm

Pobee, J. (1977). *Towards an African theology.* Nashville, TN: Abingdon.

Price-Williams, D. R., & Ramirez, M. (1971). Cognitive styles of children of three ethnic groups in the United States. *Indian Educational Review, 6,* 67-68.

Sarpong, P. (2010). *Libation.* Kumasi, Ghana: Good Shepherd.

Schmidt, P. R. (2003). *Culturally relevant pedagogy: A study of successful in service.* Paper presented at the annual meeting of the National Reading Conference, Scottsdale, AZ.

Schwarz, H., & Schwarz . Eds). (2000). *A companion to postcolonial studies: A historical introduction.* Malden, MA: Blackwell.

Tate, W. F. (1997). Critical race theory and education: history, theory and implications. *Review of Research in Education, 22*(1), 195-247.

Villegas, A. M., & Lucas, T. (2002). Preparing culturally responsive teachers: Rethinking the curriculum. *Journal of Teacher Education, 53*(1), 20-43.

Vygotsky, L. S. (1978). *Mind in society: The development of higher psychological processes* (M. Cole, V. John-Steiner, S. Scribner, & E. Souberman, Eds. and Trans.). Cambridge: MA: Harvard University.

wa Thiong'o, N. (1986). *Decolinizing the mind, politics of language in African Literature.* Oxford, England: James Currey.

CHAPTER 12

STORYTELLING AMONG THE VEEKUHANE OF CHOBE (BOTSWANA)

Social Justice, Pedagogy, and Vision 2016

Ndana Ndana and Joyce T. Mathangwane

Perhaps it is in the folktales or fables—stories centered on animals and other beings and not related to any historical events—that we have the clearest example of oral literature designed to teach specific lessons of behavior.

—Okpewho (1992, p. 117)

So why do I say story is chief among his fellows? The same reason I think that our people sometimes will give the name Nkolika to their daughters— Recalling-Is-Greatest. Why? Because it is only the story that can continue beyond the war and the warrior. It is the story that outlives the sound of war-drums and exploits of brave fighters. It is the story, not others, that saves our progeny from blundering like blind beggars into the spikes of the cactus fence. The story is our escort; without it, we are blind. Does the blind man own the escort? No, neither do we the story; rather it is the story that owns us and directs us.... The story is everlasting.... Like fire, when it is not blazing it is smouldering under its own ashes or sleeping and resting inside its flint-house.

—Achebe (1987, p. 124)

African Traditional and Oral Literature as Pedagogical Tools in Contest Area Classrooms: K-12, pages 217–231

217

The continent has its own fictive traditions; it has the tradition of story, narrated orally ... the medium through which Africa down the centuries has bared its soul, taught its (people) and entertained itself

—Ogutu and Roscoe (1974)

Introduction

In this chapter, we explore storytelling among the Veekuhane of Botswana in general, and more specifically, we wish to highlight the pedagogical potential of these narratives/stories in transmitting cultural ideas to children in an obviously mutlilingual and multicultural educational environment. More important, we also wish to stress the promotion of diversity and social justice in a world that is increasingly conflicted and polarized, due in part to the poor management and opportunistic manipulation of cultural pluralism. The case of Rwanda readily comes to mind. Put differently, in using a sample of Veekuhane narratives, the chapter seeks to show how these stories could be deployed in promoting social justice in line with the country's Vision 2016 Pillars of a moral and tolerant; safe and secure; compassionate, just and caring; and a united and proud nation (Presidential Task Force, 1997).

Using ideas from social justice, the chapter posits that narratives are one of the many tools schools can use as a starting point for children to begin to appreciate the multicultural reality of their existence and subsequently its complex dynamics. The chapter is organized as follows: we begin by justifying the choice of stories and then sketch out the theoretical background in which we highlight Botswana's language situation and how it departs from the basic tenets of social justice and its Vision 2016. We then analyze two stories to show how their teaching could be explored for the inauguration of a more tolerant and united nation.

Why Stories?

The question we are posing is why stories, and not poetry or proverbs? The choice of stories does not in any way suggest that these other genres are any less appropriate. To appreciate the choice, definitions are a good starting point. Variously known as narratives, tales, folktales, Miruka (1994) defines a story as "a prose account of people, events, places etc that may be factual or fictional" (p. 134). Implied in this definition is that human beings are not only the creators of stories, but also important actors in such tales. Human life is therefore one huge narrative to which individual narratives are conjoined and derived. As an account of people, events and places, narratives tend to be readily accessible, common, simple and therefore daily experiences and available to various sections of society without the attendant linguistic complexities found in say proverbs, idioms and riddles. For example, students sitting in a class and chanting mathematical tables are creating and participating in a narrative they will remember to varying degrees and subsequently relate to their peers and progeny. It is on the basis of their "simplicity," availability, accessibility and appeal (through fantasy and make-believe) that stories, either recorded or oral, were chosen as an appropriate means in educating and shaping young minds for social justice enroute to a tolerant nation. As Okpewho (1992) suggests, "perhaps it is in the folktales or fables—stories centered on animals and other beings and not related to any historical events—that we have the clearest example of oral literature designed to teach specific lessons of behavior" (p. 117).

Methodology

The data used in this chapter is collected from two collections. In total, two stories were selected for this analysis. One of the stories is from Jacottet's (1899) compilation, a least known, yet one of the earliest known attempts to document Chiikuhane folktales. The other one is from another collection which was recorded by Mr. Kabisa, a Mosotho who was in charge of Munga Primary School located about 10 kilometers west of Kachikau in the Chobe District, in the 1930s. He collected Chiikuhane/Subiya texts at the instruction of the then director of education, Mr. Dumbrell. Consequently, this chapter is a symbolic journey to some of the key moments in the evolution of Chiikuhane scholarship.

Theoretical Background

For sometime, Botswana has been theorized, rather uncritically, as a monolingual edifice, leading to what is known as the "homogeneity thesis" (Boikhutso, 2009). It was Botswana's presumed homogeneity some scholars had posited, that was responsible for its economic success comparable only to the Asian tigers of Japan and South Korea. Such economic success resulted in Botswana being labeled the "African Miracle" (Thumberg-Hartland, 1978). However, the reality is that from as far as human memory could recall, Botswana has been multilingual and therefore multiracial and multicultural with close to "38 indigenous languages from the Bantu and Khoesan families" (Mtenje, 2008 p. 25; Miti, 2008; Mooko, 2006; Nyati-Ramahobo, 2008a). The origin of this diversity is a matter of historical conjecture. Further, the demographics of this multiracialism are equally conjectural owing to the reluctance of government to collect data on ethnic affiliation via the national census. The last censuses to do so were the 1936 and 1946 (Schapera, 1952). Since then, questions regarding ethnic affiliation are at best treated with skepticism and suspected to be tribalistic, and therefore potentially divisive to the envisaged united nation of postindependent Botswana.

As a multilingual nation, Botswana is an excellent example of what Pratt (1991) refers to as contact zones. These are "social spaces where cultures meet, clash, and grapple with each other, often in contexts of highly asymmetrical relations of power, such as colonialism, slavery, or their aftermaths as they are lived out in many parts of the world today" (p. 35). Contact zones are thus areas of intense activity, energy and vitality leading to such processes as "autoethnography, transculturation, critique, collaboration, bilingualism, mediation, parody, denunciation, imaginary dialogue, vernacular expression" (p. 37). In contact zones that Botswana is, the various languages and cultures engage in complex and subtle relationships which would manifest in, for example, autoethnography in which people attempt to describe themselves in a manner that embrace representations others have made of them. It is also includes a process of transculturation in which members of subordinated or marginal groups select and invent from materials transmitted by a dominant or metropolitan culture and collaboration in which they act in unison to create a national culture. Each culture therefore produces its own autoethnographic texts with which to claim a space as its contribution or reaction to national or global cultures.

It should be a given therefore that in a multicultural context, the acknowledgement, recognition, appreciation and preservation of all cultures should both in theory and practice be democratic and human rights imperatives and a condition *sine qua non* in nurturing social justice. According to Asimeng-Boahene (2010), social justice is "the idea of a just society that gives individuals and groups fair treatment and just share of the benefits of society" (p. 135). He quotes Longan (1999 p. 19), as follows:

> A socially just society guarantees people who are able to exercise fair entitlement and obligation in the course of their living. Its members are concerned with treating other people in the way that they themselves want to be treated. It is about ensuring a fair go for everyone. (as cited in Asimeng-Boahene 2010, p. 435)

In Africa and Botswana in particular, fairness, tolerance, equality, peace and justice, all tenets of social justice, are central to our value system. They are so central that they are part of the human imagination and the subjects of various tales, proverbs and idioms. For example, among the Vekuhane, the proverb **"masiwa a vambeene ka a vulyi kulyi gunka,"** literally, "tripods next to one another will always rub against each other", is used to encourage people to always expect differences from one another and thus fostering tolerance and patience. Similarly, in Setswana, *"Mafoko a kgotla a mantle otlhe"* (all words at a community gathering are "good," encourages respect and tolerance for divergent opinions.

In general, there is consensus that Botswana is indeed democratic. Molutsi (2005) considers Botswana and Mauritius as "among the oldest and stable democracies with an impressive economic growth and overall development" (p. 14). Evidence of its democratic credentials includes the holding of elections every 5 years and operating a multiparty system (Nyati-Ramahobo, 2008b). However, there is concern that some of Botswana's laws "permit discrimination on the basis of ethnicity, language and culture" (p. 3). These laws are: "a) Sections 77 to 79, 15 (4) (d), 15 (a) of the Constitution; b) Sections 2 of the Chieftainship Act and c) the Tribal Territories Act" (p. 3). Sections 77-79 establish the House of Chiefs and its composition as follows: 8 ex-officio, 4 elected, and 3 specially elected. The ex-officio members of the House of Chiefs shall be such persons as are for the time being performing the functions of the office of Chief in respect of the Bakgatla, Bakwena, Bamalete, Bamangwato, Bangwaketse, Barolong, Batawana, and Batlokwa Tribes, respectively. The elected members of the House of Chiefs shall be elected from among their own number by the persons for the time being performing the functions of the office of Sub-Chief in the Chobe, North East, Ghanzi and Kgalagadi districts, respectively (*Constitution of Botswana*). The contention from marginalized groups was that these sections discriminated against them by denying their chiefs permanent membership to the House. The review resulted in the Bogosi Act of 2008 which although increased the number of the members to "from 15 to a maximum of 37" (Nyati-Ramahobo, 2008b, p. 2), the discrimination remains very much in place because only Chiefs from the eight Tswana-speaking tribes retain permanent membership and the others have to be elected every 5 years.

The effect of these laws, (Nyati-Ramahobo, 2008b) contends, is to soil what has been largely an impressive international showing characterized by the rule of law, regular elections, and stable political environment. The impact of these laws on the marginalized groups are manifest, ranging from political, economic and psychological manifestations of "regional economic disparities and poverty; imposition of chiefs, sub-chiefs and headmen, cultural erosion and assimilation" (pp. 4-6). In spite of the many languages spoken in Botswana, only English and Setswana are emphasized as official and national languages respectively. Botswana does not have a languages policy (Mtenje, 2008) to guide the utilization and management of its language resources. Mooko (2006) describes Botswana's situation thus:

> When Botswana gained independence from the British in 1966, a political decision was taken to designate English as an official language and Setswana, one of the indeginous languages, as a national language. This move disregarded the multilingual nature of Botswana society. Furthermore, although not explicitly stated, the use of other languages was, in effect, prohibited, especially in the school setting and other official arenas. Whereas the government undertook deliberate measures to promote the use of Setswana, no efforts were made by government to cater for other languages spoken in Botswana. As a result, some of the latter languages have died whilst others have survived. (p. 109)

It is therefore not hard to imagine why the use of only these two languages is believed to be the source of poor results, high dropout rates as some students are confronted by not only a language different from the one used at home, but also content that excludes their cultures (Nyati-Ramahobo, 2008b). Thus at an early stage, students are not taught about their own cultures and languages, and this is partly responsible for the development of negative attitudes towards their own language, which in turn results in language shift and language death (Mooko, 2006; Nyati-Ramahobo & Chebanne, 2001). For example, Mooko (2006) notes signs of language death in Botswana with "some Khoesan languages ... no longer in use" (p. 112). He further notes that "the supremacy of English and Setswana has also resulted in some speakers of the other indigenous languages developing a negative attitude towards their own languages" (p. 112).

Perceived to be discriminated against, marginalized groups have formed cultural nonovernmental organizations (NGOs) whose mandate is to agitate for the recognition of their languages and cultures; lobby for their inclusion in the educational and public spheres and eliminate all discriminatory laws. These they believe, will enhance the political stability that Botswana is known for and will help the country to attain the goals of Vision 2016 of unity, security and tolerance. One such NGO is *RETENG: The Multicultural Coalition of Botswana*, a coalition of 13 individual organizations which was formed in 2000 as a reaction to the debate sparked by the Presidential Commission tasked to review sections 77 to 79 of the Constitution so as to render them tribally neutral and remove any construction that may be deemed discriminatory. Discovering one another, these organizations saw wisdom in working together for a common goal. *Re teng*, a Setswana word/phrase which translates to "we are here" is an appropriate autoethnographic metaphor with which these groups attempt to theorize a space in a context whose laws exclude them. By this label, they assert their presence and entitlement to enjoy all the rights and privileges that go with being a citizen of Botswana.

The Veekuhane

The people from whom these stories are obtained call themselves *Veekuhane* and their language *Chiikuhane*. This nomenclature derives from *Ikuhane*, whom legend holds that he was the second king of Veekuhane after taking over from his father known as Iteenge, the first known king of Veekuhane (Ramsay, 2002). Thus Veekuhane means the followers of King Ikuhane. Iteenge is not only the name of a king, but also the name of the Veekuhane. The Veekuhane's geographical extent included the Victoria Falls in present Zimbabwe, parts of Zambia, Angola, Namibia and most of northern Botswana from Nata up to Maun. Further, Iteenge is also the name of the present Chobe/Zambezi river system. In the literature, they are known as Basubiya, a term Shamukuni (1972) believes to be a derivative of *subira*, to mean light-skinned. Their language is also known as *Subiya*.

The origins of the Veekuhane are shrouded in mystery as historical records by their nature can only begin somewhere to the exclusion of other data. However, they are believed to be part of the Bantu migration from Central Africa which migrated southwards (Gumbo, 2002; Likando, n.d; Ndana, 2011; Ramsden, 1977; Samunzala, 2003; Shamukuni, 1972) claims that the Veekuhane and the Mbukushu are recorded to have arrived in the Zambezi valley in the 1440s. Thus the Veekuhane are a riverine people who have adapted to swampy conditions, no wonder they are settled along major river systems from which they derive their staple diet of fish (**nswi**), water lilies (**masiko**) and building materials such as reeds (**mpe**) (Ndana, 2011). In Botswana they are mainly found in the Chobe, Ngamiland, Okavango and Boteti areas, with a large concentration in Chobe. Veekuhane speakers are also found in the Caprivi Strip in Namibia and further north in Zambia (see Andersson and Janson, 1997; www. ethnologue.com). This language is classified by Guthrie (1967-71) as K.42 in Botswana. Some scholars consider the language as belonging to the Tonga group of languages spoken in western and southern Zambia and along the Zambezi River, east of Victoria Falls (see Ohanessian & Kashoki, 1978). According to Ohanessian and Kashoki (1978), the other languages found in this group include *Ila*, *Tonga* and *Totela*. The exact number of speakers of this language in Botswana is not known because population census in Botswana is not by ethnic group. Several estimates from different sources have come up over the years and these are: 7,000 speakers (see Andersson and Janson, 1997) The Botswana National Census (2001) estimated 6,477 speakers across three districts. However, estimates by RETENG: The Multi-Cultural Coalition of Botswana puts the number of speakers at 16,000 (see http://www.geocities.com/reteng_we_are_here).

In the scheme of things we have sketched out above, the Veekuhane are a part of the socially constructed linguistic and cultural minorities in

Botswana whose language is not part of the educational curricula nor is their exact number a matter of public knowledge. The following selected stories will illustrate our contention.

Analysis

This story (and other Chiikuhane texts) were collected by teacher H. L. Kabisa under the instruction of H. J. E. Dumbrell in 1935 and was passed to, among others, Professor Lestrade of the University of Cape Town and subsequently to Dr. van der Merwe via Prof Schapera of the same university in 1943.

Unkombwe no Lyimbe

Ku veengana ko Lyimbe ne Nkuku kuzwa he ntuungo yo Lyimbe. Lumwi lusiku Unkombwe na kumbira intuungo yo Lyimbe kuti a sumisa irebo. Unkombwe chokusiya intuungo ne nguvo hanze ha valyi kusumina naya mwi rapa. Inkuku ne vaana vayo ni yeza ku gana hamasumino. Nkukwana ni zalama intuungo yo Lyimbe mwivu ni ya zova. Ulyimbe na keza ku ku hinda intuungo yakwe ku Unkombwe, na wana nkukwana chiza isoha. Ulyimbe na veenga na lwira Unkombwe kuti mbu ni kwi haya vaana vaako nsiku zoonse mukuti mba va va sohi intuungo yaangu. Chaani tu vona nkuku igana isaka intuungo yo Lyimbe ne lilyiahano zi chi isaka mukuti zi chi vengeene ne lilyiahano Ulyiimbe uchi haya nkukwana. Nko ku vengana ko Lyiimbe ne Nkuku.

Translated as:

The Cock and the Hawk

The hatred of the Hawk and the Cock was caused by the needle belonging to the Hawk. One day the Cock borrowed a needle from the Hawk in order to sew his kaross. While sewing, Cock went into the yard, leaving the needle and the kaross outside where he was sewing. Hen and her chicken came and scratched the place where Cock was sewing. In the process, the needle got lost having been buried under the sand. When Hawk came for his needle, he found out that it was lost. He became angry and told Cock that henceforth he will kill chickens everyday because they lost his needle. That it is why even today we see chicken scratching the surface because they are still looking for Hawk's needle, and Hawk continues to kill chickens. This is the hatred of the Hawk and the Cock.

This tale demonstrates social conflicts using animals as the key characters. As with many stories, it takes us to the fantasy world in which animals spoke like humans. The fantasy world it creates helps in the suspension of disbelief and thus appeal to both young and adult audiences. Told to children by an accomplished story-teller, this story could be entertaining and a source of great amusement. Taught in schools, the story could be explored to serve various functions. Other than entertaining, the actual teaching of such stories is consistent with the concept of *re teng*, "we are here," in which each and every linguistic community is allowed space to contribute to the collective good. This would enhance self pride in the respective communities as they feel they have a role to play in national affairs, and therefore reverse cultural assimilation in the current situation where some feel ashamed of their languages.

This tale also serves aetiological functions by explaining why Chicken continue to scratch the earth's surface in what might appear as a search for food and also why Hawk continues to terrorize chicken. This story thus illustrates how Veekuhane attempt to make sense of their universe. Several such stories are available to explain the current state of affairs in the Veekuhane surroundings. The following are some of the examples: **Z'embizi** (The Story of the Zebra) and **Za bangwena n'mbolo** (The Story of Crocodile and the Iguana) both recorded by Jacottet (1899) explain why the Zebra has no horns and the Iguana has two tongues respectively. Exposed to the Biblical creation myth, which has overshadowed other creation myths, Chiikuhane learners would begin to appreciate the multiplicity of available opinions in attempting to understand the natural phenomena to which human life is inextricably connected. It stands to reason therefore that privileging one myth over the others is unjust as it is likely to lead to an inferiority-superiority complex, something that a tolerant and democratic nation should not entertain. The curriculum will therefore be enriched by the availability of various myths which in turn will inculcate a feeling of equality among the various languages. In the metaphorical language of an *Ila* proverb, "all eggs in a nest are the same and no one should feel superior over the other."

The tale could be further exploited for peace building purposes. Put into smaller groups, students could be asked to pass moral judgment on both Hawk and Cock with regards to the im/morality of vengeance and the virtue of forgiveness. Put differently, using the story, students could be asked to deal with serious moral questions such as: which of the two do you agree with and why; would you do the same under similar circumstances and why; for how long should one be angry; is forgiveness a good thing; how is Hawk's vengeful attitude a danger to peace and stability of any nation? Surely, without condoning Cock's presumed carelessness, Hawk's revenge is exaggerated beyond the value of the lost property. Such hardened attitudes run counter to some of the pillars of Vision 2016 which encourage tolerance, compassion and safety. Should this tale be established in another language community, it could provide an opportunity to show the students how seemingly different communities share certain fundamental ideas about their cosmos. With its cultural diffusionist trappings, we could begin to theorize on how and when these communities came into contact and the possible effects of such contacts.

The second tale, titled *Za Sikulokubuzuka*, comes from Jacottet's collection (1899, pp. 121-122).

Za Sikulokobuzuka

Sikulokobuzuka muntu ya vena musamo ahulu; ava lyi kuti ha wana ingoombe za vaantu cho zi sivira murozi. Lyiahanu ha zi zuwa vulyio, zonse chi zi talanina kwa lyi zonse, ku kangaa ne zi shala ku valyisana. Lyiahanu iye Sikulokobuzuka cho zi kava. Lyiahanu zi wira inzira iya ku rizo. Lyiahanu vaantu ha va vona vuyio, chi va mu hindika. Lyiahanu mwanakazi wakwe wina ku muzi cho ya kwi riizo. Lyiahanu mukwame wakwe cho sika ne'ngoombe ziingi-ziingi. Lyiahanu mwanakazi wakwe cho ambira lwiizi, alu kavi ne kadaba, Lyiahanu lwizi chi lu hanzakana. Lyiahanu Sikulokobuzuka cho hita ne ngoombe zakwe: Lyiahanu lwizi chi lu voola lu sinkana. Lyiahanu vaantu zire va tandanya Sikulokobuzuka chi va zima he rizo; lyiahanu chi va lyi volyera ku muzi wa vo. Diahanu iye Sikulo-kobuzuka cho ava inyama mbwene a vena vaanakazi votatwe. Mazina a vo ngaa :zumwi nje Bumba, ne Mozo, ne Kubeza. Lyiahanu mwanakazi uzo ya va lyi ku mu vona, nja va lyi ku lyia makondo e ngoombe. Avo va va lyi kwi kala vulyio, va va lyi ku lyia inyama i nunite ya mafuta. Nkwera vumwe vusiku a yendi. Nkwera aka lyeti zimwe ngoombe; nkwera va mu tandanya. Nkwera mwanakazi uzo a ngatulyi lwizi; lyiahanu nkwera a hiti ne ngombe za kwe. Nkwera ha sika ku muzi, cho ha makondo mwanakazi wakwe, inyama cho ha vaangi.

Lyiahanu mwanakazi wakwe a ti vuti : U mu lyeke suun. Lyüahanu mukwame a yendi, a ka saki ngombe; lyiahanu a ka ziwani, lyiiahanu a zi twalyi. Lyiahanu vaantu vamu hindiki; lyiahanu a zisiviri murozi, lyiahanu a siki ha lwizi. Lyiaha-nu Sikulokobuzuka a suumpi mwanakazi wa kwe kuti eze a kave menzi ne kadaba kakwe. Iye a kani ku kava menzi. Lyiahanu vaantu va mu wondi, va mwi hayi, va twalyi ingoome zakwe, va lyi yenderi nazo.

Lyiahanu vanakazi va ti vuti: Njeni yo za ku vusa mukwame wetu? Lyiahanu uzo ya va lyi ku lya makondo e ngoombe, vumwe vusiku mwanakazi uzo ati vuti: Tu vusa uzu mukwame wetu. Lyiahanu a twalyi vulungu, a vumbi-vumbi; Lyiah-anu a sanduki muuntu. Lyüahanu a vuuki. Nkwera a yendi ku ka lyeta ingoombe. Mwanakazi wa kwe ha a vona kuti ingoombe chi za sika, cho kukava lwizi ne kadaba kakwe; lwizi chi lu hanzakana. Sikulokobuzuka cho kuhita ne ngoombe zakwe. Nkwera haa ka sika ku muzi cho wi haya ingoombe imwe. Nkwera cho ha makondo mwanakazi uzo.

Lyiahanu mwanakazi ati vuti: Sunu mbu va mwi hairire. Lyiahano a yendi a ka zi lyeti; mwanakazi a kaani ku kava lwizi. Lyiahano va mu wondi, va mwi hairiri. Mpu zi manina.

The Story of Sikulokubuzuka

Sikulokubuzuka was a powerful medicine man. When he found other people's cattle grazing, he will whistle. Upon whistling, all the cattle will follow him with nothing remaining with the herdsmen. Sikulokobuzuka would then trek the cattle to the river. Upon seeing this, the people would chase after him. His wife would then come and talk to the river, and using her **kadaba** (a cloth tied around one's waist to cover their nakedness) beat the water and the water opens up to allow Sikulokobuzuka and his loot to pass. Having crossed, the water reconnects and prevents his pursuers from crossing. Defeated, they return to their homes. It turns out that Sikulokobuzuka had three wives named Bumba (the one with magical powers), Mozo and Kubeza. Sikulokubuzuka would then slaughter the cattle and share the meat with his wives. The one who was assisting him was only given the hooves, while the other two enjoyed the juiciest and fattest portions. One day he went away and brought many cattle, the people once more pursued him and the wife separated the river and once more he gave her the hooves and the other wives the best meat. One day the aggrieved wife said "let him, today they will kill him." As usual the husband went out to look for cattle, found and trekked them to the river with the people in pursuit. Upon arriving at the river, Sikulokubuzuka called for his wife to come to his rescue, but she refused. His pursuers arrested, killed him and reclaimed the stolen cattle. One day the wives asked: "who will bring our husband back to life?" One day Bumba said: "let us resuscitate our husband." She then took beads, made the body and it turned into a human being and the husband came back to life. He then went to loot cattle. When she saw that he has brought cattle, with her **kadaba**, she split the water and allowed Sikulokuzubuka to cross. Upon arriving at home, he slaughtered a cow and gave his accomplice wife the hooves and the other two the fat meat. The wife who was given the hooves said: "today they are going to kill him for good." Again he went and brought herds of cattle, the wife refused to split the river and Sikulokubuzuka was arrested and killed for good. That is the end.

Like the first story, the story of Sikulokubuzuka demonstrates social disease and some of its causes. Unlike the first one, this story uses real people with real names and relationships, both at family and community levels. Sikulokubuzuka's family (consisting of Sikulokubuzuka, the husband, and his three wives Bumba, Mozo, and Kubeza) becomes a microcosm of society and its belief in polygamous marriages and the need to manage such marriages. It is also clear that any society has competing interests and they need to be managed in part by the adherence to a value system. Any deviations from such values bring about conflicts which can lead to death. Central to this value system are justice and fairness. When Sikulokubuzuka does not reward Bumba for her loyalty and assistance, he precipitates jealousy and anger, already simmering in a polygamous marriage, which are characterized by injustice and are a war waiting to erupt. Thus the husband treats his wives unequally, does not reward Bumba who always comes to his assistance but instead rewards lazy and unproductive wives with the tastiest portions. The hooves he gives to Bumba would suggest the low esteem in which he holds her. Yet she is willing to give her an opportunity to mend his ways by giving her a second chance. But when he scorns her further, she withholds her assistance and he is killed for good in act of poetic justice. As a human being, Bumba has a right to decent food and humane treatment. From a labour point of view, she deserves to be rewarded handsomely for assisting her husband in providing for the family, however unfair their practice was to others in the community.

Mozo and Kubeza are equally participants in unjust practices. As beneficiaries, they do not raise a finger against their husband for the injustice he is committing against Bumba, yet their very survival depends on her happiness and satisfaction. They are myopic in that they focus on immediate gratification and not on long term interests. Their dependence on the man becomes evident at his first death, and yet they seem not to have any means of assisting him to treat Bumba fairly. As women, they participate in the oppression of fellow women. Thus womanhood is not necessarily a unifying factor, but a manipulable concept in a divide and rule/conquer strategy.

As her husband's accomplice, Bumba commits injustice against the people whose cattle her thieving husband impoverishes. By giving her hooves (not the tastiest meat), Bumba is being punished for aiding what is in fact a fugitive. Bumba and her husband's injustice is greater, as it affects not only the cattle owners, but also their families. The Sikulokubuzuka family, with the magical powers it is endowed with, is a metaphor of the socially privileged classes who use their power and influence to tyrannize their fellow human beings. Such power becomes addictive as to lull the people having into thinking it is eternal. But as the family learns, power so abused and for selfish ends akin to political dictatorships is soon taken away by the greater powers that granted it in the first place. His name therefore becomes a warning that the day of **kuvuzuka** (startling) is ever present and contained in one's behavior of the moment. The story could be used to address pertinent moral questions such as: was the wife right to refuse to assist her husband? Was Sikulokubuzuka justified in giving Bumba hooves only? Who is to blame, Sikulokubuzuka, Bumba or the sources of supernatural powers? Who benefits from Sikulokubuzuka's death? And how could this story promote peace in the family and the society at large?

Conclusion

In this chapter, we set out to demonstrate, using two stories from Veekuhane, how indigenous knowledge systems can be utilized to promote social justice. We made the point that Botswana's language situation promotes injustice and violations of human rights against cultural minorities in the educational and public spheres. Left with only two years before 2016, it will be quixotic to think that Botswana will attain its vision, in particular the promise that: "There will be no disadvantage suffered by any Motswana in the education system as a result of a mother tongue that differs from the country's two official languages" (Presidential Task Group, 1977, p. 3). We argue that the teaching of and about folklore from various language communities is a step towards the attainment of a "proud and united nation" that tolerates its diversity. The two stories show that such folklore is imbibed with, among others, concepts of social justice and human rights. A Mwikuhane child will feel part of the school and the entire nation, when his or her oral traditions are appreciated and shared by all.

REFERENCES

Achebe, C. (1974). *Anthills of the savannah*. Oxford, England: Heinemann.

Andersson, L.-G., & Tore Janson. (1997). *Languages in botswana: Language ecology in southern africa*. Gaborone, Botswana: Longman.

Asimeng-Boahene, L. (2010). Counter-storytelling with African proverbs: a vehicle for teaching social justice and global understanding in urban, U.S. schools. *Equity & Excellence in Education*, *43*(4), 434-445. Retrieved from http://www.tandfonline.com/loi/ueee20

Boikhutso, K. (2009). *Ethnic identity in a homogeneous nation state* (Unpublished PhD thesis). Cape Town, South Africa: University of Cape Town.

Gumbo, G. B. (2002). *The political economy of development in the chobe: Peasants, fishermen and tourists, 1960-1995* (Unpublished MA Dissertation). Gaborone: University of Botswana.

Guthrie, M. (1967-71). *Comparative bantu: An Introduction to the comparative linguistics and prehistory of the bantu languages* (4 vols.). Farnborough: Gregg Press.

Guthrie, M. (1948). *The classification of the bantu languages*. London: Oxford University Press for the International African Institute.

Jacottet, E. (1899). *Etudes sur les languages du Haut-Zambeze: Textes origaux recueillis et traduits en France et precedes D'une esquisse grammaticale*. Paris: Ernest Leroux, Editeur.

Likando, E. S. (n.d.). *The Caprivi: A historical perspective.* (Unpublished manuscript).

Molutsi, P. (2005). Botswana's democracy in a southern regional perspective: Progress or decline? In Z. Maundeni (Ed.), *40 years of democracy in Botswana 1965-2005*. Gaborone: Mmegi Publishing House.

Mooko, T. (2006). Counteracting the threat of language death: The case of minority languages in Botswana. *Journal of multilingual and multicultural development*, *27*(2), 109-125.

Miti, L. (2008, November). Language rights as a human rights and development issue in southern Africa. *Openspace*, *2*(3), 7-18.

Miruka, O. (1994). *Encounter with oral literature*. Nairobi: East African Educational Publishers.

Mtenje, Al D. (2008, November). Language policies in the SADC region: Stocktaking and prospects. *Openspace*, *2*(3), 24-31.

Ndana, N. (2011). *The indigenous praise poetry of the veekuhane: Culture, memory and history*. Casas book series no. 83. Cape Town: Printing Solutions. SED.

Nyati-Ramahobo, L. (2008a, November). Ethnicity and language: Lessons from botswana. *Openspace*, *2*(3), 49-54.

Nyati-Ramahobo, L. (2008b, December). Minority tribes in botswana: The politics of recognition. *Briefing: Minority Rights International*.

Nyati-Ramahobo, L., & Chebanne, A. (2001, November). *The development of minority languages for adult education in Botswana: Towards cultural diversity*. Paper presented at The International Literacy Conference, Breakwater Lodge, Cape Town.

Ogutu, B., & Roscoe, A. A. (1974). Keep my words. Nairobi: Heinemann. In O. Miruka (Ed.), *Encounter with oral literature*. Nairobi: East African Educational Publishers.

Okpewho, I. (1992). *African oral literature: Backgrounds, character and continuity*. Bloomington and Indianapolis: Indiana University Press.

Pratt, M. (1991). Arts of the contact zone. *Modern Language Association*, pp. 33-40. Retrieved from http://www.jstor.org/stable/25595469

Presidential Task Group for a Long Term Vision for Botswana. (1997, September). *Vision 2016: Towards prosperity for all: A summary*. Gaborone, Botswana: Associated Printers.

Ramsay, J. (2002, January 25). Builders of Botswana: The bekuhane or basubiya. *The Botswana Daily News*, p. 5.

Ramsden, J. F. (1977). *The basubiya* (Unpublished BA Dissertation). Gaborone, Botswana: University of Botswana.

Republic of Botswana. (1933. Revised 1987). *The chieftainship act*. Gaborone, Botswana: Government Printer.

Republic of Botswana. (1933 Revised 1997). *The tribal territories act*. Gaborone: Government Printer.

Republic of Botswana. (2008). *Bogosi act*. Gaborone, Botswana: Government Printer.

Republic of Botswana. (n.d.) *Constitution of Botswana*. Gaborone, Botswana: Government Printing and Publishing Services.RETENG (n.d.). Retrieved from http://www.geocities.com/reteng_we_are_here/

Schapera, I. (1952). *The ethnic composition of tswana tribes*. London, England: London School of Economics and Political Science.

Samunzala, S. (2003). *The social aspects of life of the basubiya of chobe, 1928-1991* (Unpublished BA Dissertation). Gaborone, Botswana: University of Botswana.

Shamukuni, D. (1972). The basubiya. *Botswana Notes and Records*, *4*, 161-183.

Thumberg-Hartland, P. (1978). Botswana: An African growth economy. In I. Taylor (Ed.), Growing authoritarianism in the "African Miracle": Should Botswana be a cause for concern? Danish Institute for International Relations. Boulder, CO: Westview Press.

CHAPTER 13

GRIOTS AND MARKET SQUARE PEDAGOGY

Performative Storytelling in the Classroom

Vivian Yenika-Agbaw

Introduction

Indigenous ways of knowing have always existed in Africa; however, with the advent of colonialism they somehow fell out of favor from the public sphere. More importantly, they ceased to be of relevance to formal education practices in most schools in West Africa where the official curriculum is heavily influenced by Western ideas, traditions, and ideals. Thus, the content of the curriculum oftentimes mirror those of the specific country's colonial master's. This inadvertently created a system of intellectual dependency creating situations whereby some African educators within the continent find themselves relying more and more on the West for curricular guidance, and curricular materials (Altbach, 1991) needed to serve their local constituencies.

African Traditional and Oral Literature as Pedagogical Tools in Contest Area Classrooms: K-12, pages 233–243
Copyright © 2014 by Information Age Publishing
All rights of reproduction in any form reserved.

In the United States indigenous practices of parallel cultures have also been left out of the official school curriculum, a curriculum, which Ladson-Billings (1998) posits, is deeply informed by Anglo Saxon traditions. If this is the case, the majority of the world's children must contend with the fact that knowledge based of significance and for social mobility is dictated by Eurocentric vision. And with the push for more testing to assure that America's children can compete with their peers from other countries in the global economy, practices not considered mainstream continue to be overlooked. But of late there has been some interest in indigenous practices, including indigenous ways of knowing, seeing, and expressing, and how these can indeed impact learning in positive ways. While this recognition of aspects of old cultural practices stirs controversy among certain groups of scholars, others have embraced it as legitimate (Ciaffa, 2008). For these folks, culturally relevant curriculum and pedagogy is necessary not only because it acknowledges learners as cultural beings, but also because it creates contexts where mentoring can occur. Such contexts include a nurturing learning community where teachers/mentors guide learners also considered apprentices, as they navigate familiar and unfamiliar materials relevant for their intellectual, social, and emotional well-being. In this way, there is often collaboration between the teacher and the learner, and also between learners whom together experiment with ideas and strategies to problem solve. In regards to literature, pedagogy that is informed by indigenous practices can expand the repertoire of response models; for example through talk, chants, talk backs, performance and more. But the challenge for some skeptics of "cultural revivalist" framework of learning remains how one can effectively translate such practices in formal settings in the 21st century. Thus, the issue becomes how these kinds of learning experiences can be quantified as evidence in a society that is driven by test scores!

Jay Ciaffa (2008) captures this tension eloquently in his article, "Tradition and Modernity in Postcolonial African Philosophy," where he outlines the key issues in the debate between what he refers to as "cultural revivalists" and what I infer as pro-modernists. While the arguments posited by each group in support of its case have merit, I find the idea from the pro-modernists that, "a call for a nostalgic return to the past is not merely naïve and romantic, but positively dangerous" (p. 122) provocative. I would theorize that a lot depends on which aspects of the indigenous practice are being revived, and why. For example, as a scholar of children's literature, I know that storytelling is one of several art forms that has always been identified with Africa in general; but I am also aware of the fact that stories serve different purposes in different ethnic groups albeit its entertainment value that is universal. These stories, whether spoken, read aloud, chanted, performed at informal gatherings or formal settings have some educational value. Some of these values may appear in the stated morals, and/or the messages conveyed in the story; or it could be a commentary on larger issues of social justice, or possibly political statements cleverly woven into spontaneous oral narratives, or "nonsense" narrative verses. The benefits are many!

With griots and/or storytellers called by different names across the continent, indigenous storytelling as a revived practice in a literature-based literacy curriculum can never be "positively dangerous!" Rather, it may offer opportunities for students to experiment with different response models and tools, as they play with oral narratives perhaps in much more sophisticated ways than some teachers have seen occur in their classrooms, or than what is typically observed at make shift "market squares" with little structures. This may subsequently raise the bar of literary responses to reflect their sociocultural worlds and thus validate them as learners who consciously apply ways of knowing from their varied multicultural and social worlds to bear on their literary responses. These responses made visible in a formal classroom context can be empowering to learners as they celebrate their humanity; and enlightening to the teacher/mentor who can recognize the different tools and strategies that went into creating the variety of responses—spoken, written, video, song, and so forth—to selected oral tales. Therefore, I believe traditional storytelling as a form of pedagogy can create ample opportunities for students to respond and grow as speakers, readers, writers, visual artists, performers and more; but as Galda and Beach (2001) observe, a lot would depend on the "contexts for response" (p. 64).

In this chapter, I do not profess to review how literature is "treated" generally in schools, for Galda and Beach (2001) have covered that in their article. I am more concerned with the response possibilities opened to students in classroom settings that approach storytelling from an indigenous perspective. I also believe that responses for these students could initially be natural but may possess great potential to evolve into other forms depending on how the teacher scaffolds the experiences and the classroom atmosphere. But first let me clarify my use of indigenous storytelling in this paper. To me, these are practices that evoke "traditional" modes of narratives that may include "call and response," and impromptu response strategies that allow for participatory discourses that are spontaneous but at once structured. That is, practices that are not stifling to "authentic" responses to tales spoken, read aloud, viewed on a screen, chanted, and/or performed, for these same narrative modes lend themselves to multiple response models. The kind of teacher I envision here sees him/herself as a mentor, a griot, an artist, and an educator and thus must take some risks, be imaginative, and be prepared to deviate from scripted materials that are dictated by the school's curriculum even in this era of the Common

Core. With such a teacher in mind the classroom can become a metaphorical market square where learners gather to listen and participate in storytelling events, responding to stories in a variety of modes.

Response Theory

Galda and Beach (2001) in their review of response theory also posit that "studies have focused on (a) text, or how various texts affect response; (b) readers, or how experiences and attitudes situated in readers affect response, and (c) the context in which response is generated" (p. 64). My chapter is more concerned with the last claim, for it is my belief that a griot, *the master storyteller* within the context of what I refer to as a "market square," through "call and response" and other talk strategies can enable child listeners to respond to traditional tales, spoken, read aloud, chanted, viewed on new screens in meaningful ways that do not only serve their individual purposes, but extend their understanding of stories and the places of stories in human lives. From the informal context of the market square to the formal context of the classroom, and the teacher assuming a griot-like role acting and mentoring the learners/apprentices as they immerse themselves in literature, oral tales, the practices of indigenous storytelling and its loose structure may provide ample opportunities for learning in general, and deeper responses.

My belief in storytelling and market square pedagogy stems from my childhood experiences with griot-like figures in my local community (Lobe Estate, Cameroon, West Africa) who showed me how to love stories and to reflect on their significances given my reality at any given time. Looking back to those childhood years, I have often wondered how such encounters with oral tales at informal gatherings that eventually grew to have a makeshift structure can be translated into "good" pedagogical practices within a modern day American classroom setting. And now I have come to admit that formal classroom settings in the 21st century, with all their structural restrictions and trappings of a scripted literacy curriculum that is test driven, can still benefit from such a simple idea practiced by wise knowledgeable teachers, historians, and custodians of cultures at informal gatherings in the "market square." Storytelling, being a participatory discourse has tremendous potential to generate a spectrum of responses from personal to sophisticated, as learners grow and are supported within the community.

Thus, having students experience literature in the classroom with a griot as was done in the past in some ways echoes Vygotsky's (1978) notion of learning as social. With the teacher/mentor facilitating learning, and the learner/apprentice immersing in storytelling practices and learning the nuances of narrative discourses stories come alive in the classroom. That is, he/she enables the learner to begin to contemplate stories, their relevance, and the contradictory responses they sometimes elicit in us (listeners, readers, writers, viewers, cultural artists). First, who is a griot really? Or what are some ideas of griots do we hold, especially as one reflects on the multiple roles they play in traditional West African societies. I discuss this briefly next.

The Griot: Storyteller, Historian, Teacher, *and/or* Mentor

Griots are storytellers and historians in West African countries (Asimeng-Boahene, 2012). They are highly respected because of their cultural knowledge about the specific clan or ethnic group. They are walking libraries with an up-to-date history of their local community, and are also considered poets, praise singers and from my experience, mentors. Oling-Sisay (2012) adds that,

> In some parts of Africa, "griots" were variously regarded as storytellers, living dictionaries, and oral historians. Their primary function was to use their extensive historical knowledge to promote interethnic harmony and reduce the potential for wars among Africans. (p. 217)

Thus, within traditional settings these educators serve multiple audiences and in multiple roles. With the global focus on diversity, the idea of a griot becomes necessary in the classroom for the endless possibilities it may create for students confined within the formal educational establishment.

Perceived as knowledgeable and as great orators, griots capture the attention of their audience and hold it fast till the end of each performance. The participatory nature of their performance makes learning about one's history or any subject not only enjoyable but democratic too giving opportunities for participants to engage in conversations about culture, stories, and important historical events in a respectful manner. These conversations may involve participants posing questions for further clarification of aspects of the narratives just heard, or attempt to fill in gaps deliberately left out in such narratives, and hence expanding the discourse. The "market square" being a physical place in the past, where people gathered to learn a little more about their communities in addition to listening to stories and other gossips can become a metaphorical space in the classroom where learning can occur too.

Market Square Pedagogy and Responses to Oral Tales

If we consent a teacher in the classroom being a griot acting as a mentor to his/her students/apprentices as together they create a storied world responses to other storied worlds texts, we would begin to see how this idea echoes Vygotsky's (1978) notions of learning as a form of socialization. Such an approach to storytelling then establishes possibilities for all kinds of learning starting with the overall quality of responses to the tales spoken by individuals, read aloud by the teacher, viewed, chanted, and/or produced by the community. What these scenarios offer are ideas of the importance of responses in and of themselves, as well as "a transaction between texts and readers stances and identities within larger sociocultural contexts" (Galda & Beach, 2001, p. 66). Furthermore, "Research shows that many types of discussion are valuable, depending on the desired outcome" (p. 68). If some desired outcomes in a literature-based classroom context that implements a market square pedagogy are to (a) "demonstrate the use of language and genre within the students' zone of proximal development" (Wells, 1991 as cited in Galda & Beach, 2001, p. 68); (b) have children participate in cultural literary practices that foster "call and response" strategy; (c) encourage performance as aesthetic response to oral, written, and visual narratives, then there is no reason why market square pedagogy cannot not be explored as an alternative to a standardized classroom pedagogy, which typically encourages lots of worksheet activities! Let us pursue this idea further using a classic African trickster, Anansi and a few of his tales to illustrate the point.

First, I present a series of scenarios to enable the teacher or what I may refer to as a griotlike figure, guide learners to transform tales. In the transformation process the classroom community would then realize the myriad of possible responses that can be generated, indicating that storytelling, market square style still has a lot to offer contemporary curriculum. I present four possible scenarios, which may enable teachers to rethink indigenous ways of learning as a viable approach to storytelling in a literacy curriculum.

Scenario #1a: Spoken Word

The griot tells the story from memory spontaneously embellishing the plot and performs as necessary. After listening to the tale, students are then asked to respond by telling their own versions of the story from memory as well. Thus, they respond in a spoken/oral format with audiotaped, chanted, video taped while others take note on how each version differs from the "griot's" or their peers. Later, as a whole class they create a chart and note these differences having individuals explain how and why they might have embellish the plot the way they did.

Scenario #1b: Spoken Word and Call and Response

The griot opens the tale, and based on the students' knowledge of tricksters, he/she asks individuals to create a befitting conflict. The griot carries on developing the conflict around the character but pauses to ask students what should come next. and so forth. For example: "What should we do with this spider? Should we make him a human or leave him an animal? Should we name it/him, 'Anansi' or change the name? What names would be appropriate and why? Where do we want the character to go? Who should he meet on the way? What challenges do we envision it/her/him to encounter [or would like her/him/it to encounter] on the journey? How do we want him to handle the challenge or conflict? and so forth" With each prompt, students are expected to call out responses, which help to develop and complicate the plot. The griotlike figure [teacher] can note the responses on the board or have one student volunteer record the responses on a smart board. Later, during the normal writing workshop, students in small groups work to develop new versions of the story, writing and revising the pieces until they are satisfied with the final versions, which are then published at the back of the class or in a local newspaper or newsletter.

Scenario #2: Spoken Word and Retelling in Dialectal English

12. Grace Before Meat

a. Monkey and Anansi. *Samuel Christie, St. Anne's Bay.*

Anansi and Monkey were travelling; they were two good friends together. Anansi ask Monkey, "Brer Monkey, how much cunnie you have?" Said, "Brer, me have plenty plenty!" Anansi said, "Brer, me only have one one-half; I keep the one fe meself an' give me friend the half."

Trabble on, trabble on, until they see Tiger in one deep hole. Anansi say, "Brer Monkey, you have plenty cunnie an' long tail; sen' down tail into the hole an' help Brer Tiger!" While him sen' down him tail, Anansi climb one tree. Tiger come out of the hole now, lay hold on Monkey, say, "I nyam you t'-day!" Anansi on the tree laughing. Monkey into a fix now, don't know how to get away. So Anansi call out to Tiger, "Brer Tiger, you ketch Monkey now you gwine eat him?" Tiger say, "Yes, I gwine eat him." Anansi say, "Do like me, now. Open you two hand an' clap wid joy, say, 'I get Monkey!'" That time he open his two hand, Monkey get free. Tiger run after Monkey, Anansi mak his way down from the tree, go home. (Beckwith, 1924)

b. Goat and Anansi. *Henry Spence, Bog, Westmoreland.*

Anansi and Tiger go out hunting one day. Tiger catch one wild goat, Anansi no catch one. Anansi say to him, "Brar Tiger, wha' you say when you catch dis goat?" So Tiger say, "Not'ing!" Anansi say, "Brar Tiger, nex' time when you catch goat so, you mus' put goat under yo' arm an' knockey han' at top say, 'T'ank de Lord!'" An' Tiger did so an' de goat get away gone; de two lose. (Beckwith, 1924)

After *telling* one of these Anansi tales, the griot can then ask volunteers to retell the story in the regional variety of English with which they are familiar. That is, have students retell the story, as members of their cultural community or neighborhood would like to hear it. These sessions should be videotaped as a cultural artifact that locates communities in practice. They also have the option to act out the stories to reflect gestures from their communities. Other retold stories can also be audio/video recorded for further activities in the classroom, empowering students to be proud of their heritage. In another lesson, the teacher can then have groups of students view or listen to the tales and discuss the strengths of the different performances, while making comparisons in approach and how these impact the story contents. Students who profess to not having dialectal varieties that are different in their neighborhood could be asked then to retell one of the stories in British or Australian English. They can work in groups and work on a draft and then appoint one person to tell the story orally in class with a backdrop landscape of the country.

Scenario #3: Performing Anansi Tale

13. Day-Time Trouble

a. Rabbit and Anansi. *Susan Watkins, Claremont, St. Ann.*

Brar Nansi and Brar Rabbit went for a walk one day. Brar Rabbit ask Brar Anansi to show him 'daytime trouble'. An' while dey go on, Brar Anansi saw Tiger den wid a lot of young Tiger in it. Brar Anansi took out one an' kill it an' give Rabbit a basket wid a piece of de Tiger's meat to carry for de Tiger's fader, an' took Rabbit along wid him to Tiger's house an' tol' Brar Rabbit to han' Tiger de basket. Anansi run, an' Tiger catch at Rabbit to kill him, but he get away. Brar Anansi run up a tree an' say, "Run, Brar Rabbit, run! run fe stone-hole!" Took a razor an' give it to Rabbit. An' Tiger got up a lot of men to get Rabbit out de hole an' Tiger sent for Reindeer to dig him out, as he had a long neck to put down his head an' dig him out; but Anansi tol' Rabbit when Reindeer put down his head in de hole, he mus' tak de razor an' cut it off. A lot of people gadder to see Reindeer tak Rabbit out of de hole, but instead, Reindeer head was taken off an' he drop an' was dead an' de whole crowd run away wid fright.

After Rabbit come out, Brar Nansi say to him, "Brar Rabbit, so 'daytime trouble' stay. So, as long as you live, never ask anybody to show it to you again!"

b. Rat and Anansi. *Moses Hendricks, Mandeville.*

Rat and Anansi went out one day. They came across Tiger's four children,— Anansi knew exactly where they was. He had a handbasket, Rat had one. So Anansi said, "Brer, two fe me, two fe you!" Anansi tak up one, mak the attempt as if he going to kill it but he didn't do so, put it in his basket alive. Rat t'ot Anansi kill it, an' he tak up his now an' kill it an' put it in his basket. Anansi did the same with the second one,—didn't kill it, put it in his basket. Pat took up the other one an' him kill it. So Rat had two dead ones an' Anansi had his alive.

Anansi knew exactly which way Tiger would walk coming home. They met Tiger. Said, "Brer Tiger, I see yo' baby them Crying hungry, I tak them up come meet you. I carry two, Brer Rat two." Tiger lay down now to nurse them. Anansi took out one alive. Rat took out one dead, got frightened. Tiger looks cross. Anansi took out the other one alive. Rat took out his dead. Tiger got into a temper an' made a spring at Rat to catch him. Rat was running. The track was along the side of a wall. Anansi call, "Brer Pat, 'member stone-hole!" Tiger say, "What you say, Brer Nansi?" Anansi say, "Tell you mus' min', him go into dat stone-hole now!" Rat hear now, get into de stone-hole. Tiger wheel roun' to revenge himself on Anansi. Anansi get under de dry trash. That is the reason why rat so fond of stone-hole, an' Anansi, always find him under dry trash an' rubbish. (Beckwith, 1924)

The griot can perform his/her interpretations of these tales and have students in small groups to create a script with each one of them as characters in the Readers Theater. After going over the guidelines for developing a Readers Theater script—what goes into such a script and how it differs from dramatic interpretations of stories, the griot then asks students to develop their own scripts with each member of their group ascribed a role. Next, groups perform one of their stories and peers respond—serving as judges with a clear set of criteria on what they believe is working in the performance or not.

Scenario #4a: YouTube Rendition

The griot provides a title of what he/she purports would be the next story to listen to. He/she then introduces the character and setting only, and asks students to transform the tale however they see fit with the stipulation that they be ready to explain what they have transformed. And have it uploaded in YouTube. Students can then post their comments to the YouTube for public reaction.

Scenario #4b: Tales Transformed in Media of Choice

Students in small groups select one of the shared tales and transform in a variety of media or in different modes and peers respond orally, in digital format, or as a musical choreographed by the group. These are just a few ideas for transformative practices that are linked to traditional oral tales. Each response adds a different dimension to the story as interpreted by a particular listener/reader, in groups or individually, prompted or spontaneous.

In a research done with sixth graders, Sipe (1993) demonstrates other ways traditional tales are transformed by children. To him, "Transformations maybe parallel, deconstructed, or extended versions of the original tale, or the tale may be transformed through the illustrations" (p. 19). Further, "transformations are also distinguishable from retellings, in that a retelling attempts to be faithful to the original story, while the transformation can range farther afield" (p. 19). In market square pedagogy, transformation of traditional tales lend themselves to these original stories. Students are given the opportunity to transform traditional tales heard being spoken spontaneously, read aloud by their teacher and peers, performed by other members of their community, and/or viewed on screens in groups. When they recreate market square experiences telling tales orally through the spoken word, video, audio, and through other visual modes to encourage participatory discourses that encourage democracy and are typical of the "call and response" strategy, they transform stories as the stories transform them. As Galda and Beach (2001) observe, "Readers employ language, genres, signs, images, drama, visual art, or discourses as tools to share responses in communities of practice—such as classrooms" (p. 68). Indeed, this is what market square pedagogy promises and offers, we only need to give it a chance in the classroom as we tap on indigenous practices to inform our experiences with stories to further enrich our lives as learners and educators.

REFERENCES

Altbach, P. (1991). Textbooks: The international dimension. In M. Apple & L. Christian Smith (Eds.), *The politics of the textbook* (pp. 242-258). New York, NY: Routledge

Asimeng-Boahene, L. (2012). African traditional education and citizenship development. In O. Ukpokodu & P. Ukpokodu (Eds.), *Contemporary voices from the margin: African educators on African and American education* (pp. 67-83). Charlotte, NC: Information Age Publishing,

Beckwith, M. W. (1924). Jamaica Anansi Stories/Grace Before Meat. In *Jamaican Anansi Stories*. New York, NY: American Folk Lore Society. Retrieved from http://en.wikisource.org/wiki/Jamaica_Anansi_Stories/Grace_before_Meat and http://en.wikisource.org/wiki/Jamaica_Anansi_Stories

Ciaffa, J. (2008). Tradition and modernity in postcolonial african philosophy. *Humanitas, XXI*(1 & 2), 121-144.

Galda, L., & Beach, R. (2001). Response to literature as a cultural activity. *Reading Research Quarterly, 36*(1), 64-73.

Ladson-Billings, G. (1998). Just What is critical race theory and what's it doing in a *nice* field like education? *Qualitative Studies in Education. 11*(1), 7-24.

Oling-Sisay, M. (2012). Cultural socialization and primary educational perspectives in three Eastern African countries. In O. Ukpokodu & P. Ukpokodu (Eds.), *Contemporary voices from the margin: African educators on African and American education* (pp. 213-224). Charlotte, NC: Information Age Publishing.

Sipe, L. (1993). Using transformation of traditional stories: Making the reading-writing connection. *The Reading Teacher, 47*(1), 18-26.

Vygotsky, L. S. (1978). *Mind in society: The development of higher psychological processes*. Cambridge, MA: Harvard University Press.

CHAPTER 14

AFRICAN DRUMMING

A Pedagogical Tool for Social Justice and Cultural Diversity in Urban Classrooms in the United States

Ernest Opong

Introduction

The growing racial and cultural diversity in urban schools in the United States demands a fair and equitable system of education that reflects the growing reality on the ground. In this chapter, the author examines the adoption of African drumming as a pedagogical tool for teaching for social justice in urban schools in the United States. It could serve as one of the main tools of culturally relevant education inherent in which is the development of better educated minority students in urban America. It also has the potential for mainstream middle class America to benefit and to contribute to a mutual understanding among various ethnic groups

African Traditional and Oral Literature as Pedagogical Tools in Contest Area Classrooms: K-12, pages 245–261
Copyright © 2014 by Information Age Publishing
All rights of reproduction in any form reserved.

Schools in urban areas in the United States are directly affected by the existing overall political and economic conditions. In addition to lack of essential equipment and teachers, students in urban high schools are burdened with curriculum that disregards their cultural heritage. Referring to Anyon (1997), Lalas (2007) writes that most residents of large urban areas across the United States happen to be African American and/or Latino. In New York, Chicago, Los Angeles, Atlanta, Detroit, and Miami, they are in a majority of an average of 65%. The same applies to other metropolitan cities, such as Baltimore, Cleveland, El Paso, Memphis, San Antonio, San Francisco, San Jose, and Washington, D.C. In addition to being isolated from the mainstream of middle class America, the schools are starved of social justice and culturally diverse friendly curricula. Furthermore, the introduction of a multicultural curriculum, embracing racial pride and heritage, in urban areas is needed to match the continuous growth of minority populations as a result of the influx of people from other non-European countries. Hence, it is important that urban schools implement culturally relevant curricula that address issues of social justice (Lalas, 2007). As things stand now, the continuous decline in the quality of education in urban areas is a sad indication of the failure of the objectives of social justice in education in the United States.

The introduction of African drumming in inner city schools as suggested in this chapter will not only positively impact minority students, especially African Americans, it will also benefit the mainstream population as well. African drumming, as one component to the implementation of a multicultural curriculum, holds a commitment to the ideals of equity enshrined in the provision of well-trained and experienced instructional staff (Johnson, 2011). Moreover, a mutual respect is developed between the communities and the school authorities, and has the potential to help close the gap between schools in mainstream predominantly white neighborhoods.

This chapter will also examine the issue of social justice in education, and explore how African drumming can be used as a measure to address the matter. A theoretical framework for using African drumming the characteristics and types and types of African drumming and the rationale for adopting African drumming as a pedagogical tool as well as culturally relevant pedagogy will be examined with a view to justify the need for social justice in education in urban areas in the United States.

Theoretical Framework for Using African Drumming as a Pedagogical Tool to Teach for Social Justice

What is Social Justice?

Social justice is one concept that has been subjected to a variety of definitions, all of which point to the need for equity and fairness in society. Plato in *The Republic* postulated that the four virtues of wisdom, courage, moderation and justice should be the basis for the ideal state. From justice, the word "social" was added to connote a societal responsibility for fairness and justice (Heinaman, 1998). Christian theological movement on the concept of social justice, led by Thomas Aquinas avers that justice flows from God before whom all men are equal and must therefore treat each other with respect (Wenar, 2012). Many philosophers in later centuries including Immanuel Kant believed in the rightness of an action so long as it is motivated by duty devoid of any personal interest or profit. Kant is among the first philosophers to influence the utilitarian movement that developed later in the 20th century that justice is only relevant if it is universally beneficial (Wenar, 2012). Twentieth century's John Rawls adds further information to build upon theories from where Bentham and Mills left off; he mentions several institutional features that all liberal political conceptions will share: fair opportunities for all citizens (especially in education and training); a decent distribution of income and wealth; government as the employer of last resort; basic health care for all citizens; and public financing of elections (Wenar, 2012).

Addressing Social Justice and Cultural Diversity in Urban Schools in the United States

Due to the complex nature of society, the pursuit of social justice in the modern state is the joint effort of the governor and the governed. In the constitutions of most countries in the world, provision is made for basic individual human rights. Among the rights mentioned are education, health care and justice among others, yet in most cases those rights are honored in the breach. As the strive to achieve social justice continues, so does the struggle for rights. Lalas (2007) references Anyon (1997) who describes the kind of education provided in urban areas as "ghetto schooling," and Kozol (2005) also mentioned by Lalas, describes as "savage inequities" (p. 17) the insensitive approach to inner city education. He adds that "the more experienced instructors teach the children of the privileged and the least experienced are sent to teach the children of minorities" (p. 17).

Knudson (2011) states that inequality in America's education system is not surprising, because as is provided now, it ignores socioeconomic peculiarities of the urban population and its concomitant multicultural characteristics, but is dedicated more to maintaining the status quo than to fostering flexibility. As the status quo is driven more by political motivations, the principal objective of the mainstream is to perpetuate an underclass to support industry. Obviously social justice is not served in inner city and urban education. Knudson (2011) again concludes that in 21st century America, the ever-widening gap between the haves and have-nots and a steady decrease in the middle class remains unaddressed. Social justice requires that all students be given access to qualitative education and the only way to achieve that is to identify the peculiarities of the complexities in society and address them equally.

Critical Race Theory

Critical race theory (CRT) as it relates to education addresses the racist component in the delivery of education in urban America. The theory stems from studies addressing the relationship among race, racism and power (Delgado & Stefancic, 2001). The initial premise for the theory is its endorsement of multiculturalism in education as a means of addressing racism which is rampant in American society. The first proposition of critical race theory is that racism is endemic in American society and thus appears natural and ordinary (Delgado & Stefancic, 2001). In this regard, the theory supports the adoption of a school curriculum that recognizes the socioeconomic and cultural milieu in which it is applied. Lemon-Smith (2010) in her review of Jaqueline Leonard's (2007) *Culturally Specific Pedagogy in the Mathematics Classroom, Strategies for Teachers and Students*, agrees with Leonard's proposition. Boutte and Hill (2006) also aver that it is important to understand how culture, experiences and preferences influence teaching and learning. They add that trivializing and overgeneralization of cultural information about students are not advisable. Referencing Boutte (2002) and Banks (2006), Boutte and Hill (2006) conclude that educators and administrators need to recognize that "curriculums and standards are not culture-free" (p. 314). Just as Asimeng-Boahene (2010) endorses African proverbs as a pedagogical tool for social studies, it would be equally appropriate to recommend African drumming in much the same manner.

Leonard (2007), as referred to by Lemon-Smith (2010), articulates a theoretical backdrop for culturally specific teaching. Among her reasons, culturally specific education promotes connections to the real world and fosters positive beliefs about the need for the lessons being learned by the student.

We are reminded by Delgado and Stefancic (2001) that because White supremacy is taken for granted, White people have been allowed to make colored people accept their color differentiations and therefore their place in society. This further promotes the challenge to White scholars to engage in the CRT to make them aware of committed to critically interrogating their own racial privilege and unmasking the invisibility of racism (Rollock & Gillborn, 2011).

Critical race theorists place particular importance on the voices of the people, something Ladson-Billings and Tate (1995) describe as "naming one's own reality" (p. 57). This involves, according to Ladson-Billings and Tate, the use of parables, chronicles, stories, counterstories, poetry, fiction, and revisionist histories to illustrate the false necessity and irony of much of current civil rights doctrine.

Asimeng-Boahene (2010) argues for the inclusion of an alternative epistemology in the form of landscapes of the nondominant cultures' narratives, and African drumming is part of the reality of people of African descent. Ong (1977) describes African drumming as a highly developed acoustic speech surrogate ever. He adds further that acoustic speech is a code not unlike the Morse code used on an old-style telegraph. Against the historical background of its being feared as a potential tool of incitement of mutiny among African slaves in the 17th century (Gavidia, 2012), African drumming holds a pride of place in the African American community.

Ladson-Billings and Tate (1995) suggest as does Delgado (1989) that there are three reasons for naming one's own reality in legal discourse, (a) Much of reality is socially constructed; (b) Stories provide members of outgroups a vehicle for psychic self-preservation; and (c) the exchange of stories from teller to listener can help overcome ethnocentricism and the dysconscious conviction of viewing the world in one way. Furthermore, Carter G. Woodson (1933) laments the rejection of anything African in the education of the Negro:

> In the study of language in school pupils were made to scoff at the Negro dialect as some peculiar possession of the Negro which they should despise rather than directed to study the background of this language as a broken-down African tongue—in short to understand their own linguistic history.... The philosophy in African proverbs and in the rich folklore of that continent was ignored to give preference to that developed on the distant shores of the Mediterranean. (p. 19)

African drumming has assumed a global perspective because of its versatility as a medium of communication. Its adoption in urban school curricula would not be an aberration; it would help to increase understanding and solidarity among people of African ancestry as well as the mainstream.

Culturally Relevant Pedagogy

The thrust of the argument for critical race theory in education is equity and social justice. Kincheloe (2004) as referenced by Lalas (2007) asserts that urban education has always been embroiled in crisis and may continue to be so in the foreseeable future. It is therefore necessary to develop a powerful urban pedagogy and a rigorous urban education. It is in the same vein that Ladson-Billings (1995) identifies pedagogical excellence as good teaching which she describes as culturally relevant. She goes on to describe culturally relevant pedagogy as resting on certain criteria or propositions: Among these are "students must experience academic success; (b) students must develop and/or maintain cultural competence" (p. 159).

Academic success depends largely on how students develop the various skill needed for their future. Drawing on examples from the work of several teachers Ladson-Billings (1995) concludes that the success of their students rested on the demands and the reinforcement of academic excellence from students. Ladson-Billings makes reference to Fordham and Ogbu's (1986) observation of some behaviors among African American students toward their peers who maintain academic excellence and conclude that those students who are culturally confidence and whose teachers utilize their [the students'] culture are always successful. In addition to developing cultural competence, teaching in the language of the student provides an atmosphere of cooperation between teacher and student.

If, as observed by Ladson-Billings (1995), a White teacher's adoption of rap music in the teaching of poetry facilitated understanding and interest, using African drumming as a pedagogical tool in teaching world cultures, for instance, could equally generate interest in the subject. It would also engender self-esteem among African American students and respect and understanding among White mainstream middle class students. An 18-month pilot program introduced in Milwaukee in 1996 by the World Music Drumming including African drumming introduced in middle school (and Grades 3-5, 9-12) in Milwaukee by Will Schmid, students were observed to have developed understanding, respect and value for African and Caribbean cultures. They also demonstrated greater respect for the people represented by the musical traditions they studied (Schmid, 1996).

One of the goals of culturally relevant pedagogy is the development of critical thinking skills that allows the student to develop sociopolitical consciousness including a sense of social responsibility and empowerment (Ladson-Billings & Tate, 1995). The application of culturally relevant pedagogy has been known to affect positively schools in blighted areas that have long been ignored. Esposito and Swain (2009) write that the concept enforces social justice as it provides marginalized students with the tools that help effect change and social justice.

African Drumming?

Notwithstanding the cultural diversity of the African world, it is a world that is essentially culturally united; and one indicator of the foundation of Pan-African consciousness in the African world is the role of the drum (Johnson, 2011). The uniqueness of African drumming makes it inappropriate to define it as a mere musical instrument. The drum in Africa plays sociocultural and religious roles in society. Principally, as many researchers have indicated, the drum is an instrument of communication. But much more than that, as Bebey (1999) describes, the drum is ubiquitous in every region of Africa playing different roles amongst the various peoples. The versatility of the drum makes it a "cultural emblem" of the African World culture, says Johnson (2011). According to Barrett as cited by Johnson (2011), the drum is Africa's heartbeat. Most would consider it a communication tool, because the African drum speaks to, and for African peoples. As Finnegan (2012) further opines:

> A remarkable phenomenon in parts of West and Central Africa is the literature played on drums.... Although its literary significance has been overlooked in general discussions of African literature ... expression through drums often forms a not inconsiderable branch of the literature of a number of African societies. (p. 467)

The importance of the drum in African society is manifested in the esteem in which master drummers are held. Among the Asante people of Ghana, the master drummer is called *Odomankoma Kyerema* (Divine Drummer). The Yorubas call their drummers, *Jeli* (teacher or griot). Among the Mandes and Wollofs, the master drummer must have given his whole life to the *djembe* and *dunun* drums. One can attain the title of master drummer after a long career as a drummer. He must be highly skilled and knowledgeable about African drums, and must have learned from a master drummer. He must be able to play all types of drums and know all the songs that go with each rhythm (Nketia, 1963). He plays lead drum rhythm among his peers. He must be what in Western terms is described as a true professional.

Characteristics of the African Drum

Traditional African music is characterized severally, but essentially, as a medium of communication. Wilson (2006) as cited in Nketia (1963) puts the communication role of Asante drumming in three fundamental modes: dance, speech, and signal. Drums come in several types, and among the

Asante and Yoruba of West Africa, drums are designed to provide tonal sounds that correspond to their tonal languages.

Finnegan (2012) concludes that there are two types of communication through drums. The first is through a conventional code where prearranged signals represent a given message without any direct linguistic basis for the communication. The other is communication based on direct representation of the spoken language that can actually be translated into words.

Among the Asante the talking drums known as *Atumpan* come in pairs— one with a high tone and the other a low tone. They are designed to mimic the tonal language of the Asante. Finnegan (2012) writes, "The two drums are played with a steady flow of beats, often lacking in regularity or phrasing to mimic the highs and lows of the local *Twi* language, which is a tonal language" (p. 468). Dancers to *Atumpan* drums dance or express themselves on the dance floor in response to the messages the drums convey to them. At the same time, they do deliver messages to onlookers. African languages are highly tonal. Meanings of words are distinguished not only by their tones, but by their phonetic elements. Thus drums like *Atumpan* are designed to provide the needed tones with the appropriate phonetic sounds (Nketia, 1963).

Rationale for Using African Drums as Pedagogical tools

The role of African drumming in religion makes it an appropriate tool for teaching world religions. The drum is believed to communicate with the supernatural. Drums are known to transmit messages between God and people, and also an essential instrument in the ritual healing (Nketia, 1963). It [the drum] plays a prominent role in ceremonies, rituals, and rites as pace setter for dance and praise. The people follow the drum's rhythm and their collective energies create an "unseen" link with the ancestors (Sowande, 1969). The drum is therefore a suitable tool for teaching comparative world religions. This feature is also prominent among Native Americans who call on the deity with the drum. Africans on both sides of the Atlantic use the drum in their religious practices. The drum is prominent in inducing spirit possession among worshippers of *Voodoo* (Haiti and Americas), *Santeria* (Cuba), *Canbomble* (Brazil), and *Rastafari* (Jamaica) (Johnson, 2011).

Among the Asante, drumming at the shrine does not only communicate with the people to bring them to the shrine, the accompanying music also calls the deity to possess the priest. Wilson (2006) writes that available literature is clear in agreeing that drums are used to beckon the gods in much the same way as they use to call in worshippers. While drumming may not be essential to religious ceremonies, it is believed that music helps the gods to work hard. Nketia (1963) states that among the Asantes, "gods are supposed to be sensitive to the language of music and would come down to see 'their children' if they heard music they liked" (p. 99). Wilson (2006) draws a similarity with church music and concludes that music helps create the environment, be it fetish or the Christian church. Evidence from research at an Asante fetish grove indicates that some selected rhythms played at shrines are called *okomfo twene* or fetish drums. They are considered effective because they expedite possession of the priest by the deity.

Similar to Native American use of smoke as a medium of communication, the sociopolitical role of the drum is its use to signal the start of the day, signal milestone events in the community, notify the public of important information and /or to assemble the community for important political issues. In days when allied communities lived within earshot of each other, drums were the main media of communication. Bebey (1999) writes that "each group's 'drum language'" is influenced by the geographic topography, the style of drum, material, number of drums, size of the drum, and rhythm/beat pattern" (p. 2). In modern journalistic terms drums can be used as a source of breaking news in the community. It calls forth the elders for a meeting at the palace for important community parley.

Scholars of African oral literature now include drum language as a relevance that is often ignored, especially by non-African researchers. It makes the drum a suitable pedagogical tool for world cultures. As Finnegan (2012) points out, the drum is a medium of specific literally forms, proverbs, panegyrics, historical poems, dirges and announcements for forthcoming events, funerals, hunts, deaths, marriages and games. Drum language is classified among what Okpewho (1992) calls orature to emphasize the oral nature of African. He defines oral literature as:

> those utterances, whether spoken, recited or sung, whose composition and performance exhibit to an appreciable degree the artistic characteristics of accurate observation, vivid imagination and ingenious expression. (p. 5)

African drumming can also be used as a pedagogical tool for teaching history. At kings' courts and events such as funerals, it is not uncommon among the Asante and Yoruba to hear literally communication expertly played out of the drum. Drum language at such events, invokes the valor of kings and leaders and prominent citizens (Nketia, 1963). Name recognition and appellations by griots and drummers are common in most African communities, south of the Sahara. The Hausa and the peoples of the Sahel, including the Wollof, Fulani and Mandes among several of them, have griots or praise singers who use big and important events to drum the praises. The importance of the information talking drums turn out is its education value. People, mostly the young in society who are not able to decipher drum language learn from the interpretation of the language, usually proverbs, by elders who are capable of translating (Finnegan, 2007). It is also a source of historical information. African history has a long oral tradition and within that tradition the rhythm of the drum plays an important role (Sexton, 2007).

Knowledge of the African drum was brought to the Americas through the Trans-Atlantic Slave Trade. Wherever enslaved Africans settled in their numbers in the Americas, they made important cultural contributions to the new environment. They developed their religious and secular rituals, festivals, and social gatherings on the foundations of song, dance, and rhythm they invented to cope with and express their New World realities (Ani, 1980).

The African drum played a prominent role in the Trans-Atlantic Slave Trade. In Africa it was used to alert villages that were being raided by slave traders. In the Diaspora, African slaves developed practical uses for the drum not dissimilar to their kin in Africa. Among the Maroons in the Caribbean and Brazil, the drum was used in war to signal a charge and over long distances to synchronize guerilla operations (Johnson, 2011). According to Rath (2000), the importance of the drum in communication in the Americans can best be judged by the fear expressed by Europeans in the New World of the drum culminating in the enactment of drum laws in the 16th and 17th centuries. Drumming was used to hatch escape plans (Gavidia, 2012). Taylor (2012) also affirms that Jazz has its roots among the African slaves who were transported to the Americas.

Primarily a musical instrument, the African drum also features prominently as a tool for teaching musical arts. It also has become the basis for such musical traditions as Reggae in Jamaica, Samba in Brazil and Ramba in Cuba and share the basic musical concepts with African music that include syncopated beat rhythm that aims to emphasize the lyrics; drum/beat maintaining timing relationship with vocals; initiating and synchronizing dancer; leads call and response; and repetition throughout the track (Davis, 1992; Sowande, 1969). Johnson (2011) observes that the African influence in the Diaspora is apparent in the "heterogeneous ideal." It is apparent in Hip Hop as it is in Jazz music. Both musical forms as well as others in other parts of the Americas share the same musical traditions with African music in which the drum features quite prominently.

The drum continues to be the central point of communication among peoples of African descent. Johnson (2011) compares the commonality of the drum among African peoples to Hip Hop culture which is called from "hood to hood" (neighborhood) as the Ghetto Boys state, "the world is a ghetto." The historical uses of the drum have developed into modern day African American drum corps across the country. Barber (2007) writes about the pride shown by African American youths who participate in to-day's drum corps. He however doubts if the young Black men and women have any knowledge of the history of the drum corps which was once held in high esteem by the African American community. The drum constitutes a cultural bridge between Africans in the diaspora and the continent. It is a source of pride that binds together spiritually peoples of African descent.

Types of African Drums

African drums are categorized by the sounds they are designed to produce, their assigned roles and the occasions on which they are played. Essentially the African drum is an instrument of communication, size notwithstanding. Unlike Western drums that are only designed for rhythm, African drums are designed to both communicate and provide rhythm. The difference, however, is that rhythm in Africa goes well beyond merely providing music. The rhythm has a level of language of its own (Sexton, 2007).

Figure 10.1. *Fontonfrom* drums in the background. Photo from www.motherlandmusic.com

Figure 10.2. Atumpan Drums. Photo from www.motherlandmusic.com

It is important that the diversity of Africa be emphasized further to the misconception of Africa as a country. Despite the commonality of rhythm as a characteristic of African drumming, each diverse ethnic group possesses its own drum culture and musical tradition (Njai, 2012). A description of various types of drums in Africa below shows the differences that exist. In some cases, however, the differences in design look and sound may be quite slight. The Akan in Ghana is the collective name for a number of ethnic groups who share a similar culture and traditions, principally language (Nketia, 1963). They include, Adanse, Akyem, Aowin, Asante, Asin, Bono or Brong, Denkyira, Fante, Kwahu, Nzima, and Sehwi or Sefwi.

The Akan language belongs to the Kwa group in the Gulf of Guinea in West Africa. Akans are a little less than 50 percent of the population of Ghana per the census of 2010 (Ghana Statistical Service, 2010). As in other African groups, the Akans of Ghana share the traditions of the talking drum. Among the ensemble of drums and musical instruments, the Akan have *fontonfrom,* which are state drums played during occasions like funerals of chief and potentates, weddings and at fetish groves. In response to messages remitted by the drummers, dancers interact with bystanders making faces, smiling and gesturing (Nketia, 1963).

The most important talking drum among the Akan is the atumpan. As cited by Finnegan (2012) in Nketia (1963), only the odomankoma kyerema (master/divine drummer) plays the atumpan drum and that the divine drummer is considered the greatest of all drummers because of the breadth of his knowledge, the skill which his work demands and the role he plays as a leading musician in all ensembles in which the atumpan drums are used.

From a personal observation, other lesser drums include the *dondo,* an instrument common to most ethnic groups in West Africa is quite popular among the northern peoples of Ghana. As in other ethnic groups, the drums are played among an ensemble that may include other instruments and vocals. It is similar to the Yoruba *dundun* drums. In the West African nations of Mali, Sene-Gambia, Cote d'Ivoire, Guinea, Burkina Faso, Sierra Leone and Liberia are found the Mandinka. A very ancient people, the Mandinka have three major drums, *sabaro* (lead) drum, *kutiriba* (bass) and the *kutirinding* (rhythm). The Fulla from Guinea play the *djembe* drum. It is also traditional in several countries in West Africa, particularly among the Mandinka in Mali, Sene-Gambia, Burkina Faso, Sierra Leone and Liberia. The Wollofs from SeneGambia also play the *djembe,* as well as the Jolla and the Balanta also from Guinea (Njai, 2012). (See Figure 10.3.)

The *djembe* drum shaped like a chalice is popular among the Mande-speaking peoples of West Africa. It is a talking drum that is used to sing the praises and recite poems and history of the kings of ancient Mande empires like, Ghana, Mali and Songhai. It comes in a variety of sizes but the shape is the same (Njai, 2012).

The Yoruba of Nigeria

The Yoruba, one of the largest groups in the region play a drum ensemble collectively referred to as *Dundun* (see Figure 10.4). It is an hour-

Figure 10.3.   Photo from www.offbeat-musical-instruments.com

Figure 10.4: *Dundun* drums (photo/www.flikr.com)

glass shaped drum that can be adjusted on its sides by arm-pressure to produce the desired tonal effect. The *dundun* is a talking drum used for appellations for kings at palaces and at ceremonies. It is also played at funerals, weddings and parties. The *dundun* is also popular in Nigeria music and is a common feature in *Juju* and *Fuji* (Bebey, 1999).

Interdisciplinary Connections for Using African Drumming in Social Studies Classrooms

Integrating drumming into the social studies classroom can be fun and educational. There are many ways that drumming can be used to address the National Council of Teaching Social Studies Standards. These include the the importance of integrating social studies across subject areas to support content area literacy. This is a sample interdisciplinary map for Grades 2-5.

Figure 10.5.   Source: Tony Stead's RAN Chart

To begin, it is important to activate students' background knowledge about Africa. Teachers will want to collect multiple texts about Africa, drumming, and folk tales. Using the RAN strategy developed by Tony Stead (2007) (see Figure 10.5), students brainstorm *what they think they know* about Africa. These ideas are written on individual post-it notes and placed in the first column of a table. The teacher can then use a nonfiction selection of literature to read about Sub-Saharan African. As students find a confirmation in the text, the post-it note is transferred to the second column of the table (Figure 10.5). After they read the text, students and teacher review the chart. They attend to any misconceptions they may have had about the content and they re-read to discover any new information they want to add. During instruction, it will be important to emphasize that Africa is a continent with 53 countries. For purposes of the drumming workshop, select a region from Africa, preferably Sub-Saharan Africa.

a. obtain a number of African flags and select a country to display the drums that originate from there
b. obtain and play a taped recording of drums from the different countries; or
c. obtain and watch a video of drumming from the different African countries
d. explain to students the different African drums available either in the pictures; or
e. show students sample of drums available at the workshop
f. explain the characteristics of each drum type
g. explain the language group of country of origin of drum being used as the pedagogical tool
h. play the various drums individually and explain to students message being drummed up
i. explain message to studentsp
j. ask students to play any message they of their choice
k. The above activity may be accompanied by a model of an African village using wide tubes and cones for roof. Add raffia or twigs for the thatch and paint the walls with African symbols. Fence the village with a cardboard and use different colors to represent trees, fruits and vegetables. Sample of activity can include the use drum as a religious, communication, dramatic performance to teach history, religion, social studies. As a way of using community as resource, it is appropriate to invite people from the community to come and talk about African drumming and also to perform the dance that goes with the drum beat.

Conclusion

For far too long, education in urban America has been deficient of social justice even as national and state education policies seek to address the inadequacies. The introduction of African drumming into social studies classrooms would therefore ensure that the proper climate is created for students to be able to appreciate their own sociocultural and linguistic backgrounds, as well the cultures of others. Embracing African drumming in classroom teaching therefore offers a potential, positive step in the direction of ensuring social justice.

REFERENCES

Anyon, J. (1997). *Ghetto schooling: A political economy of urban educational reform.* New York, NY: Teachers College Press.

Ani, M. (1980). *Let the circle be unbroken: The implications of African spirituality in the diaspora.* New York, NY. Nkonimfo Publications.

Asimeng-Boahene, L. (2010). Counter-storytelling with African proverbs: A vehicle for teaching, social justice and global understanding in urban, U.S. schools. *Equity & Excellence in Education, 43*(4), 434-445.

Banks, J. A. (2006). *Cultural diversity and education: Foundations, curriculum and teaching.* Boston, MA: Pearson/Allyn & Bacon.

Bebey, F. (1999). *African music, A people's art.* Lawrence Hill Books.

Barber, H. C. F. (2007). African-American drum and bugle corps: then and now. Retrieved from http://www.dci.org/news/print.cfm?news_id=9fc7acc4-6285-4104-a66.

Boutte, G. S. (2002). *Resounding voices: School experiences of people from diverse ethnic backgrounds.* Boston, MA: Allyn & Bacon.

Boutte, G. S., & Hill, E. L. (2006). African American communities: Implications for culturally relevant teaching. *The New Educator, 2,* 311-329.

Davis, S. (1992). *Reggae bloodlines: In search of the music and culture in Jamaica.* New York, NY: De Capo.

Delgado, R. (1989). Symposium legal storytelling, *Michigan Law Review 87,* 2073.

Delgado, R. and Stefancic J. (2001). Critical Race Theory, An Introduction. London UniversityPress New York and London.

Esposito, J., & Swain A. N. (2009, Spring). Pathways to social justice: Urban teachers' uses of culturally relevant pedagogy as a conduit for teaching for social justice. *Perspectives on Urban Education,* 38-46.

Gavidia, J. (2012). "Roots of Jazz, African Drumming and Congo Square" speech at Toronto, Canada.

Ghana Stastical Service. (2010). Census. Retrieved from http://www.statsghana.gov.gh/docfiles/pop_by_region_district_age_groups_and_sex_2010.pdf

Finnegan, R. H. (2012). Oral Literature in Africa, Retrieved from http://www.openbookpublishers.com January 13, 2013

Heinaman, R. (1998). Social justice in *Plato's Republic.* Retrieved from discovery.ucl.ac.uk

Johnson, R. (2011). The Drum as indicator of cultural unity in the African World, From Hip Hop to Africa. Retrieved from http://ourlegaci.com/the-drum-as-an-indicator-of-cultural-unity-in-the-african-world

Knudson, B. (2011). A liberal education. Retrieved from http://www.brigitteknudson.wordpress.com

Ladson-Billings, G. (1995). Culturally relevant teaching, theory into practice, *34*(3), 159-165.

Ladson-Billings, G., & Tate, W. F., IV (1995). Toward a critical race theory of education. *Teachers College Record, 1*(97) 47-68.

Lalas, J. (2007, Spring). Teaching for social justice in multicultural urban schools, conceptualization and classroom implication. *Multicultural Education,* 17-20.

Leonard, J. (2007). *Culturally specific pedagogy in the mathematics classroom: Strategies for teachers and students.* New York, NY: Routledge

Njai, B. (2012). African Drumming. Retrieved from http://www.africandrumming. com/africa_drums htm

Nketia, J. H. K. (1963). *Drumming in Akan Communities in Ghana.* Edingburgh, England: Thomas Nelson.

Ong, W. J. (1977). *African talking drums and oral noetics.* Baltimore, MD: Johns Hopkins University Press.

Okpewho, I. (1992). *African oral literature, backgrounds, character and continuity.* Bloomington, IN: Indiana University Press.

Rath, R. C. (2000). Drums and power, ways of Creolizing music in coastal South Carolina and Georgia, 1730-1790, in Creolization in the Americas. In S. Reinhardt & D. Buisseret (Eds.), *Cultural adaptations to the new world* (pp. 99-130). Arlington, TX, Texas: A&M Press.

Rollock, N., & Gillborn, D. (2011) Critical Race Theory (CRT), British Educational Research Associationonline resource. Retrieved from http://www. bera.ac.uk/files/2011/10/Critical-Race-Theory.pdf

Schmid, W. (1996) Dancing Drum. Retrieved from http://www.dancingdrum.com/ programs/k12/k12-ip.html

Stead, T. (2007) Tony Stead Presentation at SAISD. Retrieved from http://edsupport.cc/mguhlin/share/index.php?n=WorkshopNotes.TonyStead10262007

Sexton, T. (2007). An ethnomusicological analysis of traditional african drum. Retrieved from http://voices.yahoo.com/an-ethnomusicological-analysis-traditional-african-149876.htm)

Sowande, F. (1969). The role of music in african society. Speech at Howard University, Washington, DC.

Taylor, B. (2012). Jazz geography. Retrieved from town.hall.org/places/Kennedy/ Taylor/bt_afric.html

Wenar, L. (2012). "John Rawls." In E. N. Zelta (Ed.), *The Stanford Encyclopedia of Philosophy.* Standford, CA: Standford University.

Wilson, B, (2006). The drumming of traditional Ashanti healing ceremonies. Retrieved from http://www.ethnomusic.ucla.edu/pre/Vol11/Vol11html/ V11Wilson.html. January 18, 2013

Woodson, C. G. (1933). The mis-education of the Negro. Asmara, Eritrea: African World Press.

ABOUT THE EDITORS/AUTHORS

ABOUT THE EDITORS

LEWIS ASIMENG-BOAHENE is an associate professor at The Pennsylvania State University-Harrisburg. He is a teacher educator and researcher who teaches social studies education, world regional geography, comparative education and foundations of curriculum. He has authored several journal articles and book chapters in his field. He coedited *Strangers in new Homelands: The Social Deconstruction and Reconstruction of "Home" among Immigrants in the Diaspora.* His research interests include African oral traditional literature as pedagogical tools in content area classrooms, social studies education, multicultural education and international comparative education. Dr. Asimeng-Boahene has led workshops and presented both at the U.S. and international schools and conferences.

MICHAEL BAFFOE is an associate professor of social work at the University of Manitoba, Winnipeg, Canada. His areas of specialization and research are world refugee movements, settlement and integration issues affecting new immigrant population groups in host societies, local and international community development. He has published several articles in this area. His other interest areas are the social and educational inclusion of persons with disabilities. He is the chief editor of a book of the proceedings on an international conference on immigrants in the

Diaspora titled *Strangers in new Homelands, The Social Deconstruction and Reconstruction of "Home" among Immigrants in the Diaspora* published by Cambridge Scholars Publishing in 2012,

ABOUT THE CONTRIBUTORS

AKOSUA OBUO ADDO, associate professor of music, believes that knowledge grows when everyone is involved in the process. Addo's research interests include issues in arts education, collaborative and comparative research on the way children create and respond to community and culture through arts play. Community engagement and active learning strategies are vital components of Dr. Addo's campus courses and global seminars. She is an associate professor of music education at the University of Minnesota, Twin Cities, MN.

LEWIS ASIMENG-BOAHENE is currently an associate professor at The Pennsylvania State University-Harrisburg. He is a teacher educator and researcher who teaches social studies education, world regional geography, comparative education and foundations of curriculum. He is an author of several journal articles and book chapters in his field. He coedited *Strangers in new Homelands: The Social Deconstruction and Reconstruction of "Home" among Immigrants in the Diaspora.* His research interests include African oral traditional literature as pedagogical tools in content area classrooms, social studies education, multicultural education and international comparative education.

MICHAEL BAFFOE is an associate professor of social work at the University of Manitoba, Winnipeg, Canada. His areas of specialization and research interest are world refugee movements, settlement and integration issues affecting new immigrant population groups in host societies, including integration issues of children and youth in educational settings, local and international community development. His other interest areas are the social and educational inclusion of persons with disabilities. He has published several articles in these areas including lead-editing a recent book on the social deconstruction and reconstruction of the concept of "home" among immigrants in the diaspora (Cambridge Scholars Publishing, 2012).

DEANNA DAY teaches undergraduate and graduate literacy courses for Washington State University, Vancouver. Previously she was a classroom teacher for 15 years. One of her goals as an elementary teacher was to help students become lifelong readers and to critically think about what they were reading. She has continued this goal as a professor, helping teachers become readers and to pass their love of literacy into their classrooms. Her scholarly interests have centered around children's literature, including interviewing authors and illustrators, critically examining books and researching literature circles in different settings.

RACHEL A. GRANT is an associate professor of education at the College of Staten Island-City University of New York. Her research interests include application of critical pedagogies focusing on intersections of race, class, culture and gender in first and second language literacies, literacy teacher education, and urban education.

NANCY L. HADAWAY has almost 40 years of experience in K-12 schools and university classrooms and has taught courses in language and literacy and multicultural education. She has coauthored and coedited several books about teaching English learners. She has also served on several children's book award committees including the Orbis Pictus Committee, the Notable Books for a Global Society Committee, the Outstanding International Book Committee, and the National Council of Teachers of English Excellence in Poetry for Children Award Committee.

KIMETTA R. HAIRSTON is the sole proprietor of Critical Diverse Interventions. She also currently serves as the Curriculum and Instruction Specialist/Professor at Bowie State University in Maryland. She received her doctoral degree from the University of Hawaii at Manao; with a focus in qualitative research, diversity and disability studies. Her 15 years of teaching experiences range from public school to higher education. She has conducted over 1,000 diversity training sessions nationally and internationally. She is an active researcher and has coauthored books and published in numerous education journals, encyclopedias, newspapers, and more. Currently her research interest is: Infusing diversity and technology in teacher preparation courses; while utilizing the Common Core Standards.

JOYCE T. MATHANGWANE is professor of linguistics in the Department of English, University of Botswana. She has published widely in the areas of Bantu phonology and morphology, sociolinguistics, comparative linguistics and onomastics. Her current research interests include research on the social aspects of HIV/AIDS especially regarding the use of minority languages in the fight against HIV/AIDS and the different labels of this disease. For the past 3 years, (April 2010-April 2013), Prof. Mathangwane was appointed an honorary professor at the Institute for African Renaissance Studies, University of South Africa (UNISA).

OSEI A. MENSAH is currently interrelated special education teacher with Clarke County School District, Athens, Ga. He received his doctoral degree in Religious Studies from University of South Africa in Pretoria. He also is Oracle Certified Database Administrator and Associate of Chartered Institute of Marketing, England. He has taught in secondary and tertiary institutions in Ghana, Nigeria and South Africa. Before relocating to United States, Osei taught religious studies and social studies education at the University of Transkei (now Walter Sisulu University) in South Africa. He is coauthor of *Digging Up Our Foremothers: Stories of Women in Africa.* (Unisa Press: Pretoria).

NDANA NDANA is a senior lecturer of literature in the Department of English at the University of Botswana. His research interests are in Shakespeare, translation theory and practice, and African oral literature, with special emphasis on Subiya oral literature.

KWADWO ASAFO-AGYEI OKRAH is an associate professor of education in the Department of Secondary and Foundations Education and director, Center for Global Education at Indiana University South Bend. He has an extensive teaching record at Elementary, Middle, and high schools in Ghana as well as college and university teaching. He also worked with the Center for National Culture in Ghana as both research officer and Traditional Norms and Practices consultant. His most distinguished accomplishment in his country Ghana was Dr. Okrah's appointment as the National and Presidential Poet Laureate (The State Linguist of the Republic of Ghana) in 1992, which placed him on the Ghanaian list of precedence. Dr. Okrah is the author of numerous books and articles on African culture and Education.

ERNEST OPONG is a graduate of Southern Illinois University, Edwardsville. He was for a decade an adjunct lecturer at the Borough of Manhattan Community College (City University of New York). He is currently the publisher and editor-in-chief of *Amandla* newspaper, an African community publication in the New York area. Mr. Opong is also the director of diaspora strategy and engagement at the Center for Media and Peace Initiative, a New York think media tank and research organization.

THERESA TUWOR was trained as a teacher at Abetifi Teacher Training College, Ghana, and earned her bachelor's degree in social studies education at the University of Education, Winneba, Ghana. She has master's and doctoral degrees in social studies from the University of Kentucky. She has worked at Lincoln Memorial University, Harrogate, TN and Saint Augustine's University, Raleigh, NC in the Office of Institutional

Planning and Effectiveness and also taught as adjunct professor in both universities.

BARBARA A. WARD is the former chair of the NCTE Excellence in Poetry for Children Award Committee Barbara A. Ward spent 25 years teaching English language arts in New Orleans, Louisiana. Currently, she teaches children's literature and literacy courses at Washington State University. She enjoys sharing her passion for reading and writing as well as performing poetry with her students. Her research interests relate to gender, race, and power issues during literature discussions.

JOSEPHINE WILSON holds a doctorate in curriculum and instruction/ early childhood education from the University of Maryland, College Park, Maryland and chairperson of the Department of Teaching, Learning and Professional Development, associate professor of education and director of teacher education council in the College of Education at Bowie State University. Her research interests include the study of preservice teachers preparation; family literacy using technology; and electronic portfolio for professional development. Dr. Wilson has presented at Oxford Round Table, national and state conferences.

VIVIAN YENIKA-AGBAW is an associate professor at Pennsylvania State University, where she teaches Literature for Children and Young Adults. An assistant editor of *Sankofa: Journal of African Children's and Young Adult Literature*, she has published numerous journal articles and serves on Children's Africana Book Award committee. Her books include *Representing Africa in Children's Literature* (Routledge, 2008), and (with Mary Napoli) *African and African American Children's and Adolescent Literature* (Peter Lang, 2011), and *Fairy Tales with a Black Consciousness: Essays on Adaptations of Familiar Stories* (McFarland, 2013 with Ruth McKoy Lowery and Laretta Henderson). Her *African Youth in Contemporary Literature and Popular Culture: Identity Quest* (with Lindah Mhando) is forthcoming.

TERRELL A. YOUNG is a professor in the Teacher Education Department at Brigham Young University where he teaches graduate and undergraduate courses in children's literature. His research focuses on children's literature and English learners. He has also served on several children's book award committees including the Orbis Pictus Committee, the Notable Books for a Global Society Committee, the Notable Children's Books in the Language Arts, the Outstanding International Book Committee, and the National Council of Teachers of English Excellence in Poetry for Children Award Committee

Made in the USA
Middletown, DE
03 January 2017